To Aaron,
Blessings and Peace,
Dwayne Adams
Luke 19:10

The Sinner in Luke

The Evangelical Theological Society Monograph Series

❖

VOLUME 4
Did Jesus Teach Salvation By Works?
The Role of Works in Salvation in the Synoptic Gospels
—Alan P. Stanley

VOLUME 5
Has God Said?
Scripture, the Word of God, and the Crisis of Theological Authority
—John Douglas Morrison

VOLUME 6
The Light of Discovery:
Studies in Honor of Edwin M. Yamauchi
—John D. Wineland, editor

The Sinner in Luke

DWAYNE ADAMS

☙PICKWICK *Publications* · Eugene, Oregon

THE SINNER IN LUKE

Evangelical Theological Society Monograph Series

Copyright © 2008 Dwayne Adams. All rights reserved. Except for brief quotations in critical articles or reviews, no part of this book may be reproduced in any manner without prior written permission from the publisher. Write: Permissions, Wipf and Stock Publishers, 199 W. 8th Ave., Suite 3, Eugene, OR 97401.

Pickwick Publications
A division of Wipf and Stock Publishers
199 W 8th Ave., Suite 3
Eugene, OR 97401

ISBN 13: 978-1-55635-461-8

Cataloging-in-publication data:

Adams, Dwayne

    The Sinner in Luke / Dwayne Adams.

    Evangelical Theological Society Monograph Series

    Includes bibliography

    xxvi + 204 p. ; cm.

    ISBN 13: 978-1-55635-461-8

    1. Bible. N.T. Luke—Criticism, Interpretation, etc. 2. Bible. N.T. Acts—Criticism, Interpretation, etc. 3. Sin—Biblical teaching, I. Title. II. Series.

BS2589.6 S15 A30 2008

Manufactured in the U.S.A.

Contents

Abbreviations / vi

Introduction / ix

1 A Survey of the History of Interpretation of the "Sinner" in Luke / 1

2 Hellenistic and Jewish Concepts of the "Sinner" / 21

3 Previews of Jesus' Mission to "Sinners" in Luke / 69

4 The "Sinner" Texts in the Gospel of Luke / 105

5 The "Sinner" in Luke / 181

Bibliography / 197

Abbreviations

AB	Anchor Bible
ACNT	Augsburg Commentary on the New Testament
AER	*American Ecclesiastical Review*
ALGHJ	Arbeiten zur Literatur und Geschichte des hellenistischen Judentums
ANTC	Abingdon New Testament Commentaries
ATR	*Anglican Theological Review*
AUSS	*Andrews University Seminary Studies*
BAGD	Bauer, Walter. *A Greek-English Lexicon of the New Testament and Other Early Christian Literature.* Translated by William F. Arndt and F. Wilbur Gingrich. 2d ed. revised and augmented by F. Wilbur Gingrich and Frederick W. Danker. Chicago: University of Chicago Press, 1979
BDF	Blass, Friedrich, Albert Debrunner, and Robert W. Funk. *A Greek Grammar of the New Testament and Other Early Christian Literature.* Chicago: University of Chicago Press, 1961
BECNT	Baker Exegetical Commentary on the New Testament
BZNW	Beihefte zur Zeitschrift für die neutestamentliche Wissenschaft
CBQ	*Catholic Biblical Quarterly*
CIG	*Corpus inscriptionum graecarum.* Edited by August Boeckh, Johannes Franz, Ernst Curtius, and Adolf Kirchoff. 4 vols. Berlin: Akademie der Wissenschaften, 1828–77
CRINT	Compendia rerum iudaicarum ad Novum Testamentum
CTM	*Concordia Theological Monthly*
ESEC	Emory Studies in Early Christianity
ETL	*Ephemerides Theologicae Lovanienses*
ExpTim	*Expository Times*
GBS	Guides to Biblical Scholarship
HALOT	Koehler, Ludwig, Walter Baumgartner, and J. J. Stamm. *The Hebrew and Aramaic Lexicon of the Old Testament.* Translated and edited under the supervision of M. E. J. Richardson. 5 vols. Leiden: Brill, 1994–2000
HTR	*Harvard Theological Review*
HUCA	*Hebrew Union College Annual*
HvTSt	*Hervormde teologiese studies*
JAAR	*Journal of the American Academy of Religion*
JBL	*Journal of Biblical Literature*
JJS	*Journal of Jewish Studies*
JQR	*Jewish Quarterly Review*
JR	*Journal of Religion*
JSNT	*Journal for the Study of the New Testament*

Abbreviations

JSNTSup	Journal for the Study of the New Testament: Supplement Series
JSOTSup	Journal For the Study of the Old Testament: Supplement Series
JTS	*Journal of Theological Studies*
K&D	Keil, C. F., and F. Delitzsch. *Biblical Commentary on the Old Testament.* Translated by J. Martin et al. 25 vols. Edinburgh, 1857–78. Reprint, 10 vols. Peabody, MA: Hendrickson, 1996
LBS	Library of Biblical Studies
LCL	Loeb Classical Library
LSJ	Liddell, George Henry, Robert Scott and Henry Stuart Jones. *A Greek-English Lexicon*. 9th ed. with new supplement. Oxford: Clarendon, 1977
NAC	New American Commentary
NCB	New Century Bible
Neot	*Neotestamentica*
NIBCNT	New International Biblical Commentary on the New Testament
NICNT	New International Commentary on the New Testament
NIDNTT	*New International Dictionary of New Testament Theology.* Edited by Colin Brown. 4 vols. Grand Rapids: Zondervan, 1975–85
NIGTC	New International Greek Testament Commentary
NovT	*Novum Testamentum*
NovTSup	Supplements to Novum Testamentum
NTL	New Testament Library
NTS	*New Testament Studies*
NTTS	New Testament Tools and Studies
OGIS	*Orientis graeci inscriptiones selectae.* Edited by Wilhelm Dittenberger. 2 vols. Leipzig: Hirzel, 1903–5
OTP	*Old Testament Pseudepigrapha.* Edited by James H. Charlesworth. 2 vols. New York: Doubleday, 1983–85
PTMS	Pittsburgh Theological Monograph Series
SBLDS	Society of Biblical Literature Dissertation Series
SBLMS	Society of Biblical Literature Monograph Series
SBLSP	*Society of Biblical Literature Seminar Papers*
SNTSMS	Society for New Testament Studies Monograph Series
StPB	Studia post-biblica
TDNT	*Theological Dictionary of the New Testament.* Edited by Gerhard Kittel and Gerhard Friedrich. Translated by Geoffrey W. Bromiley. 10 vols. Grand Rapids: Eerdmans, 1964–76
TDOT	*Theological Dictionary of the Old Testament.* Edited by G. Johannes Betterweck H. Ringgren. Translated by J. T. Willis, Geoffrey W. Bromiley and David E. Green. 8 vols. Grand Rapids: Eerdmans, 1974–
TynBul	*Tyndale Bulletin*
UJEnc	*The Universal Jewish Encyclopedia.* Edited by Isaac Landman. 10 vols. New York, 1939–43
ZNW	Zeitschrift für die neutestamentliche Wissenschaft und die Kunde der älteren Kirche

Introduction

The Need for the Study

The Term "Sinner" in the Gospel of Luke

❦ THE "SINNER" is a very important theme in the Gospel of Luke. The Greek term for "sinner," ἁμαρτωλός, is found eighteen times in Luke but only five times in Matthew (9:10, 11, 13; 11:19; and 26:45) and six times in Mark (2:15, 16 [twice], 17 [=Matt 9:10–13], 8:38, and 14:41 [=Matt 26:45]). Four of Luke's uses have parallels in the other Synoptic Gospels: (1) the question raised by the Pharisees during the banquet at Levi's house: "Why do you eat and drink with tax collectors and sinners?" (Luke 5:30=Mark 2:15=Matt 9:10); (2) Jesus' reply to the Pharisees: "I have come to call not the righteous but sinners to repentance" (Luke 5:32=Mark 2:16=Matt 9:13); (3) the description of Jesus as a friend of publicans and "sinners" in the context of his tribute to John the Baptist (Luke 7:34=Matt 11:19); and (4) the expression "betrayed into the hands of sinners" used in Matt 26:45 and Mark 14:41 in the setting of Gethsemane but used in Luke 24:7 in the context of the empty tomb.[1]

The remaining fourteen uses of ἁμαρτωλός in Luke are unique to him. Jesus mentions the "sinner" four times in the Sermon on the Plain (6:32, 33, 34 [twice]). Luke's material also includes six pericopes that focus on Jesus and his relationship with "sinners." These pericopes are as follows:

1. Luke 5:1–11 (v. 8), Peter's confession to be a "sinful" man;
2. Luke 7:36–50 (vv. 37, 39), the "sinful" woman;
3. Luke 13:2, the warning to repent or perish;
4. Luke 15 (vv. 1, 2, 7, 10), the lost sheep, coin, and son;

---

1. Biblical translations are the author's unless otherwise noted. All other English translations of the OT and NT are from the New Revised Standard Version, NRSV.

5. Luke 18:9–17 (v. 13), the Pharisee and the toll collector; and
6. Luke 19:1–10 (v. 7), the conversion of Zacchaeus.

The volume of exclusive material devoted to the theme of the "sinner" suggests its importance to Luke in understanding Jesus and his mission.

The Identity of the "Sinner" in Luke

Although the "sinner" is clearly important to Luke, there is presently no scholarly consensus regarding the identity of the "sinner" in the Gospel of Luke.[2] Who is the "sinner"? At present there are five groups with whom "sinners" could be identified:

1. Is the term "sinner" in the Gospel of Luke a synonym for the common people, the ʿam ha-ʾareṣ, who were repudiated by the Pharisees on ritual rather than moral grounds? This view became widely accepted in the early twentieth century due to the increasing use of rabbinic material in New Testament studies, especially through the commentary by Strack and Billerbeck.[3] This position is commonly associated with Joachim Jeremias and is still maintained by modern commentators such as Earle Ellis.[4] Jeremias described the "sinner" from two perspectives.[5] He held that from the point of view of the Pharisees, the ʿam ha-ʾareṣ would be labeled "sin-

---

2. Our purpose in this introduction is to survey the basic proposed definitions of the "sinner" in the Synoptics. A detailed presentation of these definitions will follow in chapters 2 and 3, where the sources used to argue each position will be given.

3. Strack and Billerbeck, *Kommentar Zum Neuen Testament aus Talmud und Midrasch*.

4. Ellis, *The Gospel of Luke*, 107.

5. The issue of Jeremias's views of the "sinner" took center stage in a debate between E. P. Sanders and Ben Meyer. The debate is found in *JBL* (1991): Meyer, "Caricature," and Sanders, "Defending." Meyer accused Sanders of misrepresenting Joachim Jeremias's view of the attitude of 1st century Jews toward non-Jews and Jeremias's conclusion regarding the identity of the "sinners." Meyer argued that Jeremias did not equate "sinners" with the ʿam ha-ʾareṣ, as Sanders suggested. Sanders, in turn, blasted Jeremias's dependence upon Billerbeck's commentary that resulted in Jeremias's misrepresentation of Pharisaic viewpoints. We will discuss the debate in chapter two of our study.

ners."[6] Craig Evans takes this approach.[7] For example, Evans defines the term "sinner" as:

> ... those who could not observe the law of Moses, particularly the oral laws and traditions of the scribes and Pharisees. The Pharisees regarded these people as having no hope for participation in the kingdom of God or the resurrection of the righteous ... [8]

James D. G. Dunn proposes a slight modification of this view.[9] Rather than using rabbinic sources to show Pharisaic concern for associating with the 'am ha-'areṣ, due to issues of ritual impurity, Dunn uses Jewish intertestamental literature to show that the term "sinner" was a label marking someone's conduct as outside the boundary of the group. Although the 'am ha-'areṣ, who does not even attempt to observe the ritual laws as defined by the Pharisees, would receive the label, the sectarian places the "sinner" label more broadly upon those who may even view themselves as pious, but whose conduct is outside the boundary of the group. It is factional, sectarian language. For example, Dunn cites 1 Enoch 82:4 where the "sinner" label is applied to those fellow Jews not using a solar calendar. The issue here is not ritual purity but what behavior is unacceptable to the group. Another example is the sectarian community at Qumran which placed the "sinner" label, not simply on the blatantly wicked, but even on those whose incorrect interpretation of the Torah brought the further description as "those who seek smooth things," commonly viewed as the Pharisees (1QH 2.14–16; 4.6–8; 4QpNah 2.7–10).[10]

2. Is the "sinner" a person who was publicly acknowledged to be immoral or a member of a profession that was despised for its reputation for dishonesty or immorality? This position is based primarily on the association of "sinners" with toll collectors in the Gospels and with links to parallels in rabbinic literature.

---

6. Jeremias, "Zöllner und Sünder," 293–300.
7. Evans, *The Gospel of Luke*, 97.
8. Ibid.
9. Dunn, "Pharisees, Sinners, and Jesus," 279.
10. Ibid.

The Sinner in Luke

Although commonly identified with the first position listed above, this was the basic position of Joachim Jeremias.[11] He held that although the Pharisee would view the common people as "sinners," the "sinner" in the Gospels must be understood from the wider perspective of the people, not the Pharisees. The "sinner" in Luke is therefore someone at whom "everyone could point a finger."[12]

Sharon Ringe uses Jeremias's definition in her recent commentary. She reveals her understanding of the definition of the "sinner" in her discussion of the "sinful" woman of Luke 7:36–50. She writes,

> . . . a woman would be called a sinner if she were known as a liar, a thief, a cheat, or any other type of sinner in her own right, or she might have simply been the wife of a man who was known to be immoral or the practitioner of any one of a number of professions looked down upon as the breeding ground of dishonesty.[13]

E. P. Sanders modifies Jeremias's argument with regard to the despised trades but affirms the basic point that the "sinner" is the truly "wicked," those who sinned willfully and heinously and did not repent, a designation shared by the wider Jewish community.[14] Sanders is the first to base his definition of the "sinner" upon the Greek term ἁμαρτωλός and its relationship to the Hebrew word רָשָׁע in the LXX and other literature. For Sanders, Jesus' uniqueness was not preaching forgiveness to genuine "sinners" but offering forgiveness without repentance as normally understood by the Pharisees.[15]

David Tiede is strongly influenced by Sanders in his recent commentary.[16] Like Sanders, he also sees Luke's "sinners" as real "sinners." For Tiede, the conflict between Jesus and the Pharisees in Luke is explained by the fact

---

11. Jeremias, "Zöllner und Sünder," 293–300. Abrahams, *Studies in Pharisaism*, 54–61, essentially agrees with this.

12. Jeremias, *New Testament Theology*, 109.

13. Ringe, *Luke*, 108. See also Marshall, *The Gospel of Luke*, 219.

14. Sanders, *Jesus and Judaism*, 177.

15. Ibid., 206.

16. Tiede, *Luke*.

Introduction

that Jesus did not demand repentance from them prior to a call to discipleship and table fellowship.[17]

Charles Talbert also holds "sinners" to be the truly wicked but speaks of them in more general Hellenistic terms as "any unjust person, whether thief, or burglar, or poisoner, or sacrilegious person, or robber of corpses."[18]

3. Is the "sinner" a Jew who has made himself as a Gentile as proposed by Norman Perrin?[19] Perrin argues that Gentiles would automatically be labeled "sinners," but the term could also be applied to those Jews, who through their association with Gentiles, were considered quislings or traitors. Perrin proposed that the "toll collectors and sinners" in the Gospels were Jews despised on political and ethnic rather than moral grounds as held by Jeremias.

4. Is the term "sinner" unrelated to any historical reference and thus to be understood only in its literary function as proposed by David Neale?[20] He bases his position first of all on what he understands to be a caricature of the Pharisee in the Synoptics. He sees Luke as utilizing a non-historical portrayal of the Pharisees as a literary device. Neale then surveys the use of the term ἁμαρτωλός in the Psalms of the LXX and Jewish intertestamental literature. He concludes from this survey that the term "sinner" is an ideological term, not a term usually used with historically defined referents. For Neale, just as Luke presents the Pharisees as the "bad guys," he portrays the "sinners" as the "good guys."[21]

5. Finally, is the term "sinner" to be understood as a part of the larger category of the "poor" as proposed by Walter Pilgrim?[22] He views the "sinner" in social terms as a part of those who are outcasts from the society. In his recent commentary, Joel Green describes the "sinner" in these terms:

17. Tiede, *Luke* 127.
18. Talbert, *Reading Luke*, 64.
19. Perrin, *Rediscovering*, 94.
20. Neale, *None But the Sinners*, 193.
21. Ibid., 190.
22. Pilgrim, *Good News to the Poor*, 81.

> It is the Pharisees who introduced the term "sinners," using it as a label. In the hands of the Pharisees, "sinners" demarcate those who associate with toll collectors as persons living outside the faithfulness of God. By means of vituperative apposition, then, toll collectors are dismissed, along with sinners, as possible friends; from the Pharisaic perspective, they are outside the boundaries, beyond the margins. In Lukan parlance, though, toll collectors and sinners would be included among "the poor," those to whom Jesus has been sent to proclaim good news.[23]

Green further defines the "sinner" as persons whose primary attribute is that they cannot be included among the righteous and are therefore persons of low socio-religious status counted among the excluded, even damned.[24]

The question remains debated. Who is the "sinner" in the Gospel of Luke? From this survey of current views, it is clear that there is a lack of consensus regarding the identity of Luke's "sinner." This lack of consensus and the importance of this theme in Luke's Gospel justify a new examination of this subject.

Several monographs and books treat various sociological features of Luke-Acts. As mentioned, Walter Pilgrim investigates the larger category of the "poor." Other works deal with the Jews in Luke-Acts.[25] Only recently has discussion of the "sinner" begun. We have already made mention of David Neale's recent monograph *None but the Sinners*. One of the significant points about Neale's monograph is that it is one of the few works focusing exclusively on this key Lucan term.

Recent research in Luke has underscored Luke's intention to write the narrative of Jesus and his followers as a continuation of the OT biblical narrative. Darrell Bock has observed Luke's concern to compare the past events of Jesus and his followers with the great salvation acts of God in the Old Testament. By comparing similar types of events, Luke can expound and proclaim the significance of Jesus and his ministry in terms of promise and fulfillment and in terms of the pattern of divine action in history.[26]

---

23. Green, *The Gospel of Luke*, 247.
24. Ibid., 570.
25. Examples include Jack T. Sanders, *The Jews in Luke-Acts*; E. P. Sanders, *Jesus and Judaism*; and Brawley, *Luke-Acts and the Jews*.
26. Bock, *Proclamation from Prophecy and Pattern*.

Introduction

Rebecca Denova argues that in Luke-Acts, Luke rewrote the entire history of Jesus and his followers in light of scripture.[27] The grand design for the structural pattern of Luke-Acts was to continue the story of Israel into the life of Jesus and his followers. Denova argues that Luke constructed narrative events from five themes found in Isaiah: (1) the prediction of a remnant (Isa 10:20–23; 14:1–2); (2) the release of the captive exiles (Isa 49:22–26; 60:1–17); (3) the inclusion of the nations who would worship the God of Israel as Gentiles (Isa 49:7; 56:5); (4) prophetic condemnation of the unrepentant (Isa 66:24); and (5) the restoration of Zion.[28] She argues that the ministry of Jesus and his disciples presented in Luke-Acts can best be understood within the context of the social injustices listed in Isaiah 59–61 and elsewhere, and emphasized throughout both books. Thus, Luke's concern for the poor and the marginalized in the narrative does not reflect an innovative "Christian" ministry, but draws upon a major theme of the prophetic oracles. Isaiah 61 provided the framework for announcing the "year of the Lord's favor" (cf. Luke 4:19), when such injustices will be righted and which Luke's Jesus proceeded to accomplish.

Denova also views Isaiah as Luke's guide for the structure of ministry in Luke-Acts. Isaiah presents the raising up of a remnant of Jacob before salvation reaches the ends of the earth (Isa 49:6). Denova suggests that Luke argued that the remnant is made up of Jesus' followers. There is no direct ministry to Gentiles in the Gospel of Luke because the pattern for fulfillment in Isaiah consists first of establishing a repentant Jewish remnant followed by the inclusion of Gentiles.[29]

It is clear that Luke emphasizes the concept of "fulfillment" (Luke 1:1). Yet no one has explored the question of how the concept of "fulfillment" might have shaped Luke's understanding of the "sinner." Does Luke see the "sinner" theme as related to OT promise and fulfillment? This question is one our research will attempt to answer.

Another question that we will attempt to address is why the "sinner" theme disappears in Acts? If it is so important to Luke, as the evidence of its use in his Gospel suggests, why is the term "sinner" not found even once

---

27. Denova, *The Things Accomplished among Us*.
28. Ibid., 26.
29. Ibid., 27. Denova's proposal will be discussed fully below.

xv

in his second volume? If, as we will argue, Luke planned the whole work as a unity, though in two volumes, then the absence of the term in the second volume is curious. In a search through various works on Luke-Acts, few make reference to this. Donald Juel says that it is a surprise that Jesus' followers seem less interested in outcasts than we might have anticipated.[30] Jack T. Sanders suggests that Luke is somehow lumping the "sinners" and the Gentiles together as those whom Sanders describes as "the originally uninvited."[31] Sanders views the connection between the "sinners" in Luke and the Gentiles in Acts to be their role as those who are responsive to Jesus and his message of salvation. The responsive "sinners" and Gentiles provide the contrast to the unresponsive Jews who reject the Gospel.[32] But does Luke's concept of fulfillment bear upon Luke's "sinner" theme in such a way as to provide insight into the question: where is the "sinner" in Acts?

The Method for the Study

The approach of this study will be to begin by surveying a history of the interpretation of the "sinner" in the Synoptics. This survey will provide a better understanding of how we have arrived at the current state of broadly diverse definitions of Luke's "sinner."

Our next step will be to re-examine the lexical and historical background of the term ἁμαρτωλός. A weakness in Jeremias's view is that he limited his analysis of the "sinner" to its relationship with the tax collector in rabbinic material. E. P. Sanders broadened his analysis to include ἁμαρτωλός but, as we will attempt to show, has defined the term too narrowly. David Neale to our knowledge has examined ἁμαρτωλός in the most comprehensive way in the literature dealing with the "sinner" in the Synoptics. However, we will attempt to demonstrate that he has minimized certain data and made sweeping judgments that the evidence will not support.

One aim in this lexical and historical analysis will be to provide the firmest possible footing for our examination of Luke's use of the term "sinner" by understanding its Hellenistic and especially its Jewish back-

30. Juel, *Luke-Acts*, 87.
31. Sanders, *The Jews in Luke-Acts*, 134.
32. Ibid., 134–35.

Introduction

ground. This approach is consistent with the recent emphasis in "Life of Jesus" research to present Jesus against the background of first century Palestinian Judaism.[33]

The last step will be to examine Luke's presentation of Jesus and the "sinner." The lexical and historical research will provide proper limits for our literary study. Our method will be intentionally eclectic.[34] Relevant pericopes are examined along the lines of literary-narrative criticism. Joseph Tyson utilizes this approach in *Images of Judaism in Luke-Acts*.[35] Robert Tannehill uses a historical-literary approach with Luke-Acts in his two-volume work, *The Narrative Unity of Luke-Acts*.[36] William Kurz applies narrative criticism to Luke-Acts with special emphasis upon how readers respond to Luke and Acts in the act of reading.[37] Our goal will be to treat the texts as they stand and to understand their meaning for Luke and his readers. Of key importance to our study will be the total portrait these texts present of the "sinner" as a category in Jesus' mission.

Recent research has also focused on the sociological interpretation of the New Testament. David Gowler brings the sociological and literary approaches together in a study of the Pharisees in Luke and Acts.[38] Gowler uses the cultural anthropologist's recognition of certain key cultural factors to shed light on the interaction between Jesus, the Pharisees, and various groups in Luke-Acts. For example, purity rules and meal fellowship play key roles in cultural interaction. The issues of purity rules and meal fellowship provide an important link between Luke and Acts. Jesus' mission

---

33. Evans, *Life of Jesus Research: An Annotated Bibliography*, 9–11. Evans cites the following examples of this emphasis: C. H. Dodd (1970), John Bowker (1973), Geza Vermes (1973, 1982), A. E. Harvey (1982), Gerald Sloyan (1983), Marcus Borg (1984), E. P. Sanders (1985), and J. H. Charlesworth (1988). To this list must be added J. Massyngberde Ford (1984), David Gowler (1991), and Joseph B. Tyson (1992).

34. The rationale for such an approach to this method can be stated no better than Talbert's defense of his own, though different, eclectic methodology found in Parsons and Tyson, editors, *Cadbury, Knox, and Talbert*, 237, when he states, "What works? What way of reading makes the most sense of the text? The combination of approaches that yields the best result is 'the' correct method."

35. Tyson, *Images of Judaism in Luke-Acts*.

36. Tannehill, *The Narrative Unity of Luke-Acts*.

37. Kurz, *Reading Luke-Acts*.

38. Gowler, *Host, Guest, Enemy, and Friend*, 15–27.

to "sinners" includes table fellowship and on this account he is met with grumbling and opposition by the Pharisees (Luke 5:30; 15:2; 19:7). In Acts, the mission to Gentiles encounters the same reaction (Acts 11:2–3).[39] A better understanding of meal fellowship at the time of Jesus will help to clarify Luke's emphasis on Jesus' meal-fellowship with "sinners." Table fellowship plays a key role in the controversy.

Our approach will be an eclectic blend of methods including historical, literary, and social science approaches as they provide insight into Luke and his use of the term and concept of the "sinner." Of special focus will be an examination of the "sinner" in view of Luke's emphasis on "fulfillment." Our research will attempt to analyze Luke's narratives for possible OT citations or allusions that may provide clues to understanding his use of "sinner."

The Unity of Luke-Acts

One presupposition of our study is the unity of Luke-Acts. Robert Maddox argues for the unity of Luke-Acts based on three primary considerations.[40] First, the same author wrote both. Second, the preface in Luke 1:1–4 introduces both volumes. H. J. Cadbury compared the opening verses of Acts with the pair of prefaces in Josephus's *Against Apion*.[41] The Acts preface reflects the usual custom for recapping a previous volume of a two-volume work. Third, the internal evidence also points to unity: (1) continuity of themes such as the rejection of Jesus' mission by the Jews and its acceptance by the Gentiles (Luke 4:16–30; Acts 28:17–28); and (2) progression of theme in that Luke 24:47–49 looks forward to Acts, especially Acts 1–2.

Mikeal C. Parsons and Richard I. Pervo have challenged the unity of Luke-Acts.[42] They observe that on the subject of unity in Luke-Acts, scholars have discussed the issue at five different levels: authorial, canonical, generic, narrative, and theological. They correct a tendency to view the books together to the neglect of each individually. They point out that

---

39. Tannehill observes this connection (*Narrative Unity*, 2:136–37).
40. Maddox, *The Purpose of Luke-Acts*, 3–6.
41. One may compare *Ag. Ap.* 1.1. (1–3) and 2.1 (1–2) with Luke 1:1–4 and Acts 1:1–2. Cadbury, *The Making of Luke-Acts*, 344–48, 358–59. Also Fitzmyer, *Luke I–IX*, 288–89.
42. Parsons and Pervo, *Rethinking the Unity of Luke and Acts*.

Introduction

there is no evidence that the books ever existed as a canonical unity and suggest that the narrative and theological unity is more presupposed than demonstrated. Finally, they suggest the removal of the dash in Luke-Acts and a return to the "and" as the appropriate connector.[43]

Although Luke and Acts are not a canonical unity, Luke-Acts may still be considered a unity at several levels. First, Luke and Acts are united in purpose. Parsons and Pervo fail to give sufficient weight to the single author's dual prefaces in Luke 1:1–4 and Acts 1:1–2. The author clearly stated his purpose to a real, although unidentifiable, person named Theophilus who was expected to read both volumes.[44] Nothing is said about what Theophilus knew outside of Luke's narrative. Consequently, to understand Luke's purpose and theology, one must, like Theophilus, be a reader of both volumes.

Second, there is a unity at the discourse level as demonstrated by parallels between Luke and Acts.[45]

Luke		Acts	
1:1–4	A preface dedicates the book to Theophilus.	1:1–5	A preface dedicates the book to Theophilus.
3:21	Jesus prayed at his baptism.	1:14, 24	The disciples prayed as they received the baptism of the Holy Spirit.
3:22	The Spirit descends after Jesus' prayer in a physical form.	2:1–13	The Spirit fills the disciples after prayer with physical manifestations.
4:16–30	Jesus' ministry opens with a sermon that gives the theme for what follows, fulfillment of prophecy, and the rejection of Jesus.	2:14–40	The church's ministry opens with a sermon that gives the theme for what follows, fulfillment of prophecy, and the rejection of Jesus.

43. Parsons and Pervo, *Rethinking the Unity of Luke-Acts*, 126–27.

44. Although some have proposed a symbolic audience based on the meaning of the name Theophilus, "lover of God," Joel Green points out that this name was common as early as the 3rd century BCE (*Gospel of Luke*, 44). In addition, if Theophilus is not intended as a real addressee, the appellation "most excellent" would be pointless.

45. Talbert, *The Genre of Luke-Acts*, 17–23.

The Sinner in Luke

	Luke		Acts
4:31—8:56	The theme of fulfillment is illustrated by examples of preaching and healing. Conflicts illustrate the theme of rejection.	2:41—12:17	The theme of fulfillment is illustrated by examples of prophesying and wonders. Persecutions illustrate theme of rejection.

Within this last general section (4:31—8:56) there are several specific parallels:

	Luke		Acts
5:17–26	A lame man is healed by the authority of Jesus.	3:1–10	A lame man is healed in the name of Jesus (cf. 9:32–35).
5:29—6:11	Conflict with the religious leaders.	4:1—8:3	Conflict with the religious leaders.
7:1–10	A centurion, well-spoken of by the Jews, sends men to Jesus to ask him to come to his house.	Ch. 10	A centurion, well-spoken of by the whole Jewish nation, sends men to Peter to ask him to come to his house.
7:11–17	A story involving a widow and a resurrection. Jesus says, "Arise" (ἐγέρθητι) . . . And the dead man "sat up" (ἀνεκάθισεν).	9:36–43	A story involving widows and a resurrection. Peter says, "Rise" (ἀνάστηθι). And the woman "sat up" (ἀνεκάθισεν).
7:36–50	A Pharisee criticizes Jesus for being touched by the wrong kind of woman.	11:1–18	The Pharisaic party criticizes Peter for his association with Gentiles.

Talbert lists thirty-two such parallels.[46] Such correspondence supports a narrative unity, at least at the discourse level.

Third, Luke sometimes uses a word to bring to mind an earlier similar incident. One such example is the witness of Peter before the Sanhedrin in Acts 4. In Acts 4:14, Luke states that because of the presence of the forty-

---

46. Talbert, *Literary Patterns*, 17–23.

Introduction

year-old healed lame man, the Sanhedrin was unable to contradict the apostles. The verb ἀντεῖπον (aorist of ἀντιλέγω) is found in the New Testament in only two places, in Acts 4:14 and in Luke 21:15, where Jesus predicted that because of their association with him the disciples would be brought before rulers. However, they were told not to fear because he would give them wisdom that none of their adversaries would be able to contradict. The description of a "witness" scene is the same in both, but Luke 21:15 is presented in the context of prophecy and Acts 4:14 in the context of fulfillment. The fulfillment of Jesus' words links the incidents in the mind of the reader, indicating an intentional narrative unity on the part of Luke.

The Genre of Luke-Acts

With regard to genre, Luke and Acts have been classified as history, biography, and novel.[47] The issue of the genre of Luke and Acts is complex but especially relates to two considerations, the nature of Luke's preface and the nature of the content of his two volumes.

Central to the issue of genre is the nature of the preface in Luke's Gospel. Luke is unique among the Synoptic writers in that he provides the reader with a preface stating his intentions. The first four verses of Luke serve as a prologue to the entire Gospel and allude also to Acts, the second volume.[48] Luke's preface has been compared to Greek classical histories such as Herodotus,[49] biographies of the founders of philosophical schools such as Laertius's *Lives*,[50] and scientific treatises such as Hero and Galen.[51]

---

47. Powell, *What Are They Saying about Acts?*, 9–13.

48. Fitzmyer, *Luke I–IX*, 289.

49. Fitzmyer mentions the classical historical prefaces of Herodotus, Thucydides, and Polybius (ibid., 288).

50. Talbert, *The Genre of Luke-Acts*, 125–34. Also Burridge, *What Are the Gospels?* 199–219.

51. Alexander, *Preface*. Although Alexander demonstrates some stylistic similarities between Luke's preface and technical literature (e.g., brevity, use of the first and second person), Luke's preface is not easily detachable as her genre category demands. Luke's emphasis on "fulfillment" suggests that the preface is essential for understanding his narrative purpose (Alexander makes little of πληροφορέω, *Preface*, 110). In addition, the content of Luke and Acts fits much closer to the narrative style of the Old Testament and later Jewish historians, such as the writers of 1 and 2 Maccabees and Josephus.

xxi

Others have observed the similarities to Hellenistic-Jewish histories such as Josephus. George Sterling has stressed that the two-volume nature of Luke-Acts must be given serious consideration.[52] For this reason, it is Josephus that provides the closest parallel to Luke.[53]

In his two-part work *Against Apion*, Josephus begins with a preface to part one: "In my history of the *Antiquities*, most excellent Epaphroditus, I believe that I have made sufficiently clear to any who would come upon that work the extreme antiquity of our Jewish race" (1.1.1–3). Josephus then states that since several people had discredited his accounts in his *Antiquities*, he sees it necessary to "devote a brief treatise to all these points" (*Ag. Ap.* 1.1.3). In the preface of the second volume of this work Josephus writes: "In the first volume of this work, my esteemed Epaphroditus, I demonstrated the antiquity of our race . . . I shall now proceed to refute the rest of the authors who have attacked us" (*Ag. Ap.* 2.1–2).

In Acts 1:1, Luke also refers back to his first volume: "The first account I composed, Theophilus, about all that Jesus began to do and teach, until the day when he was taken up, after he had by the Holy Spirit given orders to the apostles whom he had chosen." Luke's preface connects his work to historical writings of his day, especially Hellenistic-Jewish histories. But the genre issue cannot be determined simply by the presence or absence of stylistic features or stock terms (such as διήγησιν and αὐτόπται) used in various prefaces.[54] The genre issue also depends on how the terms function and the nature of the content of the writing.[55]

The content of Luke's preface suggests that Luke is making a claim to veracity, along the lines of Josephus and other historians. For example, in Luke 1:1 the term διήγησιν translated as "narrative" or "account" means "a historical report" in this context.[56] It is used this way in Diodorus Siculus 11.20.1 and Josephus, *Antiquities* 11.68. Luke also claims to use the testimony of eyewitnesses (αὐτόπται). The role of authoritative witness of Jesus' earthly ministry and resurrection is important to Luke-Acts (Luke

52. Sterling, *Historiography*, 238–40; 297–98.
53. Alexander admits that Luke's preface bears a family resemblance to Hellenistic-Jewish writers such as Josephus (*Preface*, 167).
54. Sterling, *Historiography*, 341.
55. Ibid. Alexander acknowledges this point also (*Preface*, 137).
56. BAGD, 195.

24:48; Acts 1:8; 1:22; 2:32; 3:15; 5:32; 10:39, 41; 13:31). These witnesses are "servants of the word" (Acts 26:16). The "word" (τοῦ λόγου) refers to the Christian message about Jesus, especially his acts and teachings (Acts 10:36–43). In Acts the absolute form ὁ λόγος takes on the significant overtone of "The Word of God."[57] In Acts 6:4 we read of the ministry of the word. Fitzmyer sees this as relevant for Luke 1:2.[58] These "ministers of the word" (Luke 1:2) were not propagandists for their own views of what happened with Jesus but had unreservedly put themselves in the service of his cause.[59] Luke claims that these trustworthy witnesses "handed down" (παρέδοσαν: a technical term for handing down a tradition in the early church, 1 Cor 11:2, 23; 15:3; Jude 3) this word to him.

Luke also stresses his own qualifications. He has carefully (ἀκριβῶς) followed (παρηκολουθηκότι) everything from the beginning (Luke 1:3). The meaning of παρακολουθέω is commonly understood to mean "investigate."[60] Sterling supports this meaning by citing Josephus's *Against Apion* 1.53 as a parallel text.[61] David Moessner has challenged this by surveying all of Josephus's eight uses of the verb and concluding that the meaning "investigate" is not found there.[62] Josephus's use suggests the meaning "follow closely with the mind." When the term is used of events, Josephus uses it to mean "following something as to be totally familiar with the whole affair." If Luke's use is parallel to Josephus's, Luke is either presenting himself as a contemporary who stayed actively informed about Jesus and his followers (through whatever means) from the beginning of the information circulated about Jesus, or as one who, as an insider, has complete and accurate understanding of all the events and traditions in the narratives of the "many" others. He is completely qualified to present an accurate and

57. Fitzmyer, *Luke I–IX*, 295.
58. Ibid.
59. Marshall, *Luke*, 42.
60. BAGD, 619.
61. Sterling, *Historiography*, 344.

62. Moessner, "'Eyewitnesses.'" According to Moessner, Josephus uses the verb with the meaning "physically follow or accompany" (*J. W.* 1.455; 6.251; *Ant.* 14.438) and "follow with the mind" (*Ant.* 12.259; *Ag. Ap.* 1. 218; and 2.5) or "follow events as they developed" (*Ag. Ap.* 1.53; *Life* 357).

trustworthy account.[63] Luke intends Theophilus to have confidence in the veracity of Luke's narrative.

Talbert has warned that claims by prefaces to historical accuracy cannot be taken at face value. Sometimes the use of the preface was merely a convention that was followed by a writing that was largely fiction.[64] Talbert states that the claim to veracity must be tested by what is written. This being said, Luke's preface is at least making the claim to accuracy, and he was surely as aware of the difference between truth and fiction as Josephus, to which Luke's preface clearly compares. In his *Jewish War* 1.1.1–2, Josephus claims others had written false accounts of the war with Rome based on hearsay and from a variety of malicious motives. In contrast, Josephus claims to write from the point of view of a witness (1.1.3) who knows the use of literary convention for writing histories (1.4.11) and the tendency for some to write lies (1.5.13–14). He prefers the truth of historical facts (1.5.16). Josephus's awareness of historians' fabrication can also be seen in his reference to Herod's historiographer, who colored the accounts to glorify Herod (*Ant.* 16.7.183–87). In contrast, Josephus claims to write the truth because he is of priestly lineage and does not lie (*Ant.*16.7.187). He honors the truth more than the honor of kings. One observes from Josephus that ancient writers were aware of the difference between truth and fiction. As I. Howard Marshall has observed, when Luke's claim is tested, Luke 7:21 and Acts 1:3 reveal clearly that Luke is concerned with the historical reliability of his material.[65] Luke introduces his work with a preface to underscore the reliability and accuracy of his account.

In addition to the historical veracity claims of Luke's preface, a second feature of the preface important for understanding his genre is his emphasis upon "fulfillment." Although Luke stakes a claim on the historical accuracy of his account, he is more than a secular historian. He writes concerning the "events which have been fulfilled" (Luke 1:1). These events are those included in the Gospel of Luke and the Book of Acts. The prologue of

---

63. Moessner, "Eyewitnesses," 122.
64. Talbert, *Reading Luke*, 8.
65. Marshall, *Luke*, 40.

Introduction

Acts explicitly mentions Jesus in retrospect and prepares the reader for the continuation of the story (Acts 1:1–2).[66]

The term πληροφορέω literally means "to fill completely" but is often used as a synonym for πληρόω, "fill" or "fulfill."[67] The term should be understood as "fulfill" because of Luke's emphasis in his two volumes on the fulfillment of the plan of God.[68] A few examples include: Luke 1:20, Gabriel's address to Zachariah; 4:21, Jesus' sermon in Nazareth; 9:31, Jesus' departure; 21:22, 24, Jesus' description of things to come; 24:44–47, Jesus' address to his disciples: "all things which are written about me in the Law of Moses and the Prophets and the Psalms must be fulfilled." Luke uses πληρόω with this same meaning in Acts. For example, in Acts 1:16, Peter stated concerning Judas: "the Scripture had to be fulfilled." In Acts 2, regarding Pentecost, Peter declares God's promise recorded in the prophet Joel fulfilled (Acts 2:16–36). It is God who has accomplished his plan (Acts 2:22–32). The perfect tense of the verb stresses events that have occurred in the past but their influence is continuing in the present.

From this examination of the style and content of Luke's preface and its connection to Luke-Acts, the genre of "biblical historical narrative" seems to be an apt designation of Luke's own description of his genre and his style. The historical quality of Luke's writing seems to be the Achilles' heel of Pervo's position that Luke intends his work (Acts) to be read as fiction.[69] How could it address the need for "certainty"? In addition, the entertaining nature of Luke and Acts does not rule them out as historical narratives. Dramatic elements were in common use among the historians.[70] We will use the broad idea of "biblical historical narrative" as a way of seeing the genre of Luke from Luke's point of view.[71] Kurz analyzes Luke-Acts and Luke's use of both Hellenistic historical elements (e.g., the statements of purpose in Luke 1:1–4 and Acts 1:1–2) and Jewish biblical historical patterns. Luke uses imperial dating in Luke 3:1–2, but does so in a manner

66. Fitzmyer, *Luke I–IX*, 289.
67. BAGD, 670.
68. Bock, *Luke 1:1—9:50*, 57; Fitzmyer, *Luke I–IX*, 293; Talbert, *Reading Luke*, 234–40.
69. Pervo, *Profit With Delight*, 135, 138.
70. Sterling, *Historiography*, 320.
71. Kurz uses the phrase "biblical narrative" (*Reading Luke-Acts*, 1–5).

that imitates the dating of the OT prophets like the LXX of Jeremiah 1:1.[72] Kurz also observes that the unusual expression, "events that have been fulfilled (πεπληροφορημένων)" in Luke 1:1, suggests that Luke intended to connote the fulfillment of biblical promises and prophecies. Luke's narrative belongs to the tradition of the Jews as well as to the tradition of the Greek professional writing. The dramatic shift in style at Luke 1:5 to a type of biblicist Greek throughout the infancy narrative reflects an imitation of narratives like those of Samuel–Kings and 1–2 Maccabees.[73] For this reason we will use the concept of "biblical historical narrative" for our understanding of the genre of Luke–Acts.

The Contribution of the Study

An important contribution of our research toward Lucan studies will be the clarification of a key concept in Luke's presentation of Jesus and his mission. Who is the "sinner" in Luke? How does the answer to this question contribute to our understanding of the nature of the mission of Jesus and his followers? Why did the Pharisees object to Jesus' association with "toll collectors and sinners"? Why does Luke repeat this theme so often? What role does the "sinner" theme play in Luke's understanding of "fulfillment"? What role does the "sinner" theme play in Luke–Acts? Our research will attempt to answer these questions.

---

72. Kurz, *Reading Luke-Acts*, 13.
73. Ibid., 11.

1

A Survey of the History of Interpretation of the "Sinner" in Luke

The "Sinner" in Discussions from the 2nd to the 16th Centuries

❦ MOST EARLY commentators identified "sinners" in the Synoptics as those who were notoriously wicked.[1] For example, in chapter 15 of Justin Martyr's *First Apology* (151–154 CE), Justin speaks of "countless multitudes who have turned away from intemperance and learned these things (moral purity)."[2] For support he states, "For Christ did not call the righteous and temperate to repentance, but the ungodly and licentious and unrighteous. So He said, 'I came not to call the righteous, but sinners to repentance.'" Here Justin cites Luke 5:32 as evidence that Christ called the truly wicked to a life of moral purity. This can also be seen in Origen's description of the disciples as formerly "wicked."[3] Cyril of Alexandria in the fifth century also identifies "sinners" as actual "sinners."[4] He describes them as those not yet purified from their sins and profane. Cyril explains Pharisaic opposition to Jesus' association with "sinners" not

---

1. The selection of authors for the period from the second to the sixteenth centuries is a sampling of some key commentators and does not intend to be exhaustive.
2. Justin Martyr, *First Apology*, 15.
3. Origen, *Contra Celsum*, 1.62.
4. Cyril, *Commentary on the Gospel of Saint Luke*, 115.

on ritual grounds but because Jesus disregarded the Law's prohibition on association with the profane.

Augustine describes "sinners" as the opposite of the godly and mentions idolaters and drunkards as examples.[5] Augustine also interprets Luke's story of the Prodigal Son by identifying the younger brother with Gentiles and the elder brother as the people of the Jews.[6] He connects the passage to Ephesians 2:17 (*Serm. 112A.13*) and interprets the parable as an allegory treating the admission of the Gentiles into the church without circumcision. The elder brother represents the complaining of the Pharisees in Acts 15 (*Serm. 112A.8*).

Commentators of the medieval period continued to hold the view of the Fathers that the "sinner" was the truly wicked based on moral grounds. In the late eighth century, Paschasius Radbertus describes Matthew in the account of the call of Levi as "sitting as a teacher of rapine in a fire of avarice consumed by the flames of greed (Matt 9:9)."[7] He describes Levi's home prior to his call as an "office of cruelty," a "den of fraud," and a "cave of iniquity."[8] Radbertus sees a parallel between Jesus' call of "sinners" and the salvation of Rahab the harlot.[9] He views the "sinner" as morally wicked in need of forgiveness of sins. Thomas Aquinas (1225?–1274) continues this viewpoint. He cites Bede (around 600) who explains that Matthew included his own name in the account of his call so that no one might despair of salvation because of the enormity of their sins.[10] Aquinas describes Levi (Matthew) as a rapacious man, of unbridled desires after vain things.[11] Regarding the "sinners," Aquinas cites Augustine to explain that Jesus called "sinners" in order to save them from their iniquity as a physician seeks to save the sick from their sickness.[12] Aquinas cites Bede and

---

5. Augustine, *Serm. 97A.1*.

6. Edmund Hill states that Augustine's interpretation of the younger and elder brothers is in accord with almost unanimous patristic tradition. He adds that it is in all probability true to the mind of Luke (See Augustine, *Works*, 162, n.1).

7. Pascasius Radbertus, *Expositio in Matheo Libri VI*, 516 (lines 1724–25).

8. Ibid., 520 (line 1850).

9. Ibid., 526 (lines 241–50).

10. Thomas Aquinas, *Saint Luke*, 190.

11. Ibid.

12. Ibid., 192.

A Survey of the History of Interpretation of the "Sinner" in Luke

Ambrose (late fourth century) to explain that the call of Levi (Matthew) signified the faith of the Gentiles.[13] Cornelius Lapide (1600) states that the "sinners" in the expression "toll collectors and sinners" seem to have been dissolute Jews who care little for the law and the religion of the Jews, and lived in a heathen manner, or who had apostatized to heathenism.[14] John Calvin continues the designation of the Synoptic "sinner" as the truly wicked.[15] Calvin describes the "sinners" to be "men of wicked lives and of infamous character."[16]

In summary, the Synoptic "sinner" is viewed as a "real sinner" in the period prior to the seventeenth century. Although Augustine suggested a link between the Prodigal and the Gentiles, in general, the "sinner" term was understood to refer to the truly wicked.

The "Sinner" in Discussions from the 17th–19th Centuries and the Investigation of Jewish Sources

John Lightfoot in his commentaries published in 1658 titled *Horae Hebraicae et Talmudicae*, maintains the description of "sinners" as the truly wicked. Lightfoot, however, uses Jewish sources in his discussion. In his notes on Luke 7:36, he uses rabbinic literature to describe reasons Jews would designate a woman a "sinner." The reasons are based on violations of the Law of Moses and the ceremonial laws of the rabbis. However, Lightfoot rejects the latter as the basis for the designation of the woman as an ἁμαρτωλός in Luke 7. He sees her as an adulteress or generally immoral woman, based on the connection between ἁμαρτωλός and the OT term חטאים.[17] Starting in the seventeenth century Jewish sources became a primary source for discussing the meaning of the "sinner." In a note on the expression "tax collectors and sinners" in Mark 2:16, although he did not cite the source, Lightfoot identifies the "sinners" by a virtual direct quote of *m. Sanh.* 3:3.

---

13. Ibid., 192–93.
14. Lapide, *St. Matthew's Gospel I–IX*, 361.
15. Calvin, *Commentary on A Harmony of the Evangelists*, 1:400.
16. Ibid.
17. Lightfoot, *Horae Hebraicae et Talmudicae*, 3:84–85.

The Sinner in Luke

"Sinners" were "dicers, usurers, plunderers, publicans, shepherds of lesser cattle, and those who sell the fruit of the seventh year."[18]

The growing influence of Jewish sources upon the understanding of the "sinner" is evidenced in a commentary by William Trollope published in 1842.[19] Trollope defines the "sinner" based on Lightfoot's discussion:

> The word *hamartolos*, "sinner," is generally used in the Gospels, and indeed throughout the NT either to signify a *heathen*, or such of the Jews who, from their illicit practices, were looked upon in the same light as heathen. Of this later class the Talmud enumerates dicers, usurers, plunderers, publicans, shepherds of lesser cattle (swine), those that sell the fruit of the seventh year.[20]

In his treatment of John 7:49, Trollope identifies the "common people who are accursed" to be the *'am ha-'areṣ* (עַם הָאָרֶץ) the people of the earth.[21] Yet Trollope equates the "sinners" of the Synoptics with the *'am ha-'areṣ*. Trollope links the term "sinner" especially with "Gentile." In his discussion of the sinful woman in Luke 7:37, Trollope acknowledges that ἁμαρτωλός here possibly meant "adulteress" but probably meant "Gentile." Trollope bases this interpretation on the statement of Jesus in Matthew 26:45 that the Son of Man would be betrayed into the hands of "sinful men." Trollope understands the expression "sinful men" to mean "Gentiles."[22] In his discussion of Jesus' eating with "sinners" in Luke 15:2, Trollope gives a description of the "sinner" that moves toward a sectarian understanding of the term which was a precursor to view two described above.[23] He understands the reason for the Pharisees' murmuring against Jesus' receiving "tax collectors and sinners" to be Jesus' communion with people that *they* regarded as "sinners" and with whom, even though they repented, would not associate. He cites Jewish sources for support.[24]

---

18. Ibid., 2:401.
19. Trollope, *Analecta Theologica*, 2:112.
20. Ibid.
21. Ibid., II:86.
22. Ibid., I:509.
23. See the discussion on page xi above.
24. Trollope, *Analecta*, I: 548–49.

A change in the identification from actual "sinners" to the common people who failed to keep the ceremonial laws of the rabbis, seems to begin with this growing use of Jewish sources. In our research the earliest actual equating of these two seems to be by John Owen in his commentary in 1864.[25] Commenting on the expression "publicans and sinners" Owen states, "Under this expression were included all those who fell below the Pharisaic observance of the law. The publicans and common people were regarded as great 'sinners,' to eat with whom would be moral contamination."[26] In a survey of other nineteenth century commentaries, most continued to identify the "sinners" as the truly wicked, although often connecting them to the kind of people associated with "tax collectors" in rabbinic literature. For example, Heinrich A. W. Meyer describes the ἁμαρτωλοί as "in general men of immoral stamp, with whom were classed the publicans as being servants of the Roman government, and guilty of fraudulent conduct (Luke 3:13; 19:7)."[27] In his commentary on John, Meyer identifies the "common people" of John 7:49 as the 'am ha-'areṣ but did not equate them with the "sinner."[28]

Of special significance in our discussion is the commentary of Strack and Billerbeck. The Pharisees state, as recorded in John 7:49, "These common people who know not the Law are accursed." In a footnote to this verse, Strack and Billerbeck list a host of references to Jewish sources regarding the 'am ha-'areṣ.[29] In their commentary on Matthew 9:11, in a discussion of the Pharisees' complaint against Jesus' association with "sinners" in Matthew 9:9–13, Strack and Billerbeck cite rabbinic passages that speak of avoiding meal fellowship with 'am ha-'areṣ.[30] Consequently, the Pharisees are viewed as complaining over Jesus' association with "sinners"

---

25. Owen, *A Commentary*, 95.

26. Ibid.

27. Meyer, *Critical and Exegetical Handbook to the Gospel of Matthew*, 197.

28. Meyer, *Critical and Exegetical Handbook to the Gospel of John*, 252.

29. Strack and Billerbeck, *Das Evangelium*, 494–519. The important sources for this discussion will be treated in the examination of rabbinic sources below. The primary text linking the 'am ha-'areṣ with uncleanness at meals is *m. Demai* 2:2–3. The central text linking the Pharisees to the belief that the 'am ha-'areṣ were considered to be ritually unclean is *m. Hag.* 2:7.

30. Ibid., 498–99.

on the same legalistic ritual grounds as their hostility toward the common people. So in Strack and Billerbeck's commentary, the "sinner" is viewed as a virtual synonym for the common people, the *'am ha-'areṣ*. This view, described as view one above, became widely accepted, even in some Jewish circles. For example, Isaac Landman accepted the Pharisees' harsh attitude toward the *'am ha-'areṣ* as the basis for Jesus' wide appeal to the masses.[31] Strack and Billerbeck's equating of the "sinner" with the common people influenced Joachim Jeremias who is especially associated with this view as we will discuss more fully below.[32]

In summary, the "sinner" in seventeenth century discussion continued to be understood as a wicked person but the discussion began to increasingly focus on Jewish rabbinic sources. By the middle of the nineteenth century, the "sinner" began to be viewed by some authors as a Pharisaic designation for the common people who failed to fulfill the Pharisees' legalistic regulations, thus establishing views one and two as alternative definitions of the "sinner" as simply the truly wicked.

Israel Abrahams's View

The first important study of the "sinner" in the Gospels came from Israel Abrahams in his article "Publicans and Sinners" published in 1917.[33] The article is a supplement to C. G. Montefiore's commentary, *The Synoptic Gospels*.[34] Abrahams begins the discussion by demonstrating from rabbinic sources a link between toll collectors and other blatantly immoral types: murderers, robbers, and extortionists (*m. Ned.* 3:4 / *b. Ned.* 28a; *b. B. Qam.* 113a). The tax collectors were disqualified to act as judges or witnesses

---

31. Landman, "Am Ha-Aretz," 217.

32. For example, in *Jerusalem in the Times of Jesus* (266) Jeremias states, ". . . as the true Israel they (the Pharisees) drew a hard line between themselves and the masses, the 'amme ha 'ares, who did not observe as they did the rules laid down by Pharisaic scribes on tithes and purity." His footnote to this comment refers to John 7:49, Luke 18:9–14, and Strack and Billerbeck's discussion of the *'am ha-'areṣ* (266, n.71). Luke 18:9–14 is Jesus' parable of the publican and the Pharisee in which the publican is the "sinner." Jeremias clearly linked the "sinner" and the *'am ha-'areṣ* in this reference, possibly because of the influence of Strack and Billerbeck.

33. Abrahams, *Studies in Pharisaism and the Gospels*, 1:54–61.

34. Montefiore, *The Synoptic Gospels*.

A Survey of the History of Interpretation of the "Sinner" in Luke

(*b. Sanh.* 25b). Abrahams observes the parallel between this linking of "tax-collectors and robbers" with the Synoptics' expression "tax-collectors and sinners." This is the basis for his identification of the "sinner" as "not those who neglected the rules of ritual piety, but were persons of immoral life, men of dishonesty or followers of suspected and degrading occupations."[35]

According to Abrahams, rabbis avoided association with this group because of the biblical prohibitions against associating with the wicked, not because they failed to live up to the requirements of the Pharisees. Such association was especially to be avoided during meals because mealtimes for Pharisees were services consecrated by benedictions.[36] Abrahams cites *m. Abot* 3:3 to show that Pharisees viewed themselves to be in the presence of God during a meal. This Mishna states that if three have eaten at one table and spoken the words of the Law, it is as if "they had eaten from the table of God."[37] The meal table was considered an altar. He argues that this sense of worship and discussion focused around the Torah at meals was the basis for the Pharisees avoidance of notorious "evil livers." He cites the example of the table discourse of Jesus to his disciples and the later restriction of the Lord's Supper as parallels. The Pharisees simply sought to prevent the meal from turning into a party.[38] Abrahams argues that Pharisees would not have refused "sinners" from dining at the Pharisee's own table for this would have allowed the Pharisee to control the atmosphere.

For Abrahams, the "sinner" is not the *'am ha-'areṣ*. Reluctance to eat with the *'am ha-'areṣ* was based not on a fear of evil example but on a fear of neglected tithes. Avoiding Gentiles, the "heathen," was based on a fear of mixed marriage.[39]

Abrahams's central point was that the Pharisees avoided contact with notorious "sinners" because of a fear of moral lapse (*b. Pesaḥ.* 113a; *m. 'Abot* 1:8; *b. Yoma* 69b) and because they sought to avoid the loss of their reputation by suspicion through such an association. The fear of moral lapse is illustrated by *b. Yoma* 69b where Ezra the scribe was excused for pronouncing

---

35. Abrahams, *Studies in Pharisaism and the Gospels*, 1:55.
36. Ibid.
37. Danby, *The Mishnah*, 450.
38. Abrahams, *Studies in Pharisaism and the Gospels*, 1:56.
39. Ibid.

The Sinner in Luke

the Ineffable Name because he was crying out to warn of the "evil desire" that had destroyed the Sanctuary, burnt the Temple, killed all the righteous, driven all Israel into exile, and was still dancing among them. This fear of moral lapse was the justification for avoiding certain occupations that were prone to dishonesty or immorality.[40] For Abrahams the Pharisees were not prideful, they were fearful. Pharisees held a high view of the repentant "sinner" (*b. Ber.* 34b), but viewed it as virtually impossible for them to repent. The Pharisees viewed repentance in terms of giving up the sin and making restitution to the injured parties. Thus, the tax collector would have great difficulty carrying out this requirement (*b. B. Qam.* 94b).

For Abrahams, the difference between the Pharisees' and Jesus' attitude toward "sinners" was Jesus' act of taking the initiative.[41] The Pharisees took a preventive approach, attacking vice by avoiding it. Jesus approached it from the curative side, aiming to save the dishonest and the unchaste.[42]

Abrahams concludes by giving examples of rabbinic literature that actually urged men to actively seek the lost (*Midr.* Ex. 2:1–2). Abrahams speaks of Rabbi Aaron who was lauded for rescuing "sinners" (*m. Abot* 1:12). His point is that the Pharisees would not have opposed Jesus' mission to reform "sinners." It was the association, especially during meals, that violated the Pharisees' understanding of biblical warnings against evil associations.[43]

Abrahams's research is important because of his use of rabbinic sources to clarify the difference between the "sinner" and the *'am ha-'areṣ* and the basis for Pharisaic aversion to each. Aversion to eating with "sinners" was based on different concerns than eating with the *'am ha-'areṣ*. As we will demonstrate in our discussion of Luke 5:27–32, Abrahams's point is accurate and important for understanding the identity of the "sinner." He also provides insight into one aspect of difference between Jesus and the rabbis. The rabbis took a preventive approach to holiness but Jesus took a curative approach in his mission.

---

40. Abrahams, *Studies in Pharisaism and the Gospels*, 1:157.
41. Ibid., 1:58.
42. Ibid., 1:59.
43. Abrahams, *Studies in Pharisaism and the Gospels*, 1:59.

George W. Buchanan makes several criticisms of Abrahams's view.[44] He describes Abrahams's purpose as defending the portrait of the Pharisees from the negative picture presented in the Synoptics. Because this was Abrahams's purpose, Buchanan charges him with being less than objective. For example, Abrahams quotes Josephus to prove that the Pharisees were moderate in dispensing punishment, but chooses not to mention Josephus' description of the Pharisees' behavior during the time of Alexandra (76 BCE). Buchanan also criticizes Abrahams's non-critical use of rabbinic sources. Abrahams uses certain favorable descriptions of the rabbis to prove that the Pharisees lived at peace with their neighbors, but never mentions the Pharisaic messianic movements involved in assisting the overthrow of Rome. He assumes without evidence that "favorable" portions of rabbinic literature, Philo, and Maimonides represented Pharisaism without acknowledging that much of the literature was written hundreds of years after the time of Jesus and may not accurately describe the Pharisees of Jesus' day. For Buchanan, it is even more difficult to use rabbinic literature to argue that the picture of the Pharisees in the Gospels is false since the most basic sources for understanding first century Pharisaism are those composed by first century authors, the writings of Josephus, the Gospels, Pauline letters, and secondarily the Acts of the Apostles. Buchanan notes, however tendentious they are, these were written by those who lived near in time and place to the Pharisees and described them in specific terms.[45]

Joachim Jeremias's View

Joachim Jeremias presents a definition of the "sinner" in many ways identical to Abrahams. In his book, *Jerusalem zur Zeit Jesu,* published in 1923, like Abrahams, Jeremias links the "sinner" to the kinds of people connected to the toll-collector in rabbinic literature.[46] Jeremias describes these people as immoral or people involved in occupations that were suspected of dishonesty or immorality. In a highly influential article published in 1931,

---

44. Buchanan, review of *Studies in Pharisaism and the Gospels*, 415–16.

45. Ibid. In addition to Abrahams's uncritical use of rabbinic sources, Perrin pointed out the lack of use of apocalyptic or pseudepigraphic literature (Perrin, review of *Studies in Pharisaism and the Gospels* by I. Abrahams, 118–19).

46. Jeremias, *Jerusalem in the Time of Jesus*, 303–12.

The Sinner in Luke

Jeremias treats the identity of the "sinner" in more detail.[47] He observes that exegesis alternates between two understandings of the term "sinner," and that these two definitions depend on whether one sees the "sinner" in the eyes of the Pharisee or in the eyes of the common people.[48] He states that from the perspective of the Pharisee, all non-Pharisees, the *'am ha-'areṣ*, would be designated "sinners" because of their failure to fulfill the Pharisees' demands for purity and tithing. Jeremias argues, however, that one cannot understand the Synoptic "sinner" in this broad sense of *'am ha-'areṣ* because in the expression "tax collector and sinner," the concept of "sinner" is essentially narrow and concretely set as seen in Luke 19:7 in reference to Zachaeus, and in Luke 7:35–39 in reference to the "sinful woman." Jeremias states that these passages cannot possibly permit ἁμαρτωλός to be translated "non-Pharisee." He observes that in these passages, the designation of "sinner" comes not from the Pharisees based on the violation of purity rules, but by the people themselves. He argued that the term "sinner" in the expression "tax collector and sinner" must therefore be a term that is common in the mind of the people.[49] He supports this by citing the fact that the expression "tax collector and sinner" has only one article in Mark 2:16b, Matthew 9:11b, and Luke 5:30b, thereby combining "tax collector and sinners" into a single category. Like Abrahams, he compares this expression to other rabbinic passages that linked tax collectors with thieves, robbers, harlots and others.[50] Through this analogy, Jeremias concludes that the term "sinner" refers to people of ill repute, either through their immoral lifestyle or those who, in the public's opinion, were a part of a dishonorable trade.

Abrahams and Jeremias start a trend in understanding the "sinner" based on the link of the "sinner" to the "toll collector" in the NT and the rabbinic material. Jeremias introduces the idea of viewing the "sinner" from more than the perspective of the Pharisees. He repeats this description of the "sinner" in his book *The Parables of Jesus*.[51] He explains that the Pharisees complained against Jesus' association with these individuals

---

47. Jeremias, "'Zöllner und Sünder,'" 293–300.
48. Ibid., 293.
49. Ibid.
50. Ibid., 294–95.
51. Jeremias, *The Parables of Jesus*, 132.

because this action revealed that Jesus himself was an irreligious man whom his followers should avoid. Jeremias's concept of seeing the "sinner" from a double perspective is expanded in his *New Testament Theology*.[52] At one level, Jeremias continues his description of the "sinner" as those occupied in despised trades or those whose lives were disreputable.[53] Yet in contrast to his earlier position in "Zöllner und Sünder," in which he states that the "sinner" is to be viewed from the perspective of the common person, here he emphasizes that it was Jesus' opponents who placed this label on the followers of Jesus.[54] Other labels of contempt include "the little ones" and the "simple ones" emphasizing Jesus' followers as religiously uneducated, backward, and irreligious. Jeremias then summarizes with this statement:

> We can now say that Jesus' following consisted predominantly of the disreputable, the *'am ha 'aretz*, the uneducated, the ignorant, whose *religious* ignorance and *moral* behavior stood in the way of their access to salvation, according to the convictions of the time.[55]

Here Jeremias seems to lump the religiously ignorant, the *'am ha-'areṣ* into the same group as the flagrantly immoral. The "sinners" and the *'am ha-'areṣ* appear to be synonyms. This equation is made again in the next paragraph when Jeremias discusses the second perspective on the "sinner." He states that the same group described in contemptuous terms by Jesus opponents is described by Jesus himself as the poor, the hungry, those who weep, the sick, the simple, the lost, and the "sinners."[56]

Therefore, Jeremias defines the "sinner" in two ways. From the point of view of the people, the "sinner" is a person who was known to be immoral or anyone involved in a despised trade. From the viewpoint of the Pharisee, the "sinner" includes the *'am ha-'areṣ*, the common people. Unfortunately, Jeremias fails to clarify what he means by both, allowing himself to be associated with two different definitions of "sinner." For example, his concept of the "sinner" as the truly wicked or a person of a despised trade has influenced many commentators. I. H. Marshall refers to Jeremias for this

52. Jeremias, *New Testament Theology*, 108–21.
53. Ibid., 110.
54. Ibid., 109. Compare with Jeremias, "'Zöllner und Sünder,'" 294.
55. Ibid., 112.
56. Ibid., 112–13.

point.[57] However, Jeremias's linking of "sinners" to the masses, the *'am ha-'areṣ*, became a strongly popular position. Ellis in his commentary on Luke defines the "sinner" as "the Pharisees' term for people who did not keep the ceremonial regulations laid down by the rabbis."[58]

Jeremias has been criticized for his lack of analysis of his sources, especially since he was so familiar with the importance of source criticism in Synoptic studies. Jacob Neusner sharply criticizes him for taking everything the Pharisees said about themselves as objective history and combining this with rabbinic comments as late as the twelfth and thirteenth century to form a "historical" picture of first century Judaism.[59]

The most outspoken critic of Jeremias has been E. P. Sanders.[60] Sanders has little objection to Jeremias's first definition of the "sinner" as it is linked to the "tax collector." Although he criticizes Jeremias's lack of analysis of late rabbinic exaggerations, Sanders accepts the "toll collector and sinner" point as it relates to the immoral and despised trades.[61] However, Sanders attacks Jeremias's position that Jesus' opponents could call his followers either "sinners" or *'am ha-'areṣ* with no distinction in meaning.[62] Ben Meyer defends Jeremias against Sanders's criticism, arguing that Jeremias held only one view of the "sinner" as the immoral and those involved in despised trades.[63] Meyer states that Jeremias clearly identified the "sinner" as not the *'am ha-'areṣ* in many places.[64] Even though Meyer is correct in stating that Sanders presents only part of Jeremias's position, Meyer fails to acknowledge Jeremias's statements that merged the categories together.[65]

57. Marshall, *Commentary on Luke*, 219.
58. Ellis, *The Gospel of Luke*, 107.
59. Neusner, review of *Jerusalem at the Time of Jesus*, 201–2.
60. Sanders, *Jesus and Judaism*, 176.
61. Ibid., 178.
62. Ibid., 176.
63. Meyer, "A Caricature," 451–62.

64. Ibid., 458. Meyer includes the following as examples: "'Zöllner und Sünder,'" 293; *The Parables of Jesus*, 132; *Jerusalem in the Time of Jesus*, 303–12; and *New Testament Theology*, 109.

65. Sanders acknowledged Jeremias's distinction in a footnote but his discussion dealt almost exclusively with Jeremias's equation of "sinners" with the *'am ha-'areṣ* (*Jesus and Judaism*, 385, n.14). Against Meyer, we have already noted Jeremias's two definitions in the previous discussion.

It is not too much to say that Jeremias has been the most influential writer on the topic of the "sinner." Much of subsequent research in the last thirty years has used him as a starting point.

The Development of Views Since Jeremias

Since Jeremias, there have been essentially three lines of development in the "sinner" discussion. One interpretation builds upon Jeremias by a closer examination of the link of the term "sinner" to the "tax collector." Norman Perrin, John Donahue, and William Farmer represent this line of interpretation. Norman Perrin argues for three groups of "sinners."[66] The first group consists of Jews who sinned but could find forgiveness from God as Father.[67] The second group consists of Gentile "sinners" for whom hope was doubtful, because most Jews regarded them beyond the hope of God's mercy.[68] The third group consists of those Jews who made themselves as Gentiles and as a result were also virtually beyond hope; this is view four introduced in chapter one of our study. In this last category Perrin builds upon Jeremias's list of despised occupations, arguing that these occupations were despised not because of dishonesty or immorality, but because dice players, usurers, and tax collectors were considered "Gentile sinners" in the eyes of their fellow Jews.[69] Toll collectors and revenue farmers were especially hated as "quislings" or traitors because they collected taxes from their fellow Jews on behalf of hated Gentiles. He cites *m. Tehar.* 7:6 as of special importance because it states that the tax collector defiles everything within a house by entering it, as does the Gentile. He also notes the link in the Synoptics between the tax collector and "sinner" (Mark 2:15) and the tax collector and Gentile (Matt 18:17).[70] Thus, these Jewish "sinners" had become like "Gentiles" because they had renounced the covenant by their lifestyle.

66. Perrin, *Rediscovering*, 94.

67. Ibid., 91–92. Perrin cites as evidence a parable by Rabbi Meir in *Deut. Rab.* 2:24 that is similar to the Prodigal Son story given by Jesus. The Lord God as Father will accept his repentant son. He also cites *1 En.* 5:6 that promises forgiveness of sins to Jewish sinners.

68. Ibid., 94. Perrin cites *1 En.* 5:6b: "And for all you sinners there shall be no salvation, but on you shall abide a curse." The first half of this same verse promises forgiveness for Jewish "sinners."

69. Perrin, *Rediscovering*, 93.

70. Ibid., 94.

The Sinner in Luke

William Farmer also holds that the key to understanding the "sinner" was consideration of the identity of the tax collectors in the expression "tax collectors and sinners."[71] His position is similar to Perrin's but with several clarifications. In an article first given as a lecture in 1958, Farmer identifies the "tax collectors" and "sinners" in the expression "tax collectors and sinners" not as two groups but one. The term "tax collector" classifies the group according to its social, economic, and political status. The term "sinner" classifies the same group according to its religious status within the Jewish community.[72] For support, Farmer cites the linking of the expressions in Luke 18:13, where the tax collector identified himself as a "sinner," and Luke 19:7 in which the chief tax collector, Zacchaeus, was identified by the community as a "sinner." Farmer cites the positive description of John the tax collector in Josephus to argue that the tax collector was clearly not an irreligious social outcast (*J. W.* 2.14.4–5).[73] Farmer argues that the social and economic position of tax collectors brought them into regular contact with Gentiles, which inevitably led to laxity with regard to the observance of the Mosaic laws, especially the dietary cleanliness laws as strictly interpreted by the Pharisees. In this way they became transgressors of the laws or "sinners."[74] "Sinners" were Jews that lived in regular association with Gentiles and were less scrupulous with obedience to the law of Moses than the Pharisees, but they were not irreligious social outcasts. Farmer allows that this may include the *'am ha-'areṣ*.[75]

The weakness in the views of both Perrin and Farmer is that Luke presents the negative image of tax collectors to be rooted in their dishonesty and corruption (Luke 3:12–14).[76] The positive example of John in Josephus (*J. W.* 2.14.4–5) does not negate the fact that "toll collectors" were generally viewed with scorn and suspicion (cf., *m. Ned.* 3:4). As we will point out more fully in later discussion, the tax collector is vilified in the Synoptics

71. Farmer, "Who are the 'Tax Collectors and Sinners' in the Synoptic Tradition?," 67–74.
72. Ibid., 167.
73. Ibid., 168.
74. Ibid.
75. Ibid., 174 n.11.
76. See the full treatment of the "toll collector and sinner" in the discussion of Luke 5:27–32 below **121–24**.

A Survey of the History of Interpretation of the "Sinner" in Luke

on moral rather than political or ethnic grounds (cf., Matt 21:32, "tax collectors and prostitutes").[77]

John Donahue addresses the differences between Jeremias ("sinners" are the immoral and those in despised trades) and Perrin ("sinners" are Jews who made themselves as Gentiles) by reexamining the rabbinic material on tax collectors.[78] Donahue observes an important distinction regarding the tax system current in Israel at the time of Jesus. He notes that the tax system differed in Galilee and Judea. Tax collection in Galilee was under Herod Antipas's direct control and the Romans were not involved. In Judea, however, Roman officials were in charge of collecting all taxes, even though they often employed Jews for the activity. Donahue supports this point regarding the difference in Galilean and Judean taxation by citing the corresponding difference in Rabbinic attitudes toward the מוֹכְסִין= τελώνης and the גַּבַּאי. The person who was a גַּבַּאי collected the direct taxes in association with the Roman authorities. This is important because Perrin's position that the term "sinner" refers to a Jew who made himself as a Gentile rests upon his use of *m. Ṭehar.* 7:6 which states the following:

> If tax gatherers (גַּבָּאִי) entered a house [all that is within it] becomes unclean; even if a Gentile was with them they may be believed if they say ("We did not enter," but they may not be believed if they say) "We entered but touched naught." If thieves entered a house, only that part is unclean that was trodden by the feet of the thieves.

From the close connection between tax collectors here and in Matthew 18:17, Perrin asserts, "We are entitled to claim that the 'tax collectors and sinners' frequently found in the New Testament may be understood as 'tax collectors and other Jews who made themselves as Gentiles.'"[79] Perrin mistakenly equates the גַּבַּאי of the Mishna with the τελώνης of the Synoptics. Yet throughout the rabbinic literature, toll collectors (מוֹכְסִין=

---

77. Gibson, "Hoi Telōnai kai hai Pornai," 429–33, makes a case that prostitutes and tax collectors are linked primarily because they are both prime examples of collaboration with Roman forces. Kathleen E. Corley, "Jesus' Table Practice," 444–59, argues that the "sinners" associated with tax collectors are women who are viewed as prostitutes because the terms were commonly associated. She suggests that the women were not actual prostitutes but the label functioned as traditional slander by Jesus' opponents (447–48).

78. Donahue, "Tax Collectors and Sinners," 39–61.

79. Perrin, *Rediscovering*, 94.

τελώνης) are consistently despised for their dishonesty rather than for their association with Gentiles.[80] Donahue's research supports Jeremias's position regarding the moral basis for Jewish antipathy toward toll collectors. But Donahue acknowledges that in the area of Judea, concern for Gentile association may have been more at issue.[81]

E. P. Sanders's View

The second line of interpretation in "sinner" research since Jeremias is represented by E. P. Sanders.[82] Sanders attacks the position often associated with Jeremias that the "sinners" in the Synoptics were the common people, the *'am ha-'areṣ*. Along with this, he challenged two views commonly associated with this position: (1) what made Jesus unique was his offer of forgiveness to repentant "sinners," the common people, whom the Pharisees had excluded from any hope of salvation; and (2) the cause for the Pharisees' hostility toward Jesus was that he ate with the common people whom the Pharieess' viewed as unclean.[83] Sanders begins by linking his understanding of the term "sinner" to the Greek term ἁμαρτωλός as it is used in a wider range of material, connecting it especially to the Old Testament term רָשָׁע. As a result, he concludes that the "sinner" in the Gospels is not the *'am ha-'areṣ* as understood by Jeremias, but notorious "sinners," the "wicked." This is based on the understanding of רָשָׁע as virtually a technical term which means "a person who sins willfully and heinously and will not repent."[84] From this, Sanders seeks to show, along the lines of Abrahams's study, that the Pharisees' opposition to Jesus' association with "sinners" was not based on ritual grounds like hand washing. But unlike Abrahams, who understood the Pharisaic opposition to be based on biblical admonitions against association with the immoral, Sanders argues that the Pharisees opposed Jesus' offer of forgiveness apart from the kind of repentance demanded by the law.

---

80. Examples include *m. Ned.* 3:4 and *m. B. Qam.* 10:2 which are discussed on pages 121–24 below.
81. Donahue, "Tax Collectors and Sinners," 60.
82. Sanders, *Jesus and Judaism*, 174–211.
83. Ibid., 176.
84. Ibid., 177.

A Survey of the History of Interpretation of the "Sinner" in Luke

Sanders also challenges the basic portrait of the Pharisees in the Synoptics. He argues that the picture of the Pharisees policing Galilee to scrutinize a basically righteous man (Jesus) was obviously unrealistic.[85] He also argues that the Pharisees were not large enough or powerful enough to make anyone, much less the "common people," feel excluded. Lastly, he argues that the Pharisees did not view the *'am ha-'areṣ* as "sinners." The *'am ha-'areṣ* according to Sanders were viewed by the strictest of the Pharisees, the initiated *haber*, as simply ignorant and boorish, ritually unclean but not wicked "sinners." The difference is that ritual concerns could be dealt with through ritual means like hand washing or bathing. The ritually unclean person was excluded only from Temple worship, not from salvation. The "sinner" in the Synoptics was the truly "wicked." For Sanders, Jesus' offense in the eyes of the Pharisees was that he promised forgiveness to genuine "sinners" while they were still "sinners" without demanding repentance in the way the Hebrew Scriptures and the rabbis commonly understood it, namely, making sacrifice, restitution, and committing oneself to the law.[86] He states that the evidence of Jesus' preaching or demanding repentance is scant, and that the reform of the "wicked" was Luke's emphasis, not Jesus'.[87] He explains the uniqueness of Jesus and the cause of Pharisaic opposition this way:

> The novelty and offence of Jesus' message was that the wicked who heeded him would be included in the kingdom even though they did not repent as it was universally understood, that is, even though they did not make restitution, sacrifice, and turn to obedience to the law. Jesus offered companionship to the wicked of Israel as a sign that God would save them, and he did not make his association dependent upon their conversion to the law. He may have thought that they had no time to create new lives for themselves, but that if they accepted his message they would be saved. If Jesus added to this such statements as that the tax collectors and prostitutes would enter the kingdom before the righteous (Matt 21:31), the offence would be increased. The implied self-claim, to know whom God would include and not, and the equally implied downgrading of the normal

---

85. Sanders, *Jesus and Judaism*, 178.
86. Ibid., 203, 221.
87. Ibid., 206.

The Sinner in Luke

machinery of righteousness, would push Jesus close to, or over, the border which separates individual charisma from impiety.[88]

Sanders's position that the "sinner" was the truly wicked, is based upon the equating of ἁμαρτωλός with רָשָׁע. Dunn criticizes Sanders for omitting the factional use of the term "sinner" in intertestamental Jewish literature.[89] Bruce Chilton argues that Sanders's use of the LXX is incomplete and misleading. Chilton also argues that Sanders neglects Aramaic influence on the "sinner" concept, as demonstrated by the Synoptic concept of a "sinner" as a "debtor" (e.g., Luke 7:36–50).[90] Our examination of Sanders's use of the term "sinner" will follow below in chapter 3. The evidence will give support to his basic position but will show that the term is more flexible than Sanders suggests.

Sanders has also been criticized for rejecting evidence from the New Testament and Josephus regarding the Pharisees of Jesus' day.[91] Dunn criticizes Sanders for omitting the New Testament, especially since Paul's and Josephus's pictures of the Pharisees are consistent, and Paul wrote as a former Pharisee in writings recognized as early.[92] Chilton criticizes Sanders's view of Jesus and repentance. He correctly observes that Sanders simply discounts too much material and then makes too much out of the difference between individual and collective calls for repentance. Chilton notes that Jesus' use of the lost sheep parable in Luke 15:4–7 involves God as shepherd and Israel as the flock, consistent with the Old Testament metaphor (see especially Ezekiel).[93]

Chilton points out a deficiency in Sanders's lexical research but seems to make the same mistake. Chilton argues that the Aramaic term "debtor" (*hwb'*) revealed the same broad range of meaning demonstrated by ἁμαρτωλός and is therefore the most likely background for the term

88. Sanders, *Jesus and Judaism*, 207–8.
89. Dunn, "Pharisees, Sinners, and Jesus," 264–89.
90. Chilton, "Jesus," 1–18.
91. For example, Paul's self-description of himself as a Pharisee in Philippians 3:5, 6 emphasized his zeal for the Law of Moses. Paul's evidence was his persecution of the "Church."
92. Dunn, 269–70. Also, Martin Hengel and Roland Deines, "E. P. Sanders' 'Common Judaism,'" 1–70.
93. Chilton, "Jesus," 2, 4.

"sinner" in the Synoptics. He cites examples from *Targum Isaiah* (11:4; 14:4, 5; 34:2; and 54:17). Chilton is helpful in emphasizing the need for broader lexical work on the term "sinner" but fails to give sufficient weight to the role of the LXX and the Old Testament upon Luke's narrative and the influence this has on his concept of the "sinner." As Sanders suggests, Luke does use the term for people who can be classified "sinners" on moral grounds (Luke 7:36–50, the "sinful woman"; 15:13, 30, the prodigal son; and 19:1–10, Zacchaeus). Chilton helps broaden the category of "sinner" from being viewed as a technical term with only one meaning, but fails to give enough weight to the Old Testament and other Jewish literature.

Social Science and Literary Definitions of the "Sinner"

The third line of interpretation in "sinner" research since Jeremias is the move away from dependence upon a definition of the "historical sinner" and a move toward a social science or literary approach to understanding the "sinner" in the Gospels. Those who classify the "sinners" as a category of the "poor," seeing "sinners" primarily in their role as social outcasts, represent the sociological approach. This approach is represented by Walter Pilgrim.

David Neale reflects the literary approach in a recent monograph.[94] Neale argues that a historical approach to the identification of the "sinner" is misguided. The wide range of attempted definitions of the term "sinner" convinces Neale that the key to understanding the "sinner" in Luke is not history but ideology. The "sinner" is an ideological perspective of the writer, not a historically identifiable social group.[95] Neale's emphasis appears to be that the "sinner" is not a real, factual person but an idea in the mind of the person using the term.[96] He uses an analysis of the term ἁμαρτωλός to support this conclusion.

We will interact with Neale throughout our treatment of the "sinner" theme. A question raised by his approach is what understanding of the "sinner" does Luke assume on the part of his reader? If for Luke the "sinner" has only an ideological function, some conceptual background must exist

---

94. Neale, *None But the Sinners*, 14.
95. Ibid., 15.
96. Ibid.

The Sinner in Luke

for the term in order for it to serve his purpose. We will attempt to demonstrate that Neale neglects and understates the weight of certain data.

Conclusion

The question of the historical "sinner" in the Synoptics remains a matter of debate. The definition of the "sinner" directly affects the understanding of the basis of Pharisaic opposition to Jesus' association with this group and the true nature of Jesus' mission in the Gospel of Luke.

This survey of the research on this topic has revealed several weaknesses. Abrahams treats only rabbinic literature and Philo. Jeremias is uncritical in his use of rabbinic sources and ties his research almost exclusively to the "sinner" as understood by its association with toll collectors. He does not treat the use of ἁμαρτωλός in the LXX, or its primary Hebrew equivalent term רָשָׁע. Perrin, Donahue, and Farmer make this same mistake. E. P. Sanders attempts to place the understanding of the "sinner" on a stronger footing by actually examining the term "sinner" as it is used in the OT and other Jewish literature. As we will try to show, his weakness is that he fails to acknowledge the wide range of meanings of the term. Dunn seeks to correct this deficiency in Sanders by showing that Jews can label other Jews "sinners" who from their point of view act in such a way as to exclude them from their understanding of being "righteous." Dunn is very helpful in his critique of Sanders's use of sources, but fails to utilize the Synoptic narrative sufficiently to shape his understanding of the "sinner."[97] Neale, on the other hand, neglects some Old Testament evidence and understates the weight of evidence that challenges his analysis.

To resolve this question, one must examine the term ἁμαρτωλός and its related terms in a wide range of literature (e.g., Greco-Roman, Septuagint, intertestamental and rabbinic Jewish literature, and the New Testament). This research will establish the semantic categories for the term "sinner." The semantic and historical background will then be tested against Luke's own use of the term. Our approach is to combine historical and literary approaches in our examination of the "sinner" in Luke.

---

97. Dunn, *Pharisees, Sinners, and Jesus*, 282.

2

Hellenistic and Jewish Concepts of the "Sinner"

❋ AN APPROPRIATE starting point for a correct definition of the "sinner" in Luke is to establish the basic parameters of the term in the literature that may have influenced Luke's usage. This chapter will survey the use of the term "sinner" in Hellenistic and Jewish literature, as well as in some early rabbinic literature, up to the period in which Luke wrote his Gospel and the book of Acts.

Hellenistic Background of the Term

The adjective ἁμαρτωλός is formed from the verb ἁμαρτάνω and contains the basic idea of "failure." The verb is used this way in a concrete sense in the *Iliad* of a spear "failing" or "missing" its target (5.287). The adjective ἁμαρτωλός is rarely used in classical Greek. Liddell and Scott list the meaning "that which is erroneous or erring."[1] In speaking of the ethic of hitting the mean between vice and virtue, Aristotle states that of the two extremes, vice is a "more serious error" (ἁμαρτωλότερον, *Eth. nic.* 2.1109a33). For Plutarch, the "erring" is the intellectual failure of the ignorant person who "always misses the mark (ἁμαρτωλόν) in everything" (*Mor.* 25c).

The term ἁμαρτωλός also referred to moral failings and bad character. Aristophanes used ἁμάρτωλη as a description of a main character in his play, a deceiver dressed as a woman: "This is not a girl but an old (γέρων) 'sinner' (ἁμάρτωλη) and thief (κλέπτος) and huckster (πανοῦργος)" (*Thesm.* 1111f).

1. LSJ, 77.

Karl Rengstorf concluded that whenever ἁμαρτωλός is used in classical Greek, the element of failure is the basis of the meaning.[2] The ἁμαρτωλός is the characterization of a man who is the very opposite of everything that is right and proper.[3] Günther agrees that the original sense of this word group in classical Greek is "to miss the mark or failure."[4] He states that from the fifth century BCE the adjective ἁμαρτωλός and the noun referred to that thing or person who failed.[5] Aristotle described the noun ἁμάρτημα as an offence against the prevailing order (*Eth. nic.* 5.8.1135b18). It was used in the legal language of deliberate offenses.[6] The noun ἁμαρτία can mean anything from stupidity to law-breaking, anything that offends against the ὀρθόν, the right, that does not conform to the dominant ethic.[7] Günther observes that as in the Old Testament, ἁμαρτωλός and ἀσεβής can stand side by side in Plato.[8]

The term ἁμαρτωλός does not always fit into the category of "failure." It is used commonly in grave inscriptions as a warning against anyone who would disturb the tomb. For example: "May he [the one who disturbs the grave] be a 'sinner' (ἁμαρτωλός) before all the gods and Leto and her children" (*CIG* 4259 [Pinara, Lycia]). This inscription shows that the guilty party would be recognized as such by both the gods and men. The ἁμαρτωλός would incur the wrath of both, through a fine from man and through an unspecified action of the gods. The term is also used in contexts that relate specifically to the gods: "If the rulers and leaders do not fulfill the annual sacrifices (θυσίαν), let them be "sinners" (ἁμαρτωλοί) against all gods" (*OGIS* 55:30). Richard Lattimore states that these curses were not limited to tombs but were borrowed from the curse-formula attached to oaths of allegiance and treaties.[9] In the tomb inscriptions we see

---

2. Rengstorf, "ἁμαρτωλός," 319.
3. Ibid., 320.
4. Günther, "Sin," 3:577.
5. Ibid.
6. Ibid.
7. Ibid.
8. Ibid.
9. Lattimore, *Themes*, 108.

Helenistic and Jewish Concepts of the "Sinner"

ἁμαρτωλός refer to someone that could be an object of the scorn of men and the wrath of the gods.

To summarize, the Hellenistic background of the term ἁμαρτωλός emphasizes the ideas of failure and error. The error is sometimes intellectual but often ethical or moral failure. The standard against which the failure is judged is the dominant ethic of the time. Some behavior such as grave robbing appears to be widely recognized as a specific offense for which the designation "sinner" would be made. The term sometimes describes one who by certain behaviors is worthy of scorn by other men and under the wrath of the gods.

The Old Testament Concept of the "Sinner"

The ultimate aim of our study is to understand the concept of the ἁμαρτωλός in Luke. Since the LXX has greatly influenced the Gospel of Luke, our next step is to examine the Old Testament background of the term and its use in the Septuagint.[10] The "sinner" concept will then be examined as it develops through the intertestamental and early rabbinic literature.

The term ἁμαρτωλός is used in the LXX 90 times to translate the following Hebrew terms: רָשָׁע (evil one) 74 times=82%; חָטָא ("sinner", failure) 13 times=14%; and חָנֵף, חָרָשׁ, and רַע once each respectively.[11] From this analysis it is clear that the key Hebrew terms for the "sinner" are רָשָׁע and חָטָא.

The "Sinner" as רָשָׁע

Our understanding of the "sinner" broadens through an examination of both of these Hebrew terms and the Greek terms used to translate them by the LXX. We begin with the key term רָשָׁע. Brown, Driver, and Briggs translate רָשָׁע as "wicked, criminal" and list three basic uses as a noun for someone (1) guilty of a crime, deserving punishment, (2) guilty of hostility to God or his people, or (3) guilty of sin against God or man, this latter

---

10. Joseph Fitzmyer presents the detailed evidence of the influence of the LXX on Luke, especially in regard to style and vocabulary (*The Gospel According to Luke I–IX*, 107–27).

11. The following observations are based on counts taken from Hatch-Redpath, *Concordance to the Septuagint*, 1:64–65.

23

usage being a force similar to that found in the Hellenistic grave inscriptions noted above.[12] The idea of guilt is often basic to the term, especially when viewed in contrast with the primary antonym צַדִּיק (righteous). This can be illustrated in Genesis 18:23–25. The context is Abraham's discussion with the Lord about his impending destruction of Sodom. In Genesis 18:23, Abraham asks the Lord, "Will you destroy the righteous (צַדִּיק = δίκαιος) with the wicked (רָשָׁע = ἀσεβής)?" The language is clearly legal language of guilt and innocence as evidenced by Abraham's statement in 18:25: "Shall not the judge (שֹׁפֵט = κρίνων) of all the earth do right (מִשְׁפָּט = κρίσιν)?" The legal background of the concept can also be seen in Exodus 23. In Exodus 23:1, a "sinner" (רָשָׁע = ἄδικος) is one who is trying to give a false testimony against someone. The context is the law code as it pertains to justice, mercy and appropriate dealings with others, especially the poor. Exodus 23:7 continues, "Have nothing to do with a false charge, and do not put an innocent person (נָקִי = ἀθῷος) and righteous (צַדִּיק = δίκαιος) to death. For I will not acquit (צָדַק) the guilty (רָשָׁע). The 'righteous' is used in parallel with 'innocent.'"[13] The translation "to acquit" is to declare righteous or innocent, and the "guilty" is רָשָׁע. Deuteronomy 25:1–2 also illustrates the legal background of the "righteous/sinner." When there is a dispute between men, they are to bring it to the court (מִשְׁפָּט = κρίσιν) and the judges (שָׁפַט = κρίσιν) and they shall acquit (צָדַק) the innocent (צַדִּיק) and condemn (רָשָׁע) the guilty (רָשָׁע). If the guilty man is to be flogged, he is to be flogged according to (כְּ) his guilt (רָשָׁע).

The "Sinner" and the "Righteous"

As demonstrated above, one key to understanding the "sinner" in the OT is the examination of the link between the terms "sinner" and "righteous." The following data reinforces this.

1. The Hebrew term רָשָׁע is translated in the LXX (247 times) by the following terms: ἁμαρτωλός (74 times = 30%); ἀσεβής (142 times = 57%);

---

12. BDB, 957.

13. Translations are my own unless noted. All other translations of the OT and NT are from the New Revised Standard Version (NRSV).

and ἄνομος (31 times = almost 13%). The term ἀσεβής provides an important lexical link to ἁμαρτωλός through the connection with רָשָׁע. Bauer translates ἀσεβής as "godless, impious."[14] The close connection with ἀσεβής demonstrates the religious connotation that ἁμαρτωλός often takes in the OT.

2. The adjective צַדִּיק occurs 205 times in the OT and 92 times (45%) רָשָׁע is in the immediate context as an antonym (84 times in the same verse and 8 times in the adjacent verse).

3. The LXX translates רָשָׁע in these 92 uses 16 times by ἁμαρτωλός (17%); 65 times by ἀσεβής (71%); 10 times by ἄνομος (11%) and once by πονηροί (1%). The use of ἁμαρτωλός dominates in the Psalms (15 of 19 uses of צַדִּיק/רָשָׁע in Psalms) and appears 1 time (with צַדִּיק = δίκαιος) in Proverbs (24:19). The use of ἀσεβής dominates the Pentateuch (all 6 uses); the Wisdom literature (44 of 46 uses in Proverbs, all 4 in Eccl, and both uses in Job [22:18,19; 36:6,7]). The 10 uses of ἄνομος = רָשָׁע in צַדִּיק/רָשָׁע contexts, are spread out: once in Proverbs 29:27; twice in the historical books (1 Kgs 8:32; 2 Chr 6:23); and 7 times in the Prophets (5 times in Ezek 3:19–20 (one use); 18:20, 24; 21:8 (3 LXX); 9 (4 LXX); once in Isa 3:11; and once in Mal 3:18).

A significant point is that the main concepts related to the use of צַדִּיק/רָשָׁע are found regardless of the Greek word chosen for רָשָׁע. This is illustrated in Psalm 11:2–7:

> The wicked (רְשָׁעִים = ἁμαρτωλοί) bend their bows . . . to shoot from the shadows at the upright (יָשָׁר) of heart. When the foundations are destroyed what can the righteous (צַדִּיק = δίκαιος) do? The Lord is in his holy temple; the Lord is on his heavenly throne, he sees the sons of men and his eyes examine them. The Lord examines the righteous (צַדִּיק = δίκαιος) but the wicked (רָשָׁע = ἀσεβής) and those who love violence his soul hates. He will rain fiery coals and burning sulphur on the wicked (רְשָׁעִים = ἁμαρτωλοί), a scorching wind will be their lot. For the Lord is righteous (צַדִּיק = δίκαιος), he loves righteousness (צֶדֶק); the upright (יָשָׁר) will see his face.

---

14. BAGD, 114.

The term "upright" is used as a synonym for the "righteous" (11:2, 3; 11:5; 11:7). The term רָשָׁע is translated by ἁμαρτωλός in vv. 2 and 6, but by ἀσεβής in verse 5, with no apparent change in meaning.

This flexibility of Greek terms for רָשָׁע is also illustrated in Psalm 37 (36 LXX). In Psalm 37 the Hebrew term רָשָׁע is translated 10 times by ἁμαρτωλός (37:10, 12, 14, 16, 17, 20, 21, 32, 34, and 40). The same Hebrew word רָשָׁע is translated 3 times by ἀσεβής (37: 28, 35, and 38). The key to understanding the OT concept of the "sinner" is that one must look at the sinner (רָשָׁע)/righteous (צַדִּיק) concept together, regardless of which word is used by the LXX to translate רָשָׁע.

Of special significance to the Old Testament concept of the "sinner" is that the measure of רָשָׁע is the character and attitude of God. Deuteronomy 32:4 declares, "All Yahweh's ways are just (מִשְׁפָּט). Righteous (צַדִּיק) and upright (יָשָׁר) is he." Job 34:12 states, "It is unthinkable that God would do wrong (רָשָׁע), that the Almighty would pervert justice (מִשְׁפָּט)." Job 34:17 adds, "Who will condemn (רָשָׁע) the Just One (צַדִּיק)?" Verse 18 states that as judge, God shows no partiality and judges even kings and nobles. This is illustrated in 2 Chron 12:1–12. Verse 1 states that after King Rehoboam became strong, he and all Israel with him abandoned the law of the Lord. Verse 2 states that because they had been unfaithful to the Lord, Shishak the king of Egypt attacked Jerusalem and captured the fortified cities. The prophet Shemaiah came to Rehoboam and to the leaders of Judah and declared to them this message from the Lord: "You have abandoned me; therefore, I now abandon you to Shishak," (v. 5). The leaders and the king humbled themselves and said, "The Lord is just (צַדִּיק)." The leaders affirmed that the Lord's verdict was an appropriate response to their action of abandoning him. The context shows that the Lord acted as the judge between himself and his covenant people. The act of confession and humility reflected their admission of guilt. This act of confession and humility "delivered" the city and the nation from the LORD's wrath (vv. 7–12).

The remainder of the OT affirms the righteousness of Yahweh (Pss 11:7; 116:5; 119:137; 129:4; 145:17; Isa 41:26; 45:21; Jer 12:1; Lam 1:18; Dan 9:14; Zeph 3:5; and Zech 9:9). This is affirmed especially regarding his judgments (Pss 7:11; 19:9). He judges both his people (Ps 72:2) and the Gentile nations (Pss 96:13; 98:9; and Isa 62:2) in righteousness.

Helenistic and Jewish Concepts of the "Sinner"

Gottlob Schrenk states one aspect of the concept of the righteousness of God to be the idea of the consistent and normative action of God, God himself being the norm of the measure of appropriate action rather than standing under a norm outside of God or imposed upon God.[15] Of special importance to the OT is that צָדִיק implies relationship. A man is righteous when he meets certain claims that another has on him by virtue of their relationship. The righteousness of Yahweh is seen in his covenantal relationship with his people. He is faithful to the covenant because he is righteous (Ezra 9:15; Neh 9:8). Gerhard von Rad describes the relational aspect of the term "righteous" in the following way:

> Every relationship brings with it certain claims upon conduct, and the satisfaction of these claims, which issue from the relationship and in which alone the relationship can persist, is described by our term צֶדֶק. The way in which it is used shows that צֶדֶק is out an out a term denoting relationship, and that it does this in the sense of referring to a real relationship between two parties . . . and not to the relationship of an object under consideration to an idea. To some extent, therefore, the specific relationship in which the agent finds himself is itself the norm: only, it must be borne in mind that people are constantly moving in very many relationships, each one of which carries its own particular law within it. A man belongs to a family, to a political association (clan, nation), he is involved in economic life, and, if circumstances so decree, he can also come into association with foreigners. And above all these, there is the relationship which Yahweh had offered to Israel. The just man is the one who measures up to the particular claims which this relationship lays upon him.[16]

The covenant relationship with Yahweh had an impact on one's relationship with Yahweh and others. Leviticus 19 mandates laws dealing with neighbor relationships. For example, Leviticus 19:9, 10 mandates that farmers leave a portion of their crop for the poor and the alien. This mandate ends with the simple statement: "I am the Lord." The Lord established what was צֶדֶק. Leviticus 19:11–18 gives detailed description of what was improper in relationships: lying and deceiving (v. 11); false witness, especially invoking

---

15. Schrenk, "δικαιοσυνη," 2:195.
16. Rad, *Old Testament Theology*, 1:371.

The Sinner in Luke

Yahweh's name (v. 12); defrauding or robbing one's neighbor (v. 13); cursing the deaf or tripping up the blind (v. 14). Verse 14 connects the warning to the fear of God who will hold the "guilty" accountable. Verse 15 warns that justice (מִשְׁפָּט) is not to be perverted by showing partiality to the poor or favoritism to the rich. They are to judge (שָׁפַט) their neighbor fairly (lit. "in righteousness" (בְּצֶדֶק). They are to avoid slander and any action that would endanger their neighbor (v. 16). Even their attitude toward their neighbor is impacted by the covenant. They are not to hate their neighbor (v. 17) nor seek revenge against him (v. 18). They are to love their neighbor as themselves (v. 18). This command ends with the simple statement, "I am the Lord," reinforcing the source of the command. In Leviticus 19:36, commercial dealings are regulated: "There are to be scales of righteousness (צֶדֶק); stones of righteousness (צֶדֶק); an ephah of righteousness (צֶדֶק); and a hin of righteousness (צֶדֶק). This is also reinforced by the declaration, "I am the Lord, your God, who brought you out of Egypt." Leviticus 19 establishes an important link between who is "righteous" and who is a "sinner" in Israel.

The civil concept of צְדָקָה was not separated from the sphere of religion. Von Rad states that the two areas of relationships, of men with one another and of men with God, were bound together in what he calls a "pansacrality."[17] Norman Snaith called the OT idea of righteousness "theocentric."[18]

An example of how this theocentric concept of righteousness works in human relationships can be seen in 1 Sam 24:11–17. In the context, Saul and his army were pursuing David. David had entered Saul's camp as Saul slept, cut off a piece of Saul's robe, and left undetected. Far outside the cave, David called out to Saul and held up the piece of the robe to prove how the Lord had delivered Saul into his hands (24:10–11). In verse 10, David explained that he would not lift a hand against the Lord's anointed. David's actions would be appropriate and fitting in terms of how the Lord expected a person to treat the king. David declared in verse 11, "Now understand and recognize that there is not in my hand evil (רָעָה), or rebellion (פֶּשַׁע), and I have not sinned (חָטָא = ἁμαρτάνω) against you." In verse 12,

---

17. Rad, *Old Testament Theology*, 1:374.
18. Snaith, *The Distinctive Ideas*, 59.

it was the Lord whom David invoked as "judge": "May the Lord judge (יִשְׁפֹּט) between you and me and may the Lord avenge me from what you have done to me, but my hand will not touch you." David showed his innocence by his behavior. He then cited a proverb (v. 13): "From evildoers (רְשָׁעִים = ἀνόμων) come evil deeds (רֶשַׁע = πλημμέλεια)." David continues his appeal to the Lord in verse 15: "May the Lord be our judge (לְדַיָּן = κριτήν) and judge (שֹׁפֵט = δικαστήν) between me and you; may he see and consider (רִיב = κρίναι) my dispute (רִיב = κρίσιν) and vindicate me (verb form of שָׁפַט = δικάσαι, e.g. by rescuing) from your hand." In verse 17 Saul responded to David, "You are more righteous (צַדִּיק = δίκαιος) than I." The explanation that Saul gave is that he had treated David badly (רָעָה) and David had treated him well (טוֹב). This account shows how the notion of who is "righteous" and who is "wicked" is presented in legal language and is colored by 1) how one treats another in relationship, and 2) by the underlying idea that the Lord is judge. The legal language behind the term "sinner" also provides an explanation of the idea of "sinner" as a "debtor" because he has violated God's righteousness and is therefore in legal debt to God.

Survey of "Sinner" as רָשָׁע in the OT

Earlier we examined the use of רָשָׁע as it relates to צַדִּיק in the OT. Our attention now turns to רָשָׁע specifically as it relates to ἁμαρτωλός. As the statistics show, רָשָׁע makes up 3 out of 4 of the uses of ἁμαρτωλός. This demonstrates the strong influence of the OT concept of the term "righteous" (צַדִּיק = δίκαιος) on ἁμαρτωλός in the LXX. As noted earlier, the adjective צַדִּיק occurs 205 times in the OT; 92 times (45%) רָשָׁע is in the immediate context as an antonym.

The Psalms are especially significant, with ἁμαρτωλός occurring 68 times, only 4 times not translating רָשָׁע (3 times by חָטָא and one time by חָרָשׁ). The "sinner" in the Psalms is almost always found in the plural (Pss 38:1 LXX; 57:10 LXX; 81:4 LXX; 138:19 LXX). One exception is Psalm 55 in which there is an interchange between the plural and the singular with the "sinner" being identified as a former friend (singular, Ps 55:3).[19]

---

19. Psalm 55:3 is the exception to Neale's point that the "sinner" in the Psalms is always used in a plural, collective sense. See Neale, *None But the Sinners*, 79.

The picture of "sinners" in Psalms can be summarized in the following categories: (1) their identity; (2) their characteristics; (3) their future; and (4) the psalmist's relationship to them. First, who are the "sinners"? (1) They are enemies of the psalmist *within* Israel (Pss 3:7; 100:8 LXX; 108:6 LXX; 138:21 LXX). In Psalm 3:7, the "sinners" can be understood from the MT and the LXX to be identified as the co-conspirators of Absalom against David. (2) They are enemies of God (Pss 36:20 LXX; 67:2 LXX). According to Psalm 68:2, the "sinners" hate God (cf., Isa 1:24). (3) They are enemies of Israel *outside* of Israel, Gentile oppressors (Pss 9:16–18; 124:3 LXX; 128:3 LXX). Psalm 9:16–18 establishes a clear connection between the ἁμαρτωλοί and the Gentile (ἔθνοι). The ἔθνοι are caught in the destruction that they planned (v. 16). The reason is that the Lord executes judgments so that the ἁμαρτωλός is ensnared by the works of his hands (v. 17). The psalmist declares, ". . . let the ἁμαρτωλοί be driven into Hades, all the ἔθνοι that forget God" (v. 18). (4) Finally, they are enemies of the "righteous" (Ps 138:21 LXX). The "sinners" seek to harm the "righteous" (δίκαιος). They lie in wait for them (Ps 36:12 LXX) and have drawn their sword against them (Ps 36:14 LXX).

The concept of the "sinner" as the enemy of Yahweh (e.g., Ps 37:20) is rooted in the behavior of the person. As Steven Croft notes, the "sinner" is the enemy of God by virtue of his wickedness.[20] This explains why even foreigners and foreign kings can be called "sinners" and viewed as enemies of God (Ps 68:21). To commit certain offenses like oppressing the poor and perverting justice makes one רְשָׁעִים, regardless of one's national identity.[21] The king of Israel labeled his enemies רְשָׁעִים because of their improper (opposite of צַדִּיק) actions toward him, praying that the Lord would act as judge between them and condemn the guilty and vindicate him through a victory (Pss 68:21; 31:17).[22] The Davidic king played a role as warrior and judge as the Lord's anointed. To attack the anointed was also to attack the Lord, making one the Lord's enemy (Ps 2:10–12; Ps 44).

Second, what are the characteristics of "sinners"? (1) In relation to God, the ἁμαρτωλός has no regard for him (Pss 10:4; 49:22 LXX). He

---

20. Croft, *Identity*, 46.
21. Ibid., 28.
22. Ibid., 46.

provokes the Lord and does not seek him (Ps 10:4). He even verbally defies him (Ps 72:9 LXX). He trusts in himself, not God (Ps 27:3 LXX); forsakes God's Law (Pss 49:16 LXX; 118:53 LXX) and the covenant (Ps 49:16 LXX; 57:3 LXX). Psalm 49:16–22 LXX records an address from God to the "sinner" in which he asks rhetorically,

> Why do you affirm my Laws and covenant with your mouth? (v. 16)? You have hated instruction and have cast my words behind you (v. 17). If you saw a thief, you ran along with him, and have cast your portion with adulterers...I will reprove you . . . (v. 21) now consider these things, you that forget God (v. 22).

This "sinner" forgets God by neglecting his commands. Within Israel, one's negative attitude toward the law brings the designation of "sinner." This attitude is reflected in specific acts that violate specific commands of the decalogue. A. A. Anderson suggests that "cast my words behind you" (49:17 LXX) reminds one of the ten words, or decalogue (Exod 34:28).[23] He is characterized as "lawless" (ἀνόμοι, Ps 91:7 LXX) and a "transgressor" (παραβαίνοντας, Ps 118:119 LXX). This confirms Croft's statement that the "sinner" in the Psalms is defined by his conduct towards God and his law.[24] (2) In relation to others, the ἁμαρτωλός is violent (Ps 93:6 LXX), he has slain the widow and murdered the stranger (Ps 138:19 LXX), "sinners" are men of blood (Ps 36:14 LXX). The "sinner" oppresses others (Ps 54:3 LXX) and lies in wait for the "righteous" (Ps 36:12 LXX). He borrows and does not repay (Ps 36:21 LXX). The "sinner" seen in these contexts is especially viewed as violating the character and law of the Lord as it relates to the proper way to treat people. This is consistent with our study of the basic OT distinctive meaning of the "righteous/sinner" concept (cf. Lev 19:11–18; 1 Sam 24:11–17).

Third, what is the future of the "sinner"? The "sinner" shall cease to exist (Ps 36:10 LXX) for he will perish (Ps 144:20 LXX) in judgment. According to Psalm 75:8: "all the 'sinners' (ἁμαρτωλοί) of the earth shall drink the cup of God's wrath." The power of the sinner will be shattered (Pss 36:16, 17 LXX; 74:10 LXX). Salvation is far from him (Ps 118:155 LXX).

---

23. Anderson, *The Book of Psalms 1–72*, 387.
24. Croft, *Identity*, 46.

Fourth, how does the psalmist relate to the "sinner"? He destroys them (Ps 100:8 LXX) but also avoids them (Ps 1:1, 5); not dwelling in their tents (Ps 83:10 LXX) and not even eating with them (Ps 100:5 LXX).

Karl Rengstorff summarizes the picture of the "sinner" according to the Psalms in the following way.[25]

1. He is opposite of the pious, righteous, and godly (Ps 1:1, 5).
2. He boasts of his portion in the Law and the Covenant, but does not regard or follow the Law as an absolutely binding expression of the will of God (Ps 50:16ff).
3. He persistently breaks the commandments (Ps 10:7).
4. He shows no signs of repentance and boasts of his wickedness (Ps 49:13).
5. He trusts in his own wealth and power instead of God (Ps 49:6).
6. He ignores God in his life (Pss 10:4; 36:1).
7. He is lax toward the Law (Ps 119:53).

In the Psalms, the ἁμαρτωλός is one who is opposite of the righteous (δίκαιος) in both characteristics and destiny (37:10–21) and especially one who ignores the Law of God. The sinner is under divine wrath (Pss 11:6; 68:2; 75:8). Neale is correct in calling the theme of judgment the overriding theme in relation to the "sinner" in the Greek Psalms.[26]

Neale describes the "sinner" in Psalms as a religious ideological category over against the "righteous." Because of the divergent results of those who have tried to identify the historical "sinner" in the Psalms precisely, Neale suggests that it is better to leave the historical issue behind and treat the "sinner" as symbol and metaphor.[27] Although the LXX clearly uses the "sinner" as a category of a type of person, at times the specific referent is clearly identifiable. For example, Dathan and Abiram are referred to in Psalm 105:18 LXX. In Psalm 3:7 the "sinners" are the co-conspirators with Absalom. This Psalm raises an important point that Neale overlooks. The

25. Rengstorf, "ἁμαρτωλός," 325.
26. Neale, *None But the Sinners*, 82.
27. Ibid., 78–80.

presence of the superscriptions in many of the Psalms reflects a tendency to apply the Psalms to actual events and actual individuals. One need not accept the historical validity of the superscriptions to recognize that they demonstrate the tendency by early compilers of the Psalms to seek to supply historical referents. Since the superscriptions were part of the Masoretic texts that pre-dated the LXX, and since the LXX translators included these in their translations, one may conclude that the type of person that the terms "sinner/righteous" describe was commonly seen as a reference to real people.

This tendency to apply unspecific referents in the Psalms to very specific individuals and circumstances is illustrated in the New Testament. For example, in Acts 4:25, Psalm 2 is applied by Peter to Herod, Pilate, the people of Israel and the Gentiles who all had a part in the conspiracy against Jesus, the Lord's anointed. A corrective to Neale would be to acknowledge more than one referent for the term "sinner" (Israel's enemies, the psalmist's enemies, and God's enemies) and to see the "sinner" as being used sometimes as a type of person, a symbolic use of the term, and other times as an actual person who fits that description.

The "Sinner" as חַטָּא

The second important Hebrew word for "sinner" in the OT is חַטָּא. The root חטא is translated in the LXX most frequently by ἁμαρτία and its related terms. For example, the noun חַטָּא 'sin' is translated by ἁμαρτία approximately 318 of its 385 uses (also פֶּשַׁע, 20 times; עָוֹן 33 times; אָשָׁם 6 times; all others combined 10 times). The LXX uses the verb חטא 'to sin' 198 times. It is translated 185 times by ἁμαρτάνω or a related verb, 2 times by ἀδικέω; 3 times by ἀφαγνίζω and καθαρίζω each respectively; and 5 times by ῥαντίζω.

The masculine noun חַטָּא "sinner" is used 19 times. It is translated 3 times by a participle of the verb ἁμαρτάνω, 11 times by ἁμαρτωλός, one time by ἄνομος, 2 times by ἀσεβής and once by ἀνὴρ ἀσεβής. In all, 14 of 19 uses of the noun חַטָּא are translated by ἁμαρτωλός or its equivalent (the remainder are translated by ἀσεβής (4 times) and ἀνόμοι (once).

The Sinner in Luke

There is one example of a use of חָטָא = ἁμαρτεῖν in the OT that is similar to that of the classical period, namely the reference to left-handed sling throwers who never missed (Judges 20:16). Klaus Koch argues that this is probably a metaphorical usage parallel to the use in the *Iliad*.[28] Brown, Driver and Briggs also connects חָטָא to the meaning of "miss the mark."[29] Sin is to miss the goal or path of right. Ludwig Koehler and Walter Baumgartner define חטא as "to miss the mark; to wrong (morally); to be culpable; to do wrong, to sin."[30]

Koch observes that in the OT, חטא and its derivatives, from the earliest strata, provide the most common means of expressing religious disqualification of specific human acts and modes of conduct.[31] The semantic field includes above all עָוֹן (iniquity, used approximately 224 times), פֶּשַׁע (rebellion, 92 times), רַע (wicked, 648 times), and טָמֵא (unclean, 84 times).[32] The adjective הַחַטָּאָה is used of sinful men in Amos 9:8. Although here it is in the singular, it has a collective sense with the kingdom of Judah as referent. Elsewhere the adjective is found only in the plural. The term רָשָׁע appears to be more intense, being translated as "the wicked, the evildoer, the godless, the guilty, or a criminal."[33] Yet חטא can sometimes serve as a synonym for רָשָׁע (Ps 1:1 and 1:5: רָשָׁע = ἀσεβής; חטא = ἁμαρτωλός).

The Pentateuch uses the term ἁμαρτωλός only for חטא. For example, it is used to describe the men of Sodom who were 'wicked' (πονηροί = רָעִים) and "sinners" (ἁμαρτωλοί = חַטָּאִים, Gen 13:13). Although the specific nature of the sin is not identified here, the sin is clearly against the Lord (Gen 13:13). It also is used of those who rebelled with Korah against Moses and were consumed by fire. These men are "sinners" at the cost of their lives (Num 16:38; 17:3 LXX). Here we have an example in which the referent to "sinner" is clearly identified. The assembly of Israelites is

---

28. Koch, "חטא," 311. Koch argues his position based on the wide-spread religious usage of the term in the ANE.
29. BDB, 306
30. *HALOT* 2:1295.
31. Koch, "חטא," 310.
32. Ibid.
33. Ibid., 957. Also *HALOT* 2:1295.

warned in v. 26 to move away from the tents of the wicked men (רְשָׁעִים = σκληρῶν) who are identified as Korah, Dathan, and Abiram. In Numbers 32:14, Moses reminds the tribes requesting to stay East of the Jordan of the wrath of God against Israel because of Kadesh-Barnea. They are like their fathers, a combination of sinful men (ἁμαρτωλοί = חַטָּאִים) who will bring about God's wrath by turning from him (Num 32:15). Deuteronomy 29:19, in the context of covenant renewal, warns a person who hears the covenant oath but then ignores the warning against idolatry. This "sinner" says, "I will walk in the error of my heart." Moses warns that God's wrath will be against this man and the Lord shall separate him from the people and pour out the curses of the covenant breaker upon him.

In 1 Kings 1:21 (3 Kings of LXX), Bathsheba warns David as he nears death that if his son Adonijah should become king, both she and Solomon would be considered ἁμαρτωλοί (חַטָּאִים). Keil and Delitzsch understand חַטָּאִים to mean that Bathsheba and Solomon would be guilty of a capital crime and punished as though guilty of high treason as opponents of Adonijah.[34]

In the Psalms, ἁμαρτωλός = חַטָּא three times. The precarious way of the "sinner" (ἁμαρτωλός = חַטָּא) is contrasted with the enduring way of the righteous (δίκαιος = צַדִּיק, Ps 1:1, 5). The "sinner" will not stand in the day of judgment (Ps 1:5, 6). The psalmist prays that "sinners" (ἁμαρτωλοί = חַטָּאִים) may fall from the earth (Ps 103:35 LXX).

Amos uses ἁμαρτωλός = חַטָּא two times (Amos 9:8 and 9:10). The "sinners" here are God's own people who are being warned that their election will not protect them from God's wrath. The LXX of Isaiah uses ἁμαρτωλός six times: ἁμαρτωλός = חַטָּא five times (Isa 1:4, 28, 31; 13:9; and 65:20) and ἁμαρτωλός = רָשָׁע once (Isa 14:5). In Isaiah 1:4, the prophet addresses Israel as a "sinful nation" (ἔθνος ἁμαρτωλόν), a people loaded with guilt (ἁμαρτιῶν). In Isaiah 1:24–31, the prophet links the "sinner" with God's wrath against his enemies (1:24). They are associated with the rebellious (ἀπειθοῦντας) and the transgressors (ἀνόμους, 1:25) and will be crushed together (1:28, ἄνομοι καὶ ἁμαρτωλοί).

The overriding theme of the "sinner" with ἁμαρτωλός = חַטָּא is God's wrath against his enemies. One designated a ἁμαρτωλός = חַטָּא

---

34. K&D 3:21.

The Sinner in Luke

is under wrath. This meaning is consistent with the Hellenistic usage of ἁμαρτωλός in the context of a person under the wrath of the gods.

Gentiles as "Sinners" in the Old Testament

The term "sinner" is used of certain Gentiles in the OT. The men of Sodom are described as "wicked" and great "sinners" before God (Gen 13:13) and are subsequently destroyed by God (Gen 19:24, 25). These Gentile "sinners" become symbols of extreme wickedness and the destructive wrath of God against sinners. To be compared to Sodom is to be extremely wicked (e.g., Deut 32:32; Isa 1:10; Jer 23:14; Ezek 16:46–58). To compare one's fate to that of Sodom is to emphasize God's complete judgment (Deut 29:23; Jer 49:18; 50:40; Lam 4:6; Amos 4:11; Zeph 2:9). Gentile nations are associated with idolatry and sexual immorality (Exod 34:15–16; Lev 18:24; Num 25:1–3). Israel must not follow the customs of the Gentiles who were dispossessed because of their wickedness (Lev 18:24; 20:23; Deut 18:9; Josh 23:7; cf., 1 Kgs 14:24; 2 Kgs 16:3).

The "sinner" in the OT sometimes refers to Gentile enemies of Israel (Pss 9:16–18; 94:5; 125:3; 129:3–4). We have discussed Psalm 9:16 above. Psalm 124:3 LXX declares that the Lord will not allow the scepter of the "sinners" over the lot of the "righteous." The scepter is usually taken as a symbol of foreign domination (e.g., Isa 14:5).[35] Psalm 128:3–4 LXX the writer speaks of "sinners" (ἁμαρτωλοί = חֹרְשִׁים "plowers") who have made deep furrows upon his back. The Lord has cut the cords of the wicked (ἁμαρτωλοί). Israel's foreign oppressors have not prevailed. These Gentile nations are "sinners" because they have mistreated Israel (cf., Ps 128:1 LXX). Another illustration of the "sinners" being Israel's Gentile enemies is Isaiah 13:9. This is an oracle against Israel's enemy Babylon. The oracle speaks of the Day of the Lord in which God is coming to destroy "sinners" (ἁμαρτωλοῖς = חַטָּא) from the earth. These "sinners" will be punished for their "evil" (κακός = רָע) they are the "wicked" (ἀσεβέσιν = רְשָׁעִים) who will be punished for their "iniquity" (ἁμαρτίας = עֲוֹנָם), pride and insolence (v. 11). The glory of Babylon will be like that of Sodom and Gomorrah when God overthrew it (v. 19).

---

35. Anderson, *Psalms 73–150*, 862.

Isaiah 14:5 is an example of a "sinner" passage that provides a specific historical referent, the king of Babylon. Isaiah 14:4 gives this direction to the prophet: "You will take up this taunt against the king of Babylon: How has the extortioner (the king of Babylon) ceased!" Verse 5 then tells of the Lord's plans for the Gentile king: "The Lord has broken the yoke of the sinners (ἁμαρτωλοῖς = רָשָׁע)." The "sinner" here is the king of Babylon whose oppression and pride have brought him under the judgment of the Lord (Isa 14:3–5). These references along with the "sinners" of Sodom (Gen 13:13) demonstrate that the term "sinner" is sometimes used of Gentiles in the OT.

Mercy for the "Sinner" in the OT

A final observation regarding the "sinner" theme in the OT is that mercy is sometimes offered to the repentant "sinner." Neale states that one of the distinctive elements of the concept of the "sinner" (ἁμαρτωλός = רָשָׁע) is the absence of mercy for those placed in this category.[36] He states that the "sinner" in the Greek Psalms was completely beyond the pale of restoration. There is no hint of leniency or reclamation for this type of person.

This is not the complete picture. There is a hint at forgiveness even in the Psalms. For example, in Psalm 106:6, the psalmist confesses himself a "sinner" like his forefathers, declaring, "We have sinned (חָטָא = ἁμαρτάνω), like our fathers did, we have committed iniquity, we have done wickedly (רָשָׁע = ἀδικέω)." Here the psalmist confesses himself to be guilty of both חָטָא and רָשָׁע. The Psalm ends with a prayer for deliverance (106:27), reflecting the hope that forgiveness was granted and deliverance would be the result. Psalm 51 contains a confession of sin and request for forgiveness by king David because of his sin with Bathsheba and the murder of Uriah. It is true that רָשָׁע is not found in the psalm, but חָטָא, the other key Hebrew word for "sin," is found as a noun (חָטָא = ἁμαρτία) in the Hebrew text in 51:4 (50:4 LXX), 5, 7, 11, and 15, and as a verb (חָטָא = ἁμαρτάνω) in 51:6. There is also a wide range of the terms for sin, including פֶּשַׁע = ἀνομίαν (51:3, 5, 15) and עָוֹן = ἀνομίας (51:4a, 7a, 11b). In light of the use of ἁμαρτία/ἁμαρτάνω in this passage and in view of the flexibility of this language as demonstrated,

---

36. Neale, *None But the Sinners*, 86.

The Sinner in Luke

Neale makes too sweeping a statement when he states, "It is beyond question, that the 'sinner' of the Greek Psalms was completely beyond the pale of such restoration."[37] As has been demonstrated in Psalm 106:6 and 51, real "sinners" petitioned the Lord for mercy and appear to have received their request. It is also significant that the Prayer of Manasseh, which is a prayer of confession by a genuine "sinner," is clearly dependent upon Psalm 51, demonstrating that hope for the "sinner" was not completely beyond question as Neale proposes.

Apart from the Psalms, there are promises of restoration to those who repent in Joel 2:13, 14 and Jeremiah 18:8 (if they 'repent' = שׁוּב of their "evil" = רַע. There are also prayers for present forgiveness (Ps 25:11; 51; Neh 9:33, confession of רֶשַׁע; Dan 9:5, 15). In Daniel 9:5, the writer confesses: "We have 'sinned' (חָטָא = ἁμαρτάνω), we have done 'iniquity' (עָוֹן = ἀδικέω), we have acted wickedly (רָשַׁע = ἀσεβέω)." The prayer ends with a request for forgiveness (Dan 9:19). There are also prayers for future forgiveness from רֶשַׁע (2 Chr 6:37, and 1 Kgs 8:30, 47).

Mercy for the "sinner" is clearly offered to those labeled genuine "sinners" in Ezekiel 18:20, 27 and 33:12, 19. In Ezekiel 33, the prophet uses ἁμαρτωλός = רָשָׁע three times. In Ezekiel 33:8, the prophet has become the watchman responsible for sounding the alarm of God's judgment: "When I say to the sinner (ἁμαρτωλός = רָשָׁע, 'You shall surely die,' if you do not speak to warn the wicked (ἀσεβῆ) from his way, the wicked (ἄνομος) himself shall die in his iniquity but his blood I will require of you." In Ezekiel 33:8, the prophet is specifically charged to warn the wicked. In 33:9, the "sinner" receives the offer of repentance. If the "sinner" turns (ἀποστρέφω) from his way, he shall live. In verse 11, the Lord says that his desire is not the death of the "sinner" (Alexandrian of the LXX reads ἁμαρτωλός) but that the ungodly (ἀσεβῆ) should turn from his ways and live.

In Ezekiel 33:14–16, God offers forgiveness to the repentant sinner. The offer is stated clearly in 33:19: "And when the sinner (ἁμαρτωλός = רָשָׁע) turns from his iniquity (ἀνομίας), and shall do justice and righteousness, by these he shall live." This is an offer of repentance to "sinners" in Israel. Although the offer of repentance is not new (Joel 2:12, 13; Jer

---

37. Neale, *None But the Sinners*, 86.

3:12), the call in Ezekiel is unprecedented in its emphasis as an invitation from the Lord and an expression of his desire to offer forgiveness and life to the genuine "sinner." Neale acknowledges the offer of repentance in this passage but considers it irrelevant because the "sinners" do not actually repent in Ezekiel. Against Neale's point is that the lack of repentance does not diminish the fact that God does offer mercy and forgiveness to people with the genuine "sinner" (רָשָׁע = ἁμαρτωλός) label.[38]

One final text may be mentioned regarding mercy and repentance for "sinners" in the OT. In Jonah, we have an example of a mission to real "sinners," the Ninevites. Jonah 1:2 states that the wickedness (רַע = κακίας) of the Ninevites had come up to the Lord. The term רַע seems to emphasize a kind of harmful behavior, where רָשָׁע emphasizes the person who does the behavior. This is illustrated in Proverbs 15:28: "The mouth of the 'wicked' = רָשָׁע pours out 'evil' = רַע." In Ezekiel 33:11, the "wicked" = רָשָׁע are called to turn from their "evil" = רַע. In Jonah 3:8, in response to Jonah's warning the king decreed that everyone turn from their "evil" = רַע that the Lord may have compassion and relent from his judgment. Jonah 3:10 states that the Lord observed their repentance (שׁוּב = ἀποστρέφω) and had compassion upon them. Here is an example of the "wicked" being offered repentance and responding to it.

The theme of repentance for the "sinner" is not abundant, but as the evidence presented demonstrates, the theme of mercy is present and on occasion is granted to real "sinners." This corrects Neale's overstatements and also E. P. Sanders's unqualified definition of the "sinner" in the OT as a technical term best translated by the "wicked" and referring to those who sinned willfully and heinously and who do not repent.[39]

Summary

To summarize the picture of the "sinner" in the OT, the following may be said. First, the key Hebrew term is רָשָׁע. The idea of guilt is basic to the term רָשָׁע, especially when viewed in contrast with the primary antonym צַדִּיק ("righteous," Gen 18:23–25). The language is clearly legal language of guilt and innocence (Gen 18:25; Exod 23:1; 23:7; Deut 25:1, 2). The

---

38. Neale, *None But the Sinners*, 86.
39. Sanders, *Jesus and Judaism*, 177.

THE SINNER IN LUKE

overriding theme of the "sinner" when ἁμαρτωλός = חָטָא is God's wrath against his enemies. This meaning is consistent with the Hellenistic usage of ἁμαρτωλός in the context of a person under the wrath of the gods.

Second, of special significance to the Old Testament concept of the "sinner" is that the standard of רָשָׁע is the character and attitude of God (Deut 32:4; Job 34:12). He judges both his people (Ps 72:2) and the Gentile nations (Pss 96:13; 98:9; Isa 62:2) in righteousness.

Third, the concept of the "righteous" and the "sinner" was rooted in the fact that the covenant with Yahweh had an impact on both one's relationship with Yahweh and others (Lev 19:9, 10). The civil concept of צָדִיק was not separated from the sphere of religion. The two areas of relationships, of people with one another and of people with God, were bound together (1 Sam 24:11–17).

Fourth, the will of God as revealed in the law was the standard by which one was considered to be "righteous" (צַדִּיק) or a "sinner" (רָשָׁע). Faithfulness to God in the law and the covenant as it applied to one's relationship with God and human relationships was the measure. For example, the "righteous" (צַדִּיק) fears the Lord and finds great delight in his commands (Ps 112:1) but the "sinner" (רָשָׁע = ἁμαρτωλός) has no regard for God (Ps 27:3 LXX) and rejects God's law (Ps 50:22; 119:53; Ezek 18:21).

Neale states the following regarding the OT "sinner":

> The terms "righteous" and "sinner" express the psalmist's view of the absoluteness of the moral order of the universe and are means by which he organizes his world view. The term "sinners" is merely a symbol for the enemies of God, the representatives of the condemned, the identification of whom makes possible the self-identification of the "righteous." "sinners" are, after all, exactly who the psalmist, or reader *believes* (emphasis is his) them to be. They are the mental product of his world view. The category contains only people who are assigned to it by the judgment of others. For this reason it is best to speak of the "sinners" not in terms of socially identifiable referents, but as a religious "category." A world view which contains absolute conceptions of right and wrong must have such a category. It is an essential element in a system of thought

which distinguishes between good and evil; the "sinners" are the necessary counterpart of the "righteous."[40]

Neale limits the term "sinner" in the OT to symbol and metaphor. The "sinner" for him is a religious category which serves as merely the necessary counterpart of the "righteous." The "sinner" category contains those people who are assigned to it by the judgment of others. Although the "sinner" in the OT is indeed to be understood by its relationship to the concept of "righteous," Neale fails to define what actually makes a person "righteous" in the OT, and as a consequence his understanding of the OT "sinner" is presented in terms that are too general. There is no debate that the "sinner/righteous" category represents a type of person in the OT. The error that Neale makes is not clarifying the particular elements that make up this category in the OT. What has been demonstrated in our study of the use of "sinner" (רָשָׁע) and "righteous" (צַדִּיק) is that legal language undergirds the OT definition of a "sinner" as one who is guilty of acting in an inappropriate way toward God or man, and is consequently under the judgment of God, the Judge. The key to the OT understanding of the "sinner" is that the inappropriate action is measured against Yahweh's nature for those outside the covenant and against Yahweh's nature as revealed especially in the law and the covenant for those inside the covenant. One may partly explain Neale's insistence upon only a metaphorical OT "sinner" because of his neglect of the Pentateuch and historical books in his analysis of the "sinner/righteous" concept.[41]

Fifth, the identification of the "sinner" was found to be best described as a range. On one end the term "sinner" could describe a type of person and on the other end could refer to specific individuals who fit that category (Num 16:26–38 the "wicked men" (רְשָׁעִים) = ἀσεβής) are identified as Korah, Dathan, and Abiram).

Sixth, certain Gentiles were designated "sinners" either because of their wicked behavior against God (e.g., Sodom in Gen 13:13) or because they were enemies of Israel (cf., Ps 9:16; Isa 13:9; 14:5).

Seventh, mercy for the "sinner" was present in the OT but infrequent.

---

40. Neale, *None But the Sinners*, 96–97.

41. I observe only one paragraph dealing with OT material outside of the Psalms in Neales's *None But the Sinners*, 88–89.

The Sinner in Luke

Intertestamental Jewish Material

The Apocrypha

In the Apocrypha, one observes a parallel use of the key "sinner" terms used in the LXX: ἁμαρτωλός, ἄνομος, and ἀσεβής. For example, Sir 16:1–6 speaks of the heritage of the ungodly using all three of these terms for the same group, reflecting the flexibility of the terminology: this heritage is called "ungodly" (ἀσεβής,16:1, 3); "wicked" (ἄνομος, 16:4); and "sinner" (ἁμαρτωλός, 16:6a). In Sir 39:24, 25 ἄνομος is used in verse 24 and ἁμαρτωλός in the verse 25 parallel. The terms ἁμαρτωλός and ἀσεβής are interchanged in Sir 41:8 ("children of ἁμαρτωλῶν" with "children of ἀσεβῶν"). The flexibility of the terms is also seen in 1 Macc. For example, the term ἁμαρτωλός and the expression "wicked men" (ἄνδρες ἄνομοι) are synonyms in 1 Macc 2:44. In 1 Macc 7:5, this expression "wicked men" (ἄνδρες ἄνομοι) is used in parallel with the "ἀσεβῆ of Israel" (also 9:23, the "ἄνομοι of Israel" is synonymous with the "ἀσεβεῖς ἄνδρας of Israel" in 9:25).

In the Apocrypha, one observes a distancing of the "righteous" from the one designated a "sinner," possibly due to the growing fear of Hellenization. In Sir 12:4, 7, for example, the writer emphasizes that one is not to give assistance to the "sinner." It is appropriate to give to the godly, but not to help (ἀντιλαμβάνω) the "sinner." Tobit 4:17 makes the same point: "Give nothing to the wicked" (ἁμαρτωλός).

Sirach

Most of the Sirach references deal with retribution. Of the 39 references to "sinners," most sound like the wisdom literature's warnings against following the ways of the "sinner" (7:16) and avoiding association with them (8:10; 13:17).

The "sinner" in the Apocrypha can be Israelites who do not fear the Lord. For example, in Sirach, the "sinner" presumes upon the Lord and sins without fear (Sir 5:4–5). This one is in danger because the Lord's wrath rests on such a "sinner" (Sir 5:6). He heaps sin upon sin (Sir 3:27) and has a hard heart and neck (Sir 3:26, 27a). For Sirach, the "sinner" is one who has forsaken the law (Sir 41:8). In addition to this general statement, Sirach names specific sins that are violations of "righteousness," or ways in which Israelites are to treat one another that are consistent with God and his law. For example, the "sinner" sins against his neighbor (cf., Lev 19:11–18) by the following actions: digging pits and setting traps (Sir 27:26); he is violent, laying wait for blood (Sir 11:32); he is greedy and violent, willing to kill in order to gain money (Sir 11:32). His greed is illustrated in Sir 29:16. In this context, Sirach states that one is to use his money to help one's brother and friend instead of hoarding it (29:10). He should use his money according to the commandments of the Most High (29:11). This includes giving alms (29:12) and helping a neighbor by putting up surety for him (29:14). A "sinner" (ἁμαρτωλός) will overthrow the estate of his neighbor by taking back his surety and stealing his property (Sir 29:16). He also dishonors the poor (Sir 10:23). The "sinner" is characterized by a hard heart and an unwillingness to accept reproof (Sir 2:17). Sirach 35:17 declares, "the sinful man (ἄνθρωπος ἁμαρτωλός) will not accept reproof."

Tobit

In Tobit, we have the "righteous"/"sinner" theme presented in a manner consistent with the Old Testament definition. For example, in Tob 1:3, Tobit identifies himself as one who "walked in the way of truth and justice (δικαιοσύνη)." He then explains this in more detail in chapter 1:5–11: (1) he went to Jerusalem for the feasts (1:5); (2) he tithed (1:6–8); (3) he did not intermarry with the Gentiles (1:9); and (4) he ate his meal in accordance with the law of Moses, not the food of the Gentiles (1:10, 11). As in the OT, what is acceptable behavior rests on the righteousness of the Lord (Tob 2:2). Anything outside of this is considered sin (ἁμαρτία, Tob 2:3). As in the OT, the "sinner" in Tobit is opposite of the "righteous" and righteousness is measured by one's relationship with the Lord and his law. For example, in Tob 4:5, Tobit addresses his son Tobias. He calls upon him (1) to remember the Lord (4:5); (2) not to set his will to sin (ἁμαρτάνειν) or transgress (παραβῆναι) the commandments (4:5); (3) to practice righteousness (δικαιοσύνη) and (4) to avoid walking in the way of unrighteousness (ἀδικίας). As has been demonstrated, the concept of righteousness in the OT is especially a relational concept that is measured with regard to one's relation between the Lord and his human

The Sinner in Luke

relationships. In Tobit, the general measurement of the law and the commandments stated in 4:5–6 becomes more specific in terms of proper dealings with people. For example, in Tob 4:7–17 the righteous one will do the following: (1) give alms (4:7–11); (2) avoid intermarriage with Gentiles (4:12–13); (3) pay wages honestly (4:14); (4) avoid drunkenness (4:15); (5) care for the poor and hungry (4:16); honor the righteous but not the "sinners" (ἁμαρτωλοῖς).

1 AND 2 MACCABEES

There are additional specific referents for the term "sinners" in the Apocrypha. For example, in 1 Macc, Antiochus decreed that Jews were required to leave their own laws and follow his in a program of forced Hellenization (1:41). The writer of 1 Macc states that many Israelites (1) consented to his religion; (2) sacrificed to idols; and (3) profaned the Sabbath (1 Macc 1:43). In 1 Macc, those who conformed to Antiochus in this way are "sinners" within Israel. The Maccabean revolt was intended to expel Antiochus and restore Jewish political and religious freedom. Those who opposed the Maccabees, were "sinners." In 1 Macc 2:44–48, the writer describes others of Israel joining forces with Mattathias: "So they joined forces and slew sinful men (ἁμαρτωλούς) in their anger, and wicked men (ἀνόμους) in their wrath: but the rest fled to the Gentiles (ἔθνη) for help." Here, the "sinful men" (ἁμαρτωλούς) are the Jews who opposed Mattathias.

Another example of a specific designation of a "sinner" within Judaism is 1 Macc 7:5–9 in a context describing Judas Maccabee's war with the Syrians. Hellenization continues to be an issue. In 1 Macc 7:5 reference is made to the "wicked" (ἄνδρες ἄνομοι) and "godless" (ἀσεβεῖς) of Israel with Alcimus as their captain. These are Jews who allied themselves with the Syrians against the Maccabees. In 7:9, Alcimus is labeled "that wicked Alcimus" (ἀσεβής), a strong designation for a High Priest of Israel. His sin is specified and illustrated in 1 Macc 7:12–18. He is guilty of betrayal, deceit, and the murder of sixty Hasidim, having promised them safety to come and be heard (cf., 1 Macc 9:23, 25). Another illustration is 2 Macc 4:13 in which the "wicked" one (ἀσεβοῦς) is another High Priest. This time it is Jason who purchased the position of High Priest.

Gentile "Sinners" in the Apocrypha

The term ἁμαρτωλός is also used as a designation for the heathen or Gentiles in the Apocrypha. Sometimes the term "sinner" is used as a virtual synonym for "Gentile." For example, Sir 16:6 states: "In the congregation (συναγωγή) of 'sinners' (ἁμαρτωλοῖς) shall a fire be kindled, and in a rebellious nation (ἔθνει) wrath is set on fire." An analogy is then made between the old giants (16:7), Sodom (16:8), and others who died in their sins (ἁμαρτίας) in a warning to the reader to repent (16:11). Sirach 39:23b–24 applies the term "wicked" to Gentiles in general: "The Gentiles (ἔθνει) shall inherit the wrath of the Lord. The ways of the Lord are stumbling blocks to the 'wicked' (ἄνομοι)." The ἔθνει are viewed here as the "wicked." In 3 Macc 6:4, Eleazar the Priest is reported to have designated Pharoah as "wicked" (ἄνομος) and in 6:9 he speaks in general of the abhorred, lawless (ἄνομοι) Gentiles. Tobit 13:6 uses ἔθνη ἁμαρτωλῶν of the nation of the Assyrians, or possibly his own people who are in exile. In Wis 19:13 the ἁμαρτωλοῖς are the Egyptians upon whom God's punishments fell.

The term "sinner" sometimes designates specific Gentiles. For example, in 1 Macc 1:10 reference is made to Antiochus Epiphanes who is described as a "sinful root" (ῥίζα ἁμαρτωλός). In 1 Macc 1:34 the Syrian forces that occupied Jerusalem, are called a "sinful nation" (ἔθνος ἁμαρτωλόν, cf., Isa 14:5). In 1 Macc 2:44–48, the writer describes others of Israel joining forces with Mattathias:

> So they joined forces and slew sinful men (ἁμαρτωλούς) in their anger, and wicked men (ἀνόμους) in their wrath: but the rest fled to the Gentiles (ἔθνη) for help. So they recovered the law out of the hand of the Gentiles (ἔθνη), and out of the hand of kings, and they did not give triumph to the sinner (ἁμαρτωλῷ).

The "sinful" and "wicked men" in the first half of the text refer to Jewish collaborators with the Gentiles. However, the term "sinner" (ἁμαρτωλῷ) refers specifically to Antiochus Antiphanes and the term "Gentiles" (ἔθνη) to his people. They are labeled "sinners" because they are enemies of Israel who had in arrogance defiled and robbed the sanctuary, killed innocent Israelites, and forced Gentile idol worship upon Israel (1 Macc 1:21–24; 2:9, 12). They are insolent and lawless (1 Macc 2:20). Another specific use of "sinner" to refer to a Gentile is 2 Macc 12:23. The ἁμαρτωλός is Timotheus, the Gentile general, whom Judas Maccabee pursued and defeated.

The use of the term "sinner" to refer to the Gentile in the Apocrypha flows out of OT precedent (Gen 13:13; Exod 9; Pss 9:16–18; 94:5; 125:3; 129:3–4; Isa 14). The idea is general in Sirach and Wisdom of Solomon, but due to the nature of the provenance of the material, the "sinner" references to Gentiles become very specific in 1 and 2 Macc.

Mercy for "Sinners" in the Apocrypha

An important feature of the "sinner" in the Apocrypha is that the "sinner" is sometimes offered repentance. For example, in Sir 16:11, the Lord is said to be both mighty to forgive and to pour out wrath. Sirach gives a clear call to repentance in 17:24–25: "Unto them that repent (μετανοέω), he granted them to return and patiently comforted those who failed (or lacked endurance). Return to the Lord and forsake your sins (ἁμαρτίας) and petition his face." Sirach also calls upon his son to repent in Sir 21:1. In 21:6, he states that "the 'sinner' hates reproof, but the one who fears the Lord will turn and repent in his heart."

Tobit admonishes his people who are in captivity in Nineveh to repent: "Turn, sinners (ἁμαρτωλοί), and do justice (δικαιοσύνη) before him. Who knows, if he may accept you and have mercy on you" (Tob 3:6).

The Prayer of Manasseh presents the "sinner" as an individual in personal confession and penitence.[42] The first observation is that this prayer illustrates the flexibility of the language for "sin" consistent with the LXX. For example, one may observe the following in verses 8–12:

v. 8   You have appointed repentance for me the sinner (ἁμαρτωλός)

v. 9   For I have sinned (ἥμαρτον) more than the number of the sand of the sea
my transgressions (ἀνομίαι) are multipled
the multitude of my iniquities (ἀδικιῶν)

---

42. *OTP* 2:627.

v. 10   I have done evil (πονηρόν) before you
        not doing the Lord's will
        not keeping his commandments
        setting up abominations

v. 12   I have sinned (ἡμάρτηκα), Lord, I have sinned (ἡμάρτηκα)
        and I acknowledge my transgressions (ἀνομίας)

The interplay between ἁμαρτωλός/ἁμαρτάνω with ἀνομίαι, ἀδικιῶν, and πονηρόν reflect flexibility in this language. The fact that the LXX translates רָשָׁע by a variety of terms and that these terms are used with flexibility in the LXX and Apocrypha is a corrective to E. P. Sanders who states that "sinner" is a technical term (רָשָׁע = ἁμαρτωλός).[43]

Second, the prayer is an example of the "sinner" in an individual instead of a corporate context (v. 9, the dramatic use of the 1st person singular "I have sinned," ἥμαρτον). This illustrates that although "sinners" are commonly a corporate entity in Jewish literature, individual "sinners" are also identified. This corrects Neale's overstatement that "sinners" in the Apocrypha are always a corporate entity and never identified with specific individuals.[44]

Third, the standard OT concepts of the "righteous/sinner" theme are clearly present. For example, the "righteous" is one properly related to the Lord (v.1, the "righteous" seed; v. 3, the Lord is the God of the "righteous") and has not sinned (ἡμαρτηκόσιν) against the Lord (v. 3). This proper relationship is measured by the law of the Lord. For example, v. 10 states that he had not done the will of the Lord or kept his commandments. Neale states that the "sinner" in the Apocrypha is usually of a general ideological nature, part of the description of the struggle between absolute good (represented by God and the "righteous") and absolute evil (represented by the "sinners").[45] Yet the "righteous/sinner" theme is not presented in such general terms. It is presented against the background of the Lord as righteous, his demands of appropriate dealings with him and others in view of his righteousness, and those demands revealed in the law.

43. Sanders, *Jesus and Judaism*, 177. See the discussion earlier in this chapter for the LXX data.
44. Contra Neale, *None But the Sinners*, 82.
45. Ibid., 81.

Fourth, the Prayer of Manasseh is significant because it pre-dates the destruction of 70 CE.[46] This demonstrates that the idea that genuine "sinners" could repent existed in Palestinian Judaism before 70 CE. Neale suggests that this may be the only pre-Christian example of the use of "sinner" in the context of repentance.[47] This overlooks Psalm 51 to which the Prayer of Manasseh has great affinity.[48] The parallels are clear and demonstrate that the possibility of repentance for real "sinners" was present early and, contrary to Neale, not something new but something based on OT precedent.[49]

The "Sinner" in the OT Pseudepigrapha

Enoch

When we turn to the Pseudepigrapha, the initial observation is that one finds the same emphasis upon judgment and condemnation of the "sinner" that we find in the Psalms. *1 Enoch* 1:9 is typical: "He (God) will destroy the wicked ones and censure all flesh on account of everything they have done, that which the "sinners" and the wicked ones have committed against him."[50]

Many passages do not identify a specific "sinner" but refer to the type of person who is opposite of the "righteous." But even here, the OT understanding of the "righteous/sinner" is behind the generalized uses. For example, the "sinner" is not specifically identified in *1 En.* 1:1. The "sinners" are those opposite of the "righteous" and "elect" who will be removed at the judgment (*1 En.* 1:9).

As in the OT, the "righteous/sinner" theme in *1 Enoch* is understood with the background of the Lord as judge (cf., *1 En.* 22:10–12). To be a "sinner" is to be one who does not fear the Most High (*1 En.* 101:7, 9). The

---

46. *OTP* 2:627. Charlesworth notes that many scholars date the prayer to the 2nd century BC because of its Jewish language and affinity to other Jewish apocryphal works, especially the additions to Daniel. I have chosen to treat the Prayer of Manasseh in the Apocrypha section because of its inclusion in the LXX.

47. Neale, *None But the Sinners*, 92.

48. For a chart of the parallels, see *OTP* 2:630.

49. Neale, *None But the Sinners*, 92.

50. Numerous examples could be cited (*1 En.* 1:9; 81:7–8; 95:2; 100:4, et al.).

"sinner" in *1 Enoch* also maintains the OT understanding of the "righteous/sinner" theme in regard to one's relationship with others. For example, in *1 En.* 94:1, Enoch admonishes his children that the way of the "righteous" is worthy to be embraced but the way of the "wicked" will perish (cf., Ps 1:6). In vv. 6–11, he describes the way of the "wicked" in standard OT language: oppression and injustice (v. 6); the use of deception to get rich (v. 8); forgetting the Most High and committing oppression (v. 9).

In more specific terms, the "sinners" in Enoch are idolaters (*1 En.* 99:7; 104:9) and appear to be economic and political oppressors. This includes not only the Greek and Roman imperialists but also the Jewish aristocracy.[51] For example, economic exploiters are rebuked in *1 En.* 97:7: "Woe to you, sinners (ἁμαρτωλοί) whose records are evil and against you." The specific crime is stated in v. 8: "Woe to you who gain silver by that which is not just" (צַדִּיק = δίκαιος, cf., 101:7; 103:5). In *1 En.* 102: 9, like the prophets (cf. Amos 2:6, 7; Mic 6:10–12), the "sinners" are accused of robbing and impoverishing people by taking their property. An example of political oppression is found in *1 En.* 103:14, 15: "In our tribulation we brought a charge against them before the authorities, and cried out against those devouring us, but they (the authorities) neither would pay attention to our cries nor wish to listen to our voice." Verse 15 states that instead of helping the victims, the authorities helped those robbing and murdering them. It concludes, "Concerning the 'sinners' (ἁμαρτωλοί), they do not remember their sins (ἁμαρτία)." Sin is being viewed in a social context similar to the theme of justice in the Pentateuch. The theme of injustice in *1 En.* is similar to the use of רָשָׁע in the legal dispute contexts of Exodus 23:1, 7 and Deuteronomy 25:1–2. For example, in Exodus 23:1, a sinner (רָשָׁע = ἄδικος) is one who is trying to give false testimony against someone. The context is the law code as it pertains to justice, mercy and appropriate dealings with others, especially the poor. A person was to expect justice before the court in accordance with the character and law of God. Deuteronomy 25:1–2 directs a person with a dispute to bring it to the court (מִשְׁפָּט = κρίσιν) and the judges (שֹׁפֵט = κρίνων) and they shall acquit (צָדַק) the innocent (צַדִּיק) and condemn (רָשָׁע) the guilty (רָשָׁע). Yet *1 Enoch* states that the "sinners" (ἁμαρτωλοί) lied and even

---

51. *OTP* 1:9.

altered just verdicts (104:10). For Enoch, the comfort for the "righteous" is that even though the "sinner" will not remember his sin, the Lord is writing them down in his book (*1 En.* 104:5, 6).

In *1 En.* 82:4, a person is designated a "sinner" who does not reckon the calendar by the sun and by a 364 day calendar: "Blessed are those who walk in the street of righteousness and have no sin like the 'sinners' in the computation of the days in which the sun goes in its course in the sky" (*1 En.* 82:4–7). James Dunn cites this as an example of a "factional" context in which a "sinner" is someone whose conduct is outside of the boundary. He is simply guilty of conduct unacceptable to those inside the group.[52] Dunn's observation is correct regarding this usage but caution must be taken not to minimize the fact that the "sinner" so designated even here is viewed as one who has violated the law and the covenant. The term "sinner" is not applied to people simply because they are outside their narrow interpretation of a trivial rule. Also, it is misleading to suggest that this usage dominates the "sinner" theme in *1 Enoch*. This is not the case. Usually the "sinner" is defined in terms consistent with OT categories as described earlier (*1 En.* 94:1, 6–11).

Jubilees

In *Jubilees*, the "sinners" can include those within Israel as in *1 Enoch*.[53] The issue of Hellenization is an important concern in *Jubilees*. But *Jubilees* places much greater emphasis on keeping the law and the covenant in specific terms. For example, in *Jub.* 15:33–34, Israelites who fail to circumcise their sons have left the covenant and made themselves as Gentiles. As a result of this sin, they have become sons of Beliar and are condemned to eternal punishment with no hope for forgiveness. Another example is *Jub.* 23:16 in which the writer speaks of those who will be judged by the Lord because they have forsaken the covenant. In 23:19, this is defined as forgetting "the commandments and covenant and festivals and months and sabbaths and jubilees and all of the judgments."

---

52. Dunn, "Pharisees, Sinners, and Jesus," 276–77.

53. Wintermute dates *Jubilees* before 140 BCE (see *OTP* 2:44). He bases this especially on the likelihood that Jubilees was written before the split between the Maccabees and the Essenes because of Jubilees pro-Maccabee stance.

Helenistic and Jewish Concepts of the "Sinner"

This is similar in some ways to the language of Tobit who identifies himself as one who "walked in the way of truth and justice" (δικαιοσύνη, Tob 1:3). For Tobit this included:

(1) attending the feasts at Jerusalem (1:5), cf., the Feasts of Shebuot (*Jub.* 6:7–31), of Firstfruits (*Jub.* 44:1–4) and Passover (*Jub.* 49);

(2) tithing (1:6–8, cf., *Jub.* 13:25–27; 32:10–15);

(3) avoiding intermarriage with Gentiles (1:9, cf. *Jub.* 30:7–17);

(4) eating food in accordance with the law of Moses, not the food of the Gentiles (1:10, 11, cf., *Jub.* 5: 6–14; 6: 38).

These similarities suggest that there were some basic common elements included in the idea of what it meant to be "righteous" (צַדִּיק = δίκαιος) in Palestinian Judaism during this early to mid- second century of the intertestamental period. Apart from these similarities, in *Jubilees* the measure of what identifies one as a "sinner" within Israel becomes linked more closely with Temple language. For example, in *Jub.* 9:15, the sons of Noah speak of the final judgment of the Lord on those who violate boundaries. These will be judged because they have filled the earth with "sin and pollution and fornication and transgression." Another example is *Jub.* 16:5, which describes to Abraham the justification for the condemnation of Sodom: "Behold, I have made known to you all of their deeds that (they were) cruel and great "sinners" and that they were polluting themselves and they were fornicating in their flesh and they were causing the pollution of the earth." In v. 6, this condemnation is promised to all places that act according to the pollution of Sodom. The example of Sodom is also used in *Jub.* 20:6–9 in a charge by Abraham to Isaac to avoid fornication, impurity, and all corruption from sin. Abraham reminds Isaac of God's destruction of Sodom (v. 6) and calls upon him to love and follow God's commands (v. 7a) and to avoid idols (vv. 7b–9).

Another example in *Jubilees* declares that the time of Jubilee will not occur for Israel until Israel is purified from all sin of fornication, defilement, uncleanness, sin, and error (50:5). Some of this emphasis on Temple language can be explained by the probable authorship of *Jubilees* from the priestly circles of Judaism during the period of the Maccabees prior to the break with Hyrcanus.[54] Sexual sins are particularly condemned. For example, there is no greater sin than fornication (*Jub.* 33:20; cf., 9:15; 16:5; 20:6–7; 50:5). Mention is also made of incest (*Jub.* 33:13; 41:23ff).

Another feature of the "sinner" within Israel introduced in *Jubilees* is the concern over more narrow issues related to worship within Judaism. This is illustrated particularly in the concern over the use of the 364-day solar calendar for calculating the feasts and the sabbaths. For example, *Jub.* 6:34 states that to confuse the calendar will result in corrupting the fixed times, transgressing their ordinances, setting awry all the ordinances of the year. As a result, the children of Israel will forget the feasts and the covenant and walk in the ways of the Gentiles (*Jub.* 6:35). There is no reason to view this as a sectarian concern. The priestly author presents his position as the normative orthodox position. He acknowledges the periods of apostasy but expects a general return to the position which he represents (*Jub.* 23:26).[55]

Jubilees also identifies the "sinner" with the Gentile, another reflection of the fear of Hellenization. The "sinners" of Sodom have already been mentioned (*Jub.* 16:5). In *Jub.* 23:24, the expression "the Gentiles" is in direct apposition to the term "the sinners" in a clear general equating of the two groups. For the writer of *Jubilees*, Gentiles are "sinners." Another example is *Jub.* 24:28 which speaks of Isaac's curse on the Philistines to be treated as objects of wrath and anger at the hands of the "sinners," the Gentiles. The "sinners" here are the nations surrounding the Philistines that Isaac desires to be used as an instrument of God's wrath on the Philistines. In Jubilees 30:21–23 the "sinner" moves in two directions. The first direction is toward what it means to be a "righteous" person in contrast to a "sinner" within Israel. The context is the rape of Dinah by the sons of Shechem. In *Jub.* 30:17, the act of killing these men is called "righteousness" for them and written down for them as "righteousness." The patriarch Levi is one of the avengers who is then chosen for the priesthood because of his zeal for righteousness and judgment (30:20). Levi is then called a friend and a "righteous one" in the heavenly tablets (30:20b). This emphasizes righteousness in terms of a relationship with the Lord God as friend. This concept is then applied to all members of the covenant in Jubilees 30:21:

---

54. This position is stated and defended by Wintermute (see *OTP* 2:44–45). The close parallels with 1 Macc makes this position probable.

55. *OTP* 248.

> All of these words I have written to you, and I have commanded you to speak to the children of Israel that they might not commit sin or transgress the ordinances or break the covenant which was ordained for them so that they might do it and be written down as friends.

The consequences of breaking the commandments and the covenant are spelled out in 30:22:

> But if they transgress and act in all the ways of defilement, they will be recorded in the heavenly tablets as enemies. And they will be blotted out of the book of life and written in the book of those who will be destroyed and with those who will be rooted out of the land.

According to *Jubilees*, to transgress the commandments and the covenant makes one God's enemy, he is under the condemnation of God. Although the term is not used here, this one would clearly be considered a "sinner."

The second direction that *Jub.* 30:23 takes is the identification of the Gentiles as "sinners." The names of the sons of Jacob were said to have been written in heaven because they did what was right (צְדִיק) and upright and just against the "sinners" who had raped their sister Dinah. The writer of *Jubilees* generalizes this event and applies it to Israel's present concern regarding intermarriage (*Jub.* 30:10–15). It is a capital crime for which no sacrifice will atone (*Jub.* 30:10–17). This concern for intermarriage and the evil influence of Gentiles is reflected in the admonitions to separate from the Gentiles.[56] For example, in *Jub.* 6:35–38, the writer warns his readers about forgetting proper dates of the feasts because it results in a general slide that includes walking in the ways of the Gentiles, transgressing God's commandments and eating Gentile food. Every deed of humankind is "sin and evil" (*Jub.* 21:21). In *Jub.* 22:16, Abraham warns his grandson Jacob to separate from the Gentiles. He is not to eat with them, do their deeds, associate with them because their deeds are defiled, their ways contaminated, despicable, and abominable. Although the term "sinner" is not used in this text, the description here of Gentiles in general bears strong resemblance to the description of the "sinners" of Sodom (*Jub.* 16:5). In 22:17 Abraham warns Jacob not to sacrifice to their idols, which are demons. The laws

---

56. This supports Abrahams's postion as stated on page 7 above.

against intermarriage, being a capital offense with no atonement possible, are emphasized (*Jub.* 30:7; 10–17).

Sibylline Oracles

The *Sibylline Oracles* may be mentioned briefly. Book 3, which contains a relevant section, in the opinion of J. J. Collins, dates between 163–145 BCE and was written in Egypt.[57] According to the Sibyl, certain types of action lead to destruction and others lead to deliverance. Specific groups are admonished for certain behaviors. For example, the Romans are warned against homosexuality (*Sib. Or.* 3:185–86) and covetousness (3:189). The Greeks are also endangered by idolatry (3:545–55), adultery and homosexuality (3:762–66). Gentiles in general are endangered by homosexuality (3:601–607). Jews are warned that idolatry caused their exile to Babylon (3:275–85). They should avoid idolatry (3:575–90), adultery and homosexuality (3:595–600). In *Sib. Or.* 3:304, the Sibyl speaks of woes that God devised for Babylon because it destroyed his temple: "Woe to you, Babylon, and race of Assyrian men. At some time a rushing destruction will come upon the whole land of 'sinners.'"

What is significant about this section of the Sibylline Oracles for our study is that we find specific kinds of sins associated with Gentiles, especially idolatry and sexual sins. *Jubilees* made similar warnings (without the same emphasis on homosexuality) written close to the same time period. *Jubilees* was written from Palestinian Jewish circles and the Oracles from Alexandrian Jewish circles. This demonstrates that there was a widely held set of sins that the Jewish religious community associated with Gentiles.

Psalms of Solomon

The *Psalms of Solomon* represent Palestinian Judaism and pre-date the fall of Jerusalem in 70 CE. Many see these as examples of sectarian writings from either Pharisaic or Essene circles. The identity of "sinner" in the *Psalms of Solomon* are "sinners" both within Israel and without. The identity of "sinners" within Israel range from general to specific.[58]

---

57. Collins, *OTP* 1:354.

58. R. B. Wright tends to link the psalms to either Pharasaic or Essene groups because

In the *Psalms of Solomon* there is a general identification of the "sinner" within Judaism that is consistent with the OT and the Apocrypha and Pseudepigrapha. Righteousness is understood in terms of one's proper relationship with God, demonstrated by faithfulness to the law and the covenant, and one's proper relationship to one's neighbor, again measured by the law. This is illustrated in *Pss. Sol.* 14:1–6. The right relationship with God is the beginning point and this is demonstrated by one's faithfulness to the law (14:1–3): "The Lord is faithful to those who truly love him, to those who endure his discipline, to those who live in the righteousness of his commandments, in the Law, which he has commanded for our life." The devout shall not be uprooted forever for Israel is their portion and inheritance from God (14:4, 5). But the "sinner" is opposite of the "righteous" (14:6). "Sinners" (ἁμαρτωλοί) and "criminals" (παρανόμοι), who love (to spend) the day in sharing their sin, will be uprooted.

The "sinners" are those not faithful to the Lord or his law. At one level, the psalmist is concerned for Israelites who have been unfaithful to the covenant and adopted Gentile practices (*Pss. Sol.* 17:15). The citizens of Jerusalem do not practice righteousness, from the king, to the judge, to the people (17:19–20). This material lends support to Perrin's understanding of the term "sinner" to refer to "those Jews who made themselves as Gentiles."[59]

At another level, the "sinners" in the *Psalms of Solomon* can be other Jews who are not as diligent in their religious practice. For example, in 3:7–9, "The righteous constantly searches his house to remove unintentional sins" (v. 7). The one who is "righteous" actively deals with his sin according to verse 8: "He atones for (sins of) ignorance by fasting." In contrast the "sinner" (ἁμαρτωλός) stumbles and adds sin upon sin (v. 10). This is the same characteristic mentioned in Sir 3:27.

The "sinner" within Israel in the *Psalms of Solomon* can have an even narrower identification, namely the Jewish opponents of the devout. The opponents are probably the Hasmonean Sadducees who are viewed as violent usurpers of the Davidic throne and Solomon's temple. R. B. Wright

---

of its theodicy (*Pss. Sol.* 2:30, 32), and the psalmist's view of his opponents as guilty of the misuse of the law (4:8). Charlesworth argues that such a label is unwise because of a lack of clear knowledge regarding the Pharisees before 70 CE. Both of these positions are found in *OTP* 2:641–42.

59. Perrin, *Rediscovering*, 94.

observes the parallel between the catalog of sins that characterize the opponents of the Qumran community listed in the *Damascus Document*, the "3 nets of Belial," and those listed by the psalmist:[60]

CD 4:15–18	*Pss. Sol. 8:8–12*
1) lust	1) adultery
2) riches	2) stealing from the sanctuary
3) defilement	3) walking on the place of sacrifice and defiling the sacrifices as if they were common meat

The psalmist attacks a person who sits in the council of the devout, probably the Sanhedrin, as a "profaner," who provokes the Lord by lawbreaking (4:2). He is cruel and excessive in his judgments against "sinners." Josephus also spoke of the cruelty of certain council members who were extremely rigid in judging offenders (*Ant.* 20.9.1). Another example of this use of "sinner" is *Pss. Sol.* 17:5: "Because of our sins (ἁμαρτίαις), 'sinners' (ἁμαρτωλοί) rose up against us, they set upon us and drove us out." The psalmist says that these "sinners" had not received the Lord's promise, they set up a monarchy because of their arrogance, and despoiled the Davidic throne (17:6). Wright identifies these as Judeans, probably the Hasmoneans, as illegitimate usurpers of the throne and the temple.[61] Johannes Tromp, who argues that the "sinners" of *Psalm of Solomon* 17 are consistently Gentiles throughout, has recently disputed this.[62] But the "sinners" of 17:1–7a are in the third person plural. In 17:7b, the psalmist abruptly states, "There rose up against them (the "sinners" of 17:1–7a) a man alien to our race." The change in referents is from "sinners" opposed to the psalmist to a single "foreigner" whom God used to punish them, uprooting them and their descendents from the earth. The foreigner in 17:7b seems to refer to the same "sinner" identified in *Pss. Sol.* 2:1 who stormed Jerusalem. The reference is most likely to the Roman general, Pompey. This interpretation is supported by the details of Josephus's de-

60. Wright, *OTP* 2:648.
61. Ibid., 665.
62. Tromp, "The Sinners," 344–61.

scription of Pompey's attack on Jerusalem and the subsequent removal of Aristobulus from Jerusalem to Rome as described in *Ant.* 14.4. Josephus states that Pompey had the supporters of Aristobulus killed (*Ant.* 14.4.4) and Aristobulus and his family removed to Rome (*Ant.* 14.4.5).

Sometimes the *Psalms of Solomon* appear to have Israel's foreign oppressors in view. The *Psalms* open with the psalmist's plea as a "righteous" man to the Lord when "sinners" set upon him in the clamor of war (*Pss. Sol.* 1:1–2). Sometimes the "sinner" is in the singular and can be identified. For example, as discussed earlier, in *Pss. Sol.* 2:1, the term "sinner" (ἁμαρτωλός) refers specifically to Pompey and his attack on Jerusalem in 63 BCE.[63] Neale states that in the *Psalms of Solomon*, there is more certainty and concreteness with reference to actual historical "sinners" in the writer's world than in any other intertestamental literature.[64] It is against these Gentile "sinners" the psalmist hopes for the son of David, the Messiah, to come soon to purge Jerusalem from the Gentiles who trample her to destruction (17:22); to drive out the "sinners" (ἁμαρτωλοί) from the inheritance (17:23); and to smash the arrogance of the "sinners" (17:23b). At the warning of the Messiah, the Gentiles will flee from his presence and he will condemn the "sinners" by the thoughts of their hearts (17:25). Yet there is the hope that the Gentile nations will serve the Messiah under his yoke (17:30) and come from the ends of the earth to Jerusalem to see the glory of the Lord (17:31). The Messiah will show compassion to all Gentile nations who revere him (17:34). So within the strong language against the Gentile "sinner" there is also a theme of hope for Gentiles who respond properly to the Messiah when he is revealed. This evidence is a correction to Perrin's assertion that Jewish literature of this period denied all hope to Gentiles.[65]

A final note on the *Psalms of Solomon* is that the psalmist acknowledges that he almost shared the fate of death with the "sinner" (16:2). He was drawn away from the Lord (16:3) but the Lord woke him up and thus saved him from being counted with the "sinner" for his destruction. He prayed to God for mercy (16:6) and then for protection from immorality (16:7, 8), deceit and anger (16:10). This is a correction to Neale who states

63. Wright, *OTP* 2:651.
64. Neale, *None But the Sinners*, 84.
65. Perrin, *Rediscovering*, 93.

The Sinner in Luke

that the "sinner" in *Psalms of Solomon* is fully the object of God's condemnation and wrath.[66] Mercy was available. It also corrects Perrin's assertion that Jewish "sinners" were regarded as beyond hope.[67] The theme of mercy is presented in a manner consistent with Tob 3:6. Although the theme is infrequent, mercy is available for those who humble themselves and repent (*Pss. Sol.* 9:6, 7).

A significant change takes place in the literature of the Pseudepigrapha. The later Pseudepigrapha have much greater emphasis upon "sinners" as potential objects of God's mercy. For example, the *Greek Apocalypse of Ezra* (second–ninth century CE) asks for mercy on "sinners" in 1:15 and then declares "woe to the "sinners" in the world to come" in 1:24. The writer asks that the Lord pity the "sinners" (2:23) and have mercy on them (5:6).[68] The *Apocalypse of Sedrach* (150–500 CE) also requests mercy for "sinners" (5:7,8), declaring the Lord to be merciful, showing pity and grace to "sinners" (15:1). An interesting note here is that the Lord is recorded as stating that the reason "sinners" are not saved is that their hearts are like stone (15:5). This is consistent with the "sinner" as characterized by a hard heart and neck (Sir 3:26–27a) and an unwillingness to accept reproof (Sir 2:17; 35:17). The *Testament of Abraham* (200 BCE–100 CE) describes "sinners" (ἁμαρτωλοί) as those who pass their lives in sin (ἁμαρτία, 10:12). The "sinners" in the *Testament of Abraham* are viewed in universal terms, as Abraham observes the entire inhabited world (10:12, 13). From the view of a flying chariot, Abraham observes robbery and murder (10:5); sexual immorality (10:8); and home invasions for theft (10:10). Michael, the angel, chastises Abraham because of his lack of mercy on "sinners." The angel explains that since Abraham has not sinned (ἁμαρτάνω), he has no mercy on "sinners" (ἁμαρτωλοί, 10:13). Yet Abraham will later plead for mercy on behalf of "sinners" (14:11–14). The patience of God toward "sinners" is explained in 10:14: "God delays the death of the 'sinner' so that he should repent (ἐπιστρέφω) and live."

---

66. Neale, *None But the Sinners*, 91.
67. Perrin, *Rediscovering*, 93.
68. E. M. Stone dates Ezra between the second–ninth centuries CE. *OTP* 1:563.

Neale states that the concept of mercy for the "sinner" is a new view that takes place after the destruction period.[69] However, the Prayer of Manasseh and Tob 3:6 express a view of mercy for the repentant "sinner" and this view is early, having its roots in earlier declarations (e.g., Ps 51). The presence of the theme of repentance is also found in Sirach who gives a clear call to repentance in 17:24–25.

Sirach also calls upon his son to repent in Sir 21:1. In 21:6, he states that "the "sinner" hates reproof, but the one who fears the Lord will turn and repent in his heart." But the merciful view toward the "sinner" is even found in early Pseudepigrapha. For example, in the *Testament of Benjamin*, a good man is said to be merciful to all even though they may be "sinners" (ἁμαρτωλοί, 4:2).[70] Neale cites this in a footnote as one of the few references to "sinners" in the pre-destruction Pseudepigrapha.[71] If this is the case, then it is significant that it expresses mercy toward the "sinner." What occurs in the later Pseudepigrapha is not the introduction of a new theme but an entirely new emphasis on the theme of mercy for the "sinner."

A few other observations may be made regarding these later Pseudepigrapha. First, there is still maintained the OT concept of the "righteous" as being those who are properly related to God and others in accordance with God's will. For example, that which is "righteous" is weighed against the righteousness of God (*T. Ab.* 13:10). The legal language and image which informs the "righteous/sinner" concept in the OT (Exod 23:1–8; Deut 25:1, 2) is also found. For example, the picture of final judgment is a judge sitting on a throne who examines both the "righteous" (δίκαιοί) and the "sinner" (ἁμαρτωλοί, *T. Ab.* 13:3–8). Second, the use of the term "sinner" has a range of meaning. On one end it is used as a type of person. *Testament of Abraham* 10:5–10, for example, characterizes "robbers, murderers" (10:5) and the sexually immoral (10:8) as "sinners". On the other end, it is used of specific "sinners" who commit specific sins. In the *Greek Apocalypse of Ezra*, Herod is specified as a "sinner" and his specific sin is murdering infants (4:9–12).

---

69. Neale, *None But the Sinners*, 91.
70. H. C. Kee dates Benjamin in the second century BCE, *OTP*, 1:778.
71. Neale, *None But the Sinners*, 91 n2.

Summary of the "Sinner" in Jewish Intertestamental Literature

In summary, the following can be stated regarding the "sinner" theme in the Jewish Apocrypha and Psedepigrapha. First, the theme of judgment on the "sinner" observed in the OT and Psalms is present throughout this material, although emphasized more in some writings (e.g., *Jubilees*).

Second, offers of repentance are found throughout the material from Sirach to the late Pseudepigrapha. However, in the early material the theme is infrequent. In the later Pseudepigrapha, the theme of mercy for the "sinner" receives greater stress; though, even here the theme of judgment for the unrepentant "sinner" is prevalent.

Third, the "sinner" can be inside of Israel. This ranges from those who blatantly violate the law and the covenant (circumcision, intermarriage, eating Gentile food, immorality, breaking the Sabbath) to those who fail to observe the law as the writer understood its demands (e.g., the correct interpretation of the calendar, *Jub.* 6:32). The literature reflects concern over Hellenization and Gentile influence.

Fourth, "sinners" are often Gentiles, both in the Apocrypha and the Pseudepigrapha. Sometimes it refers to Gentiles in general (e.g., *Jub.* 23:23) and sometimes to specific Gentile "sinners" (e.g., Antiochus and Pompey).

Fifth, as in the OT, the term "sinner" has a range of use. On the one hand, the "sinner" can be a type of person whose qualities are emphasized. On the other hand, the term "sinner" may be applied to a specific group or individual who fit the profile. There is a range of meaning of the term "sinner," from metaphorical to concrete, depending on the context. Neale defines the "sinner" from only one end of the spectrum, neglecting to give sufficient weight to those contexts that identify actual "sinners."

Just as the OT text identified actual historical referents to circumstances in the Psalms through the superscriptions (e.g., Ps 3), which were later included by the writers of the LXX, the "sinner" in the Apocrypha and Pseudepigrapha also moves from general contexts to specific people and situations. It is this range of use that Neale fails to see because of his insistence upon the "sinner" as only an ideological category and metaphor. Steven Croft provides a helpful example of how a term like "sinner" can be understood best in terms of its range of meaning. He applies this idea to the use of the term "poor" in the OT and, as has been demonstrated

Helenistic and Jewish Concepts of the "Sinner"

in our examination of the term "sinner," this term also is used with both metaphorical and concrete uses.[72]

The "Sinner" in Rabbinic Judaism[73]

The "Sinner" and the Law of Moses

In early rabbinic Judaism, the perceptions of the sinner described in Psalms and in Sirach continue but they focus especially on the attitude of a person to the Law. For the rabbis, the "sinner" was essentially the same type of person described in the Old Testament. The term רָשָׁע is found 33 times in the Mishnah, 18 times in the plural and 15 times in the singular.[74] As in the Old Testament, the Mishnah uses the term "sinner" as a type of person opposite of the "righteous" but also as a term applied to specific individuals. As a type of person, *m. 'Abot* 5:10 describes the רָשָׁע person in comparison to three other types:

> There are four types of men: he that says, "What is mine is mine and what is thine is thine"—this is the common type, and some say that this is the type of Sodom; [he that says,] "What is mine is thine and what is thine is mine"—he is an *'am ha 'aretz*; [he that says,] "What is mine is thine and what is thine is thine own"—he is a saintly man; [and he that says,] "What is thine is mine, and what is mine is mine own"—he is a wicked man = רָשָׁע."

This Mishnah clearly distinguishes the "sinner" from the other types. Rabbi Magriso suggested that the trait describing the *'am ha-'areṣ* is that trait of mutual reciprocity where everyone wishes everyone else well and

---

72. Croft, *The Identity*, 55, 70.

73. My use of the rabbinic Jewish sources will focus on the Mishnah (compiled by 200 CE) and some use of the Midrash. This material post-dates the NT but some of the traditions of the Tannaim may represent earlier tradition. The authority of a tradition is strengthened when supported by other Jewish sources such as Josephus, Qumran, and Philo. Geza Vermes argues for this approach in "Jewish Literature and New Testament Exegesis," 361–76. Jacob Neusner's position is simple: "What we cannot show, we do not know," *Rabbinic Literature and the New Testament*, 85–94, 190. So we use the rabbinic material with the understanding that it may reflect the tradition of the Pharisees. Our use of Tannaitic sayings at least puts us on a firmer footing.

74. This count is taken from Kasovsky, *Thesaurus Mishnahe* 4:1684–85.

The Sinner in Luke

helps one another.[75] The third person wants to share what he has but requests nothing from others; this is the "saint," the *chasid*. The fourth type is the רָשָׁע, the "sinner." The "sinner" is both stingy, he will not share what he has, but also greedy, he wants what everyone else has. The contrast between the *'am ha-'areṣ* and the "saint" is one of degrees of reciprocity. The contrast between the "saint" and the "wicked" is one of moral opposites. This Mishnah clearly distinguishes between the *'am ha-'areṣ* and the רָשָׁע.

The Mishnah *'Abot* further describes the רָשָׁע as "easy to provoke and hard to appease" (5:11). When it comes to charity, the רָשָׁע type of almsgiver "is minded not to give himself and that others should not give" (5:13). He does not give and discourages others. In regard to his faith, he is described in terms similar to Psalms. There the "sinner" ignores God in his life (10:4; 36:1) and does not observe God's law (119:53). Mishnah *'Abot* describes the "sinner" as one "who neither goes (to the synagogue) nor practices (the Law)" (5:14).

But just as the type of person can be applied to actual referents throughout the literature we have examined, the Mishnah applies the term "sinner" (רָשָׁע) to specific people for specific reasons. For example, in Mishnah *'Abot* 5:19, Balaam is called *the* "sinner" (הָרְשָׁע) four times in one verse. His sin is specific, Balaam is guilty of leading others to sin (5:18).

The "Sinner" and the "Righteous"

The Mishnah is consistent with the OT and earlier material in that the primary antonym for the "sinner/wicked" (רָשָׁע) is the "righteous" (צַדִּיק). This is illustrated in *m. Sanh.* 8:5 which uses the contrast four times in one verse. For the rabbis, the "sinner" was a person guilty of violating the Law of Moses. This is supported by the fact that 10 of the 33 uses of רָשָׁע are found in Mishnah *Sanhedrin* that deals with applying the Torah to specific cases of guilt or innocence and appropriate punishment. For example, *m. Sanh.* 8:1 begins with the quotation from Deut 8:1: "A stubborn and rebellious son" and then deals with what specific behaviors make a son condemned. Specifics like age, lifestyle (drunkenness), and stealing from his parents are mentioned (8:2–4). The one who is guilty is רָשָׁע and is scourged or, if unrepentant, he is stoned.

---

75. Magriso, *Avoth MeAm Lo'ez*, 254.

The "Sinner" and the *'Am ha-'areṣ*

The "sinner" in the Mishnah is not the common person, one of the *'am ha-'areṣ*.[76] The common people were not schooled regarding the details of the Pharisaic traditions, nor concerned with maintaining the same level of ritual purity. Because of this, in the view of the rabbis the *'am ha-'areṣ* would fail to observe the details of the law because of their ignorance.

For example, *m. 'Abot* 2:5 states that an *'am ha-'areṣ* cannot be pious. Since the Pharisee sought to be ceremonially pure at all times, he had to distance himself from those who might defile him. This fear of defilement is seen especially in the Mishnah tractate *Demai*, which is concerned with the paying of appropriate tithes on produce and livestock. In *m. Demai* 2:2, for example, the text reads: "He who undertakes to be trustworthy [in the matter of tithing all his produce; *n'mn*] tithes what he eats, and what he sells, and what he purchases, and does not accept hospitality of an *'am ha-'areṣ*."[77]

The reason the *ḥaber* is not to accept hospitality from the *'am ha-'areṣ'* is because he is suspected of not being trustworthy in tithing in the way desired by a *ḥaber*. In a conflicting opinion, Rabbi Judah taught that a *ḥaber* who accepts the hospitality of an *'am ha-'areṣ* is still trustworthy and although this opinion did not hold the day, it reflects the point that, although the *ḥaber* sought to regulate his interactions with the *'am ha-'areṣ*, the *ḥaber* did not see the *'am ha-'areṣ* as cut off from Israel or under the wrath of God.

This is illustrated in Mishnah *Ṭeharot* that assumes regular social interaction between the *ḥaber* and the *'am ha-'areṣ*. The statements of *m. Ṭehar.* 7:1—8:3 make this clear. The following are summary statements from these texts: If a man gave his key into the keeping of an *'am ha-'areṣ*, his house still remains clean, since he only gave him charge of guarding the key (*m. Ṭehar.* 7:1b). As this reference makes clear, a *ḥaber* could give his key to the *'am ha-'areṣ* to guard his house for him and his house remains clean. Although the *'am ha-'areṣ* was not "trustworthy" in regards to tithe and meal uncleanness, a *ḥaber* could entrust him with his home.

---

76. Sanders, *Jesus and Judaism*, 179–82.

77. Although the term *'am ha-'areṣ* is plural, for the sake of simplicity we will use the term for individuals. The context should make the meaning clear.

But the *ḥaber* could also have an *'am ha-'areṣ* as an overnight guest, as illustrated in the next verse. *Mishnah Ṭeharot* 7:2 states: If a *ḥaber* left an *'am ha-'areṣ* within his house awake and found him awake, or asleep and found him asleep, or awake and found him asleep, the house remains clean; but if he left him asleep and found him awake, the house is unclean. According to this text, a *ḥaber* could have an *'am ha-'areṣ* as an overnight guest and everything in the home is still considered clean unless the *'am ha-'areṣ* may have touched something without the *ḥaber's* knowledge. One may observe an instructive addition to this point in the Tosefta to this Mishnah that states: "A *chaber* who was sleeping in the house of an *'am ha-'areṣ*, with his clothes folded up and lying under his head, and his sandals and his jug before him—lo, these are clean" (*t. Ṭehar.* 8:2a). Here the *ḥaber* was staying as a guest of an *'am ha-'areṣ*. The explanation is that the *ḥaber* guards his personal belongings. The examples could be multiplied. Mishnah *Ṭeharot* 8:1 makes it clear that the *ḥaber* and *'am ha-'areṣ* could be neighbors and participate in social activity, as long as the *ḥaber* brought his own vessels. After his evaluation of the evidence, Aharon Oppenheimer concluded that the *'am ha-'areṣ* was neither a separate sect nor socially ostracized from the Pharisees.[78]

The point here is that the Mishnah does not equate the *'am ha-'areṣ* with the רְשָׁעִים. The key antonym group for *'am ha-'areṣ* is not the term "righteous" but the terms *ḥaber*, "trustworthy," or the "pious." This reflects a different category than "righteous/sinner" in rabbinic usage. Sarason's definition of the term *'am ha-'areṣ* makes the same point:

> As a technical term in the Mishnah, this refers to Israelites who do not observe the laws of levitical purity when handling unconsecrated foodstuffs (*hullin*), as contrasted with *ḥaber/ḥaberim*. Such common folk also are not deemed trustworthy (*ne'eman/ne'emanim*) to separate all tithes properly from produce that they grow, eat, sell, or feed to others. In the Talmud and later literature, the term sometimes is used additionally to designate an ignorant or boorish Jew who is unlearned in rabbinic traditions, as contrasted with *hakham/hakhamim* ("a [rabbinic] sage").[79]

---

78. Oppenheimer, *The 'Am Ha-Aretz*, 224.
79. Sarason, *Demai*, 399.

The *ḥaber*, although a non-priest, scrupulously attempted to maintain the strictest level of levitical purity in his daily life, especially in regards to food.[80] Although the *'am ha-'areṣ* were, in the Pharisees' view, the religious ignoramuses of the day, they were not synonymous with the "sinner."[81] The main consequence for being a non-*ḥaber*, or *'am ha-'areṣ*, was that the *ḥaber* would need to take precautions during social interaction. In contrast, the term "sinner" applies in a more narrow way to the "wicked," those who have rejected the covenant by ignoring the Law of God and are as a consequence under God's wrath.

The "Sinner" and the Gentile

Joseph Bonsirven states that among the Jews, the right name for Gentiles was "sinner."[82] He cites several lines of support. For example, the Gentile race has a deep and inborn perversion (Wis 12:10). He also cites Paul's reference to "sinners" for the Gentiles (Gal 2:15) and his catalog of vices associated with Gentiles (Rom 1:28ff.; 1 Cor 6:9ff.).[83] Bonsirven notes that the rabbis taught that Jews should avoid Gentiles because of their bestiality and sexual perversions (*t. 'Abod. Zar.* 3:4).

Mishnah *'Abot* 5:19 contrasts the disciples of Abraham with the disciples of Balaam, who is called "the wicked." The disciples of Balaam have "an evil eye, a haughty spirit, and a proud soul." They will "inherit Gehenna and go down to the pit of destruction." The *Midr. Psalm* 55:24 applies the "men of blood and deceit" to Ahithopel and his band of rebels against David. But here in Mishnah *'Abot* 5:19, the wicked are the disciples of a Gentile. Scot McKnight concludes that Jewish attitudes towards Gentiles rested on the "religious and sociological consciousness that Israel is elect, has participated in God's covenant, and consequently must live within the bounds of the covenant-and anyone who does not live within this framework are not God's chosen and so will experience God's wrath."[84] And as our research has demonstrated, being under God's wrath makes a person

---

80. Sarason, *Demai*, 400.
81. Bruce, *New Testament History*, 81.
82. Bonsirven, *Palestinian Judaism*, 66.
83. Ibid.
84. McKnight, *A Light Among the Gentiles*, 28.

a "sinner." Thus Jewish aversion to Gentile social intercourse was based on fear of judgment by breaking the covenant.

To put the picture together, one sees the attitude of the Psalms, which portrays the "sinner" as one who rejects the Law and who is an enemy of the righteous, applied by the Pharisees to those who did not follow the Law. The term "sinner" is used of those who would be classified as "sinners" by the entire community (such as the woman in Luke 7:37).[85] Although the *'am ha-'ares* were, in the Pharisees' view, religiously ignorant and could not be pious, they were not automatically equated with the "sinner." The term "sinner" applies in a more narrow way to the "wicked," those who have rejected the covenant by ignoring the Law of God.

Conclusion

The portrait of the "sinner" gathered from our research may be summarized in the following outline.

1. Often basic to the understanding of the term "sinner" is its association with guilt because of lawbreaking, especially when viewed in contrast with its primary antonym "righteous." The language is legal language of guilt and innocence.

2. A consistent characteristic of the "sinner" in both Hellenistic and Jewish sources is that he is under the wrath of God.

3. Of special significance is that the identity of the "sinner"/"righteous" in the OT is rooted in the character and attitude of God who judges both his people and the Gentile nations in righteousness.

4. The OT concept of the "sinner"/"righteous" was also linked to the influence of Israel's covenant relationship with Yahweh upon human relationships (e.g., Lev 19). A person who did not treat his neighbor in accordance with the will of the Lord would be a "sinner."

5. In the OT and Jewish material, the will of God as revealed in the law was the standard by which one was considered to be "righteous" or a "sinner."

---

85. Abrahams, *Studies in Pharisaism and the Gospels*, 1:55.

6. The identification of the "sinner" was found to be located on a continuum from metaphorical usage to specific historical referents. The "sinner" was found inside and outside of Israel.

7. Gentiles were sometimes designated "sinners." The identification was not broad in the OT but developed more clearly in the Apocrypha and especially the Pseudepigrapha.

8. The theme of mercy for the "sinner" is present but infrequent in the OT and early intertestamental Jewish literature. The theme became more frequent in later Pseudepigrapha.

The "sinner" for the Jew was primarily a person who was the antithesis of the "righteous." The "sinner" violated the Law of God and was unwilling to repent. There is a level of consistency between the picture of the "sinner" in the LXX, the intertestamental literature, and the rabbinic material. The "sinner" is under the wrath of God. Even the *koine* inscriptions reflected this basic sense of ἁμαρτωλός. The change in the Jewish concept comes only in the development of a greater openness to the possibility of repentance for the "sinner." Neale is correct in the following statement: "The evidence of the *Prayer of Manasseh* would suggest that the view of the 'sinner' as a penitent was not unknown before the time of Jesus. Nevertheless, Jesus' call expressly to 'sinners' appears to be a considerable departure from the habit of his time. My conclusion is that the call to repentance was not new, but the call to the 'sinner' was."[86] The missing element in Neale's argument is the sinner-Gentile link. The use of "sinner" to refer to Gentiles, though sparse in the OT, is consistent throughout the material.

An important point is that the "righteous" is called upon to distance himself from the "sinner" but not simply for fear of being ceremonially defiled. This was the concern of the *ḥaberim* in their association with the *'am ha-'areṣ*. Instead, it was the fear of being associated with the wicked, being influenced by them, being judged with them (e.g., Psalm 1). This dissociation from those Jews publicly acknowledged as "sinners" and from all Gentiles who automatically fell under the label (cf. Gal 2:15) was practiced by most pious Jews, even the *'am ha-'areṣ*.

---

86. Neale, *None But the Sinners*, 95.

3

Previews of Jesus' Mission to "Sinners" in Luke

❁ HAVING EXAMINED ἁμαρτωλός in its semantic and historical backgrounds, we turn our attention to an examination of Luke's use of the term. Before turning to the texts themselves, two preliminary points will be addressed. First, did Jesus actually eat with "toll collectors and sinners"? The authenticity of this tradition has been challenged and we will examine this question. Second, what contribution do the first four chapters of Luke's Gospel make to an understanding of the "sinner" in Luke?

The Historical Reliability of the "Sinner" Tradition in the Synoptics

Luke presents Jesus as a "friend of tax collectors and 'sinners' (Luke 7:34)." According to Neale, if there is a scholarly consensus about any feature in the life and ministry of Jesus, it may be Jesus' association with the outcasts of society.[1] But, this position has not gone unchallenged. William Walker analyzes the Synoptic tradition of Jesus' association with tax collectors and "sinners" and concludes that the historical reliability of this tradition cannot be asserted with confidence but must remain open.[2] Walker presents the following six arguments:[3]

---

1. Neale, *None But the Sinners*, 191.
2. Walker, "Jesus and the Tax Collectors," 221–38.
3. Ibid., 224–37.

1. The tradition regarding Jesus' association with tax collectors is found only in the Synoptics and is notably absent from John, the fourth Gospel.
2. The Synoptics preserve traditions that suggest Jesus held a highly negative view of tax collectors.
3. The references to intimate contact between Jesus and tax collectors appear, for the most part, in the form of accusations on the lips of Jesus' critics, and it is not at all clear that these accusations are based on fact.
4. There are only two passages that actually report that Jesus did, in fact, hold table fellowship with tax collectors, and both of these can plausibly be regarded as artificial constructions.
5. The specific identification of one of the 12 as a tax collector is at least problematic.
6. The term tax collector, τελώνης, is possibly the result of an erroneous transliteration into the Greek of an Aramaic term, *telane*, meaning "playboy."

My response to Walker will be point by point. First, the presence of the tradition only in the Synoptics and its absence from John is not determinative against the reliability of the tradition. The real question is the reliability of the data in the Synoptics. The term τελώνης is found in the triple tradition (Matt 9:10, 11; 10:3; 11:19; 21:31, 32; Mark 2:5, 16; Luke 3:12; 5:27, 29, 30; 7:29, 34; 15:1; 18:10; and 19:2, ἀρχητελώνες). It is also found in a variety of layers: in sayings of Jesus (Matt 5:46, 47; 18:17; 21:31; Luke 18:10, 11, 13); on the lips of his critics (Matt 9:11; 11:19; Mark 2:16; Luke 5:30; 7:34); and in the narration of the Evangelists (Matt 9:10; 10:3; Mark 2:15; Luke 3:12; 5:27, 29; 7:29; 15:1; 19:2). The absence of the tax collector scenes in John carries little weight. Walker himself admits that arguments from silence have little value.[4] If the author of John's Gospel had different purposes and themes in mind, this could easily account for the differences.

---

4. Walker, *Jesus and Tax Collectors*, 224.

Previews of Jesus' Mission to "Sinners" in Luke

Second, that Jesus holds a negative view of tax collectors does not rule out his association and ministry to them. Jesus is presented as consistently viewing tax collectors and sinners to be in need of repentance (Matt 9:12, 13; Mark 2:17; Luke 5:31, 32). Especially Luke presents them as models of responsiveness to Jesus, in contrast with the so-called righteous (Luke 18:9–14). Here, Walker seems to want to have it both ways. That is, he disparages the material that makes up the tradition of Jesus' association with tax collectors and then uses that tradition to establish Jesus' negative attitude toward them. E. P. Sanders is guilty of the same thing, as others have noted.[5]

Third, Walker claims that the reference to Jesus' intimate contacts with tax collectors appears, for the most part, on the lips of his critics and these accusations may have not been based on fact. Specific reference is made to Luke 7:33–34 (cf. Matthew 11:18–19a). Walker observes the serious and derogatory charges leveled by the Pharisees against John the Baptist who is said to have a demon and against Jesus who is said to be a friend of tax collectors and sinners.[6] Since it is clear that the charge against John is false, the charge against Jesus is by implication also untrue. Walker also adduces other charges that are viewed as untrue: the charge of sedition and the charge that Jesus casts out demons by the power of Satan. The difference here is that the reader clearly understands John not to have been demon possessed. In fact, he is presented as a prophet (Luke 1:76; 7:26, 28; Matt 11:13). In the charge against Jesus casting out demons by the power of Satan, Jesus' casting out of demons is presented as true, but the casting out of demons by the power of Satan is clearly presented as untrue with an entire discourse presented to counter the assertion (Matt 9:32–34; 12:22–29; Mark 3:22–27; Luke 11:14–22). The charge against Jesus' association with tax collectors and sinners, however, is never refuted but defended. Jesus' association with tax collectors and sinners in Luke 7:33–34 is defended by a wisdom saying in 7:35 and the story of the sinful woman and the Pharisee in Luke 7:36–50. The same pattern is found in Luke 15:1–2 after the Pharisees complain about Jesus' association with tax collectors and sinners. Jesus defends his action through a series of parables by presenting

---

5. Hengel and Deines, "E. P. Sanders' 'Common Judaism,'" 5.
6. Walker, *Jesus and Tax Collectors*, 226, 230.

himself as the seeking rescuer who acts consistently with the mercy of God on behalf of repentant sinners (Luke 15:3–32). If the church's goal was to refute this charge against Jesus, it would be a most curious approach for the Evangelists to create so many scenes in which Jesus is presented as intimately associating with tax collectors (Matt 9:10–11; Mark 2:14–16; Luke 5:29–32; 15:1–2; 19:1–10).

Fourth, Walker argues that only two passages actually report that Jesus held table fellowship with tax collectors, and both of these can plausibly be regarded as artificial constructions.[7] The first of these passages is Matthew 9:9–13/Mark 2:13–17/Luke 5:27–32. Walker's position depends almost entirely upon Bultmann's source critical arguments. I count fifteen footnote references to Bultmann as support. Not everyone agrees with Bultmann's assessment of the source evidence. I. H. Marshall, for example, sees no real reason to reject the historical value of Mark 2:13–17 which is parallel to Luke 5:27–32.[8] If readers reject the tradition of Jesus' association with tax collectors, they are still left with the question: from where did the tradition come? Walker himself is left with the problem of explaining the origin of the tradition. His solution is to propose a theory that the references to "tax collectors" in the Synoptics are possibly a mistake based on a transliteration of an Aramaic word, *telane*, which Walker suggests may have a meaning close to our term "playboys." This Aramaic word may have been the original word in the tradition about Jesus but when translated into Greek, the word was accidentally changed because it sounded like the Greek word for "tax collectors," *telonai*.[9] This theory has little to support it. Michael Sokoloff presents the only meaning listed for Walker's suggested term as a "type of demon."[10] There is no evidence to demonstrate its use as "playboys." Even more important is the evidence in the Mishnah that tax collectors as a group are often despised, being linked, as found in the Synoptics, with other undesirable people: thieves (*m. Tehar.* 7.6), robbers (*m. B. Qam.* 10.2; *m. Ned.* 3.4) and murderers (*m. Ned.* 3.4).

---

7. Walker, *Jesus and Tax Collectors*, 233.
8. Marshall, *Commentary on Luke*, 218.
9. Walker, *Jesus and Tax Collectors*, 237.
10. Sokoloff, *Dictionary of Palestinian Aramaic of the Byzantine Period*, 225.

It also seems appropriate to consider how Luke handles source material in general. Nils Dahl analyzes Luke's use of the story of Abraham and concludes that Luke stays closer to the Old Testament narratives and references to Abraham than any Christian or Jewish writer of his time. Luke gives very little room to legendary accretions and refrains from daring theological interpretations.[11] Based upon Luke's manner of using the Abraham story, Dahl concludes, "He (Luke) keeps rather close to his sources and wants to respect what he assumes to be the historical facts."[12] It seems to be a better approach to respect Luke's presentation of Jesus' association with tax collectors and "sinners" as being a presentation of history than to reject the multiple attestation of the Synoptics to this aspect of Jesus' life and then, in its place, propose a theory with so little to support it.[13]

Previews of Jesus' Mission to "Sinners"

Luke's preface (1:1–4), birth narrative (1:5—2:52), and material that relates the launching of the ministries of John the Baptist and Jesus (3:1—4:44) each have elements that prepare the reader for Jesus' mission to "sinners."

The Preface

As noted earlier, Luke is unique among the Synoptic writers in that he provides the reader with a preface stating his intentions. The first four verses of Luke serve as a prologue to the entire Gospel of Luke and allude also to Acts, the second volume.[14] It is not our purpose to do a complete analysis of the prologue. However, several features are relevant for our understanding of Luke's presentation of Jesus' ministry in general and how we are to understand his "sinner" material in particular, namely, Luke's claim to historical accuracy, the role of "fulfillment," and the goal of "assurance."

---

11. Dahl, "The Story of Abraham in Luke-Acts," 152.

12 Ibid., 154.

13. The term ἁμαρτωλός is found in the triple tradition (Matt 9:10=Mark 2:15=Luke 5:30; Matt 9:13=Mark 2:16=Luke 5:32; and Matt 26:45=Mark 14:41=Luke 24:7 (in a different setting); in Q (Matt. 11:19 and Luke 7:34 in discourse material); and in L (Luke 5:8; 6:32, 33, 34; 7:37, 39; 13:2; 15:1, 2, 7, 10; 18:13; and 19:7).

14. Fitzmyer, *The Gospel According to Luke I–IX*, 289.

Luke introduces his work with a preface to underscore the reliability and accuracy of his account. The preface suggests that Luke intends his readers to believe that they are reading an accurate, truthful, and thoroughly historical narrative.[15] Although he stakes a claim on the historical accuracy of his account, he writes concerning the "events which have been fulfilled" (Luke 1:1). These events are those included in the Gospel of Luke and the book of Acts. The prologue of Acts explicitly mentions Jesus in retrospect and prepares the reader for the continuation of the story (Acts 1:1–2).[16]

Charles Talbert observes that the "promise–fulfillment" theme plays a major role in Luke's narrative.[17] Prophecy is understood in the sense of a prediction of things to come. Fulfillment means what was predicted has happened or is believed to have happened. Fulfillment comes from three sources: (1) from the Jewish scriptures, (2) from a living prophet, and (3) from a heavenly messenger.

Darrell Bock observes that Luke uses fulfillment not only in the sense of direct fulfillment of specific OT passages, but also through links to OT patterns, typological fulfillment, analogous fulfillment, illustrative fulfillment, legal proof uses, proof passages, and explanatory fulfillment.[18] Luke's concern is to compare past events with the great salvation acts of God. By comparing similar types of events, he can expound and proclaim the significance of Jesus and his ministry in terms of promise and fulfillment and in terms of patterns of divine action in history.

As mentioned in chapter one, Rebecca Denova argues that in Luke-Acts, Luke rewrites the entire history of Jesus and his followers in light of scripture.[19] The grand design for the structural pattern of Luke-Acts was to continue the story of Israel into the life of Jesus and his followers. Denova argues that Luke constructs narrative events from five themes found in Isaiah: (1) the prediction of a remnant (Isa 10:20–23; 14:1–2); (2) the release of the captive exiles (Isa 49:22–26; 60:1–17); (3) the inclusion of

---

15. For a discussion of the preface, its relationship to the genre of Luke, and its historical claims see the discussion on pages xxi–xxvi above.

16. Fitzmyer, *Luke I–IX*, 289.

17. Talbert, *Reading Luke*, 234.

18. Bock, *Proclamation*, 50. An updated article based on this monograph emphasizes Luke's hermeneutic in Acts (Bock, "Scripture and the Realisation of God's Promises.").

19. Denova, *The Things Accomplished Among Us*, 25–29.

the nations who would worship the God of Israel as Gentiles (Isa 49:7; 56:5); (4) prophetic condemnation of the unrepentant (Isa 66:24); and (5) the restoration of Zion.[20] She argues that the ministry of Jesus and his disciples presented in Luke-Acts can best be understood within the context of the social injustices listed in Isaiah 59–61 and elsewhere, and emphasized throughout both books. Thus, Luke's concern for the poor and the marginalized in the narrative does not reflect an innovative "Christian" ministry, but draws upon a major theme of the prophetic oracles. Isaiah 61 provides the framework for announcing the "year of the Lord's favor" (cf. Luke 4:19) when such injustices will be righted. For Luke, it is Jesus who rights these injustices in fulfillment of OT promise.

Denova also views Isaiah as Luke's guide for the structure of ministry in Luke-Acts. Isaiah presents the raising up of a Jewish remnant of Israel before salvation reaches the ends of the earth (Isa 49:6). Denova suggests that Luke argues that the remnant is made up of Jesus' followers. No direct ministry to Gentiles exists in the Gospel of Luke because the pattern for fulfillment in Isaiah consists first of establishing a repentant Jewish remnant followed by the inclusion of Gentiles.[21]

A criticism of Denova is that her method for seeing typological parallels has few controls in Luke's narrative. She explains that her controls include (1) seeing a level of coincidence between Luke's character and events and possible parallels in Scripture; and (2) observing that the context of the passage in Luke-Acts has some association with the context of the Scriptural parallel.[22] Yet these suggested parallels can be too subtle unless Luke has given some lexical or clear conceptual connection. For example, Denova suggests that the Romans in Acts are Luke's parallel to the Ninevites in Jonah because Romans make positive judgments toward Jesus and this fulfills Jesus' prediction that the Ninevites would rise up at the judgment and condemn the unrepentant Jews (Luke 11:29–32). She views Paul as a type of Jonah (Acts 27).[23] Yet these parallels, though conceptually possible, appear overly subtle and have no observable lexical links. In addition,

20. Denova, *The Things Accomplished Among Us*, 26.
21. Ibid., 27.
22. Denova, *The Things Accomplished Among Us*, 115.
23. Ibid., 110.

THE SINNER IN LUKE

Denova overlooks the eschatological nature of Jesus' statement concerning the Ninevites and the Jews. According to Jesus, the Ninevites will condemn the Jews at the eschatological judgment (Luke 11:31, 32).

This being said, Denova is correct in underscoring the importance Isaiah plays in Luke-Acts. This can be seen in the numerous allusions to Isaiah in Luke-Acts. The following references are from the margins of Nestle-Aland's *Novum Testamentum Graece* 26 (*italics* indicate allusions that contain stronger lexical links; = designates direct citations):

Luke 1–10	Isaiah	Luke 11–24	Isaiah
1:32	9:6	11:21	49:24; 53:12
1:35	4:3	12:31	41:14
1:47	61:10; 17:10	*13:6*	*5:1–7*
1:54	41:8	13:17	45:16
1:76	40:3	13:29	43:5; 49:12; 59:19
1:78	60:1	13:34	31:5
1:79	9:1; 59:8	15:5	49:22
2:14	57:19	16:3	22:19
2:25	40:1; 49:13; 52:9	19:43	29:3
2:30	*40:5*; 52:10	*19:46=*	*56:7*
2:32	*42:6*; 46:13; 49:6,9	20:9	5:1
2:34	8:14	20:17	28:16
3:4–6=	*40:3–5*	20:18	8:14
3:22	42:1; 44:21; 62:4	21:10	19:2
4:12	7:12	21:25–27	24:19 LXX
4:18=	*61:1; 58:6*	21:33	40:8
5:22	43:25; 55:7	21:34	5:11–13
6:20	61:1	21:35	24:17
6:21	61:2; 65:18	*22:37=*	*53:12*
6:25	5:22	22:62	22:4
6:25	65:13	23:29	54:1
7:22	29:18; *35:5,6*; 42:18; 26:19; *61:1*	23:34	53:12
		23:35	42:1
8:10	*6:9*	24:26	53
9:35	42:1		
10:15	14:13; 15:11		
10:18	14:12		
10:20	4:3		

Previews of Jesus' Mission to "Sinners" in Luke

Acts 1–8	Isaiah	Acts 9–28	Isaiah
1:8	49:6	10:36	52:7
2:17	2:2	10:38	61:1
2:39	57:19	10:38	58:11
3:8	35:6	10:43	33:24
3:13	52:13; 53:11	13:23	44:28
4:27	61:1	*13:34=*	*55:3*
7:48	16:12 LXX	*13:47=*	*49:6*
7:49=	*66:1*	15:17	45:21
7:51	63:10	17:29	40:18
8:27	56:3–7	18:9	41:10
8:32=	*53:7*	19:27	40:17
		26:18	42:7, 16
		28:26=	6:9–10
		28:28	40:5

These allusions are based on conceptual and lexical connections. One allusion that is missing from the list is Luke 1:17. The verse speaks of the mission of John the Baptist and is primarily an allusion to Malachi 4:5–6. But v. 17 ends with the expression "to make ready a people prepared for the Lord." Darrell Bock observes that this combination of words is unique in the New Testament and the Old. It appears to combine elements of the LXX of Isaiah 40:3 ("prepare the way of the Lord") with 2 Sam 7:24 ("you have prepared a people for yourself"). Bock prefers the latter as the key linkage because of the emphasis on a "prepared people."[24] The importance of the term "prepare" is also reflected in the later fusion of Mal 3:1 and Isa 40:3 in Luke 7:27. Isaiah 40:3 also is the background for Luke 1:76: "for you will go before the Lord to prepare the way for him." Luke 1:77 explains how John will prepare the way of the Lord, by giving his people "the knowledge of salvation through the forgiveness of their sins."

Isaiah 40:5 also provides the allusion in Simeon's declaration of praise in Luke 2:30–31 when he declares after seeing Jesus: "My eyes have seen your salvation (τὸ σωτήριον), which you have prepared (ἡτοίμασας) in the sight of all people." The expression "my eyes have seen your salvation (τὸ σωτήριον)" is a clear allusion to Isa 40:5: "all flesh (σάρξ) shall see (ὄψεται) the salvation of God (τὸ σωτήριον τοῦ θεοῦ)." In respect to

---

24. Bock, *Proclamation*, 60.

the missions of John and Jesus but also development, John will prepare the people, giving them knowledge of salvation through repentance for forgiveness of their sins. Jesus will be the instrument of God's salvation.

When Luke introduces the public ministry of John the Baptist, he uses terms similar to the launching of OT prophetic missions: "the word of God came to John son of Zechariah in the desert" (Luke 3:2; cf. Jer 1:1). The content of his preaching is 'a baptism of repentance for the forgiveness of sins' (Luke 3:3), a clear fulfillment of Luke 1:77. In Luke 3:4, Luke connects this preaching ministry directly to Isa 40:3–5. This is the first Old Testament book clearly identified by Luke. Old Testament references in Luke 2:23, 24 are simply described as "what is said in the Law of the Lord." The reference to Isaiah in Luke 3:4 is also not given by a voice in the narrative but by Luke himself. He identifies the reference in clear, specific language: "as is written in the book of the words of Isaiah the prophet." Bock labels the use of Isaiah 40 here as "typological-prophetic," understanding Luke to see in John's ministry both fulfillment and a new and ultimate repetition of the pattern of deliverance revealed in the Exodus and promised in Isaiah.[25]

In the early chapters in his Gospel, Luke alludes to Isa 40:3–5 two times and cites it directly once. The passage, combined with Mal 3:1, serves as a summary description of John's ministry seen in Luke 3:3–17. Luke does not directly allude to the passage again in his Gospel after Luke 3 except for a possible allusion in Jesus' summary comment concerning John in Luke 7:27. However an allusion is found in Acts 28:28 at the close of the two-volume work. There, "all flesh" broadens to include the Gentiles to whom the "salvation of God (τὸ σωτήριον τοῦ θεοῦ)" is sent.

Bock compares Luke's use of Isa 40 with its OT context and concludes that Luke is correct in understanding the emphasis on the moral preparation of the people through repentance as the first stage in the ultimate fulfillment of God's salvation promise.[26] Bock also observes a natural progression that is initiated in the Isaiah 40 context, namely, the calling of a repentant people (Isa 40:11, cf. 57:13–21) followed by the Lord leading them into the land (Isa 49:11; 52:12). Luke uses this Isaiah text to dem-

---

25. Bock, *Proclamation*, 99.
26. Ibid., 9699.

onstrate that the pattern of God's redemption displayed in the Exodus is about to be repeated but now with his ultimate act of deliverance to be revealed in Jesus.

The theme of salvation being 'revealed' is also found in Luke 1:77 and 78 with strong allusions to Isaiah. Zachariah speaks of the tender mercy of God 'by which the rising sun (ἀνατολή) will visit (ἐπισκέψεται) from on high' (1:78). The word ἀνατολη contains within it both the reference to a rising 'sprout' from Jesse and to a rising light. Farris sees a fusion of the images here in a way similar to Revelation 22:16, "I am the root and offspring of David, the bright and morning star." The images serve to emphasize Jesus as the Messiah of David's line.[27] Bock also sees this double reference but distinguishes the function of the branch/sprout as deliverance and the star/sun image as linked to the light metaphor in Luke 1:79, which alludes to Isa 9:1; 42:7; 49:6; 59:9 and Ps 107:10 (Ps 106 LXX).[28] Those who sit in darkness are the people of Israel as in Isa 9:1.[29] The darkness in which they sit is a symbol of their utter need and oppression, using the image of the darkness of the prison cell that serves as the OT background (Isa 42:7; Ps 107:10). Jesus as *Servant-Messiah* will announce liberty to these captives in Luke 4:18.

This language taken from Isaiah and the light imagery in Luke 1:78–79 provide a link to Simeon's reference in Luke 2:32 to Jesus as "a light for revelation to the Gentiles and for glory for your people Israel." The verse as a whole is connected to vv. 30–31 by means of the word "light" which explains the nature of the "salvation."[30] In Isaiah, "light" is linked to Gentiles (49:6; 51:5 LXX and "glory" linked to Israel, 46:13; 60:1, 19). Luke uses Isa 40:5, 49:6, and others to emphasize the universal scope of the salvation provided by the Servant-Messiah. The details of bringing this salvation are not laid out in Isaiah but the fact that John is sent to "prepare a repentant people" within Israel before the ministry of the Messiah suggests that the pattern found in Isaiah is found in Luke-Acts. The pattern consists of the "good news" concerning "peace" and "salvation" being proclaimed first to

---

27. Farris, *Hymns*, 140–41.
28. Bock, *Proclamation*, 73.
29. Farris, *Hymns*, 141.
30. Ibid., 149.

The Sinner in Luke

Zion (Isa 52:7–9) and then being revealed "in the sight of all the nations" and "all the ends of the earth will see the salvation of God" (Isa 52:10; cf. Acts 1:8; 28:28).

Simeon's reference to the "consolation of Israel" (Luke 2:25) appears in Isa 40:1; 49:13; and 51:3. The "redemption of Jerusalem" is a parallel idea in Luke 2:40 which alludes most likely to Isa 52:9. Both of these link what is happening with Jesus as fulfillment of this hope for Israel. These ideas are linked in Luke 24:21 in the expression the "redemption of Israel" revealing that these disappointed followers of Jesus had expected this hope to have been fulfilled in Jesus.[31] For Luke, the order for the promised eschatological salvation as presented in Isaiah is proclamation for the glory of Israel followed by light to the nations. This order provides the basic framework for Luke-Acts in preparing a repentant people from among all Israel followed by a broadening ministry to the Gentiles (Luke 24:47; Acts 1:8, "ends of the earth"; 13:47).

Another allusion to Isaiah serves to prepare the reader for opposition to the Servant–Messiah. In Simeon's address to Mary in Luke 2:34, he states that Jesus is appointed "for the falling (πτῶσιν) and rising (ἀνάστασιν) of many in Israel and for (εἰς) a sign (σημεῖον) to be spoken against." Jesus shall cause division within Israel. The reference apparently combines images from Isa 8:14–15 that describe God as a stone of stumbling and a "rock of falling (πέτρας πτώματι)" that causes those who refuse to put their confidence in the Lord to "fall (πεσοῦνται) and be crushed (συν–τριβήσονται)" (Isa 8:19). This image appears to be combined with an oracle against the leaders of Jerusalem in Isa 28:13–16. These leaders will "fall backward (πέσωσιν) and be crushed (συντριβήσονται)" but those who put their trust (ὁ πιστεύων) in the new foundation of Zion, the costly cornerstone, will never be ashamed (Isa 28:16; Luke 20:17). The child divides Israel into those who fall and those who rise.

The theme of resistance and unbelief continues in Luke-Acts. Isaiah 6:9 is used in Luke 8:10 and cited directly in Acts 28:26 to emphasize the theme of judicial blindness. Luke presents this as being fulfilled and illustrated in official Judaism's response to Jesus, reflected by the actions of the Sanhedrin and other leaders of Israel. Just as Isaiah served as the key

---

31. Bock, *Proclamation*, 86.

Previews of Jesus' Mission to "Sinners" in Luke

program text for John the Baptist and Simeon's address regarding Jesus, Luke also uses Isaiah to continue to define the identity and the mission of Jesus in Luke 3:15—4:19. In Luke 3:22, the voice from heaven declares Jesus to be his "beloved son" in whom he is "well-pleased." This expression is probably a fusion of allusions that include reference to Ps 2:7 but also to the Servant of the Lord in Isa 42:1 and possibly 41:8 and 44:2.

In Luke 4:18, Jesus quotes Isa 61:1–2 in explicit terms and combines it with Isa 58:6 both to explain and proclaim his Messianic mission as the herald of "release" in terms of the year of Jubilee. Yet the term for "release" (ἄφεσιν) has already been introduced by Luke as part of the mission of John in giving his people "knowledge of salvation through the forgiveness of sins" (Luke 1:77). As observed, Jesus' mission has both continuity with John the Baptist and progress. Where John is seen to be the prophet preaching a baptism of repentance for forgiveness of sins, Jesus is seen as the one who pronounces forgiveness as the Herald who brings "release." Allusions to Isa 61:1–2 are found in (1) Luke 6:20 and 7:22 where Jesus cites the fact that "the blind see" and that he is "preaching the gospel to the poor" as proof of his Messianic identity; (2) Acts 4:27 where Peter speaks of Jesus as the Lord's "holy servant" whom God "anointed"; and (3) 10:36–38 where Peter summarizes Jesus' ministry for the Gentile Cornelius by stating that the message God sent to Israel was "the good news of peace through Jesus Christ" (v. 36; cf. Luke 4:18) and how that, after the baptism that John preached, God "anointed Jesus of Nazareth with the Holy Spirit and power, and how he went around doing good and healing all who were under the power of the devil" (v. 38). Peter's summary of Jesus' ministry fits the program description in Luke 4:18–19, 31–44.

For our present purpose, it is enough to underscore that Luke 4:18–19 is programmatic for Jesus' ministry in Luke's Gospel and, as will be demonstrated, for the ministry of his followers in Acts. Just as John's mission followed directly upon the use of the Isaiah text to provide the reader with a fulfillment context, so Jesus' mission will follow immediately from his declaration at Nazareth (Luke 4:31–44). The pattern that Jesus establishes, rooted in Isaiah and supplemented with the response to rejection (Luke 4:18–30), becomes the pattern that Jesus establishes for his disciples in Luke (9:1–6; 10:8–12), which is carried out in Acts (3:1–22; 4:30; 5:12–16; 8:4–8; 9:32–43; 14:1–8).

The Sinner in Luke

Luke presents the account of Jesus and his followers as fulfillment. This fulfillment is seen not only as apologetic but also as proclamation of the salvation plan of God revealed in Jesus. His mission to "sinners" will be presented as fulfillment of the promise that "all flesh would see the salvation of God" Jesus takes the "knowledge of salvation through the forgiveness of sins" to all who humble themselves in repentance and put their trust in him as the one who brings God's salvation. For this reason, the "sinner" texts in Luke must be understood as illustrations of the fulfillment of Jesus' mission that includes conflict as promised by the birth narrative and illustrated in his Nazareth experience. Israel will be divided over Jesus. This will be part of the sifting of Israel that began with John the Baptist and was prophesied concerning Jesus (Luke 2:34; 3:17; 13:1–9). Therefore, rather than seeing the "sinner" material in Luke as primarily a literary device that provides the conflict necessary to drive the narrative forward, it is more accurate to say that mission drives the narrative and that conflict is a necessary part of Jesus' mission.[32] This conflict will include the leaders of Israel.

To summarize, Luke uses both allusions and clear citations of Isaiah in Luke 1:5—4:19 to set forth the ministry and identity of John the Baptist and Jesus and to emphasize the nature of the salvation as spiritual, eschatological and universal. He also uses allusions to Isaiah to prepare the reader for opposition and judgment within Israel. As Denova suggests, Luke uses Isaiah as a general outline for the presentation of the fulfillment of God's salvation in Jesus in Luke-Acts.

In addition to presenting the account of Jesus and his followers as fulfillment, Luke states that the purpose for his own narrative was that Theophilus may "know the certainty" of those things about which he had been instructed (1:4). The term "certainty" (ἀσφάλειαν) has the literal meaning of firmness and the figurative meaning of certainty, truth, safety, or security.[33] The verb ἀσφαλίζω is used in Matt 27:64–67 of the tomb that was to be made secure and in Acts 16:24 of the feet of Paul and Silas secured in the stocks (cf. Acts 5:23, 16:23). A significant parallel to Luke 1:4 is the use of the adverb in Acts 2:36. The adverb is placed in emphatic position there. It is found in the context of Peter's sermon at Pentecost: "Therefore let

---

32. Contra Neale, *None But the Sinners*, 100.
33. BAGD, 118.

all the house of Israel 'know' (γινώσκω, compare ἐπιγινώσκω in Luke 1:4) 'beyond doubt' (ἀσφαλῶς) that God has made him both Lord and Messiah, this Jesus whom you have crucified." In the context, Peter claims to be an eyewitness of what has recently occurred in the ministry, crucifixion and resurrection of Jesus (Acts 2:32). Luke aims to provide certainty for Theophilus regarding the ministry of Jesus and his followers.

There are several implications drawn from the prologue that affect an examination of the "sinner" texts in Luke. First, Luke intends the reader to believe that he is reading history, not fiction. This suggests that for any proposed definition of the "sinner" in Luke, one must ask if the proposal has support in the historical use of the term. Second, the narrative reflects the fulfillment of God's plan. In what way, if any, does Luke's emphasis on "sinners" in Jesus' ministry serve to reflect this fulfillment? Does this have any bearing on understanding the role of "sinners" for Luke-Acts? Third, Luke intends for Theophilus to receive assurance from the narrative. How does the "sinner" theme assist Luke in developing his stated purpose of providing assurance?

The Birth Narrative

In chapters 1 and 2, Luke presents the birth of John the Baptist and of Jesus. Luke 1:5–56 details the promise of their births. The promise of John's is described first in 1:5–25 and the promise of Jesus' birth is described in 1:26–56. The fulfillment of the births takes place in 1:57—2:7. The final section of the birth account is the testimony to the birth of the Messiah (2:8–52). Many details have already been discussed in the previous section on "fulfillment."

There are several features in the birth narrative that reveal how Luke prepares the reader for Jesus' mission described in Luke 5 and following. First, there is the deliberate use of Old Testament language, allusions, patterns, and citations to present the narrative as a continuation of the Old Testament. For example, there are parallels to angelic birth announcements in the OT (Ishmael in Gen 16:10–11; Isaac in Gen 17:15–19; Samson in Judg 13:3–21). Second, the emphasis is on fulfillment of OT promise and prophecy within the narrative. This includes John's birth; his father's deaf/dumb condition and its removal; John as filled with the Holy Spirit from birth and his witness to Jesus while in the womb; the announcement to the shepherds and the fulfillment of the signs; the promise to Simeon and its fulfillment in Jesus; and Anna's declaration of Jesus as fulfillment of promise for those hoping for the redemption of Jerusalem. Fulfillment is seen in words and actions such as the John witnessing to Jesus from the womb (Luke 1:41). Fulfillment is not merely for apologetic purposes but for proclamation of the present events as revealing God's promised salvation in Jesus.[34] Third, the miraculous births of John and Jesus are given in parallel but with a step-parallelism that points to the superiority of Jesus as the main focus.[35] Fourth, God is the key actor throughout the narrative. God sent angels (1:19, 26); He has done mighty things (1:49–54); He has visited and redeemed his people (1:68–69); and His people are led by the Spirit (2:25–27). Fifth, the focus of the narrative is Jesus. Everything points to his role and authority.[36] Sixth, the witnesses to Jesus are authoritative and reliable. They include the angel Gabriel; pious Israelites favored of God such as the devout priest, Zechariah, and his righteous wife, Elizabeth; and Mary, a humble maiden highly favored of God. Witnesses also include a host of angels, humble shepherds who obey the angels and confirm the word of the angels, Simeon, an aged prophet filled with the Spirit, and an aged, pious prophetess named Anna.

The birth narrative also emphasizes several themes relevant to the "sinner" material found later in Luke. The first theme is the identity and mission of John the Baptist as forerunner of the Messiah who is to prepare a repentant people. He is filled with the Holy Spirit from his mother's womb (Luke 1:41–44). This expression is used of great men of God (e.g., Samson in Judg 13:5, 7; 16:7), the Servant of the Lord (Isa 49:1), and Jeremiah (Jer 1:5). God set John apart for a special role in His redemptive plan. The second theme is the identity of Jesus as Messiah, son of David, son of God, Savior, son of the Most High, and Servant of the Lord. The third theme emphasizes certain aspects of the character of God: mercy (1:50, 54, 72, 78), power and sovereignty revealed in his overruling the decisions of rulers (1:51–53). The fourth theme is the present as the time of fulfillment of

---

34. Bock, *Proclamation*, 98–99.
35. Marshall, *Luke*, 49.
36. Coleridge, *The Birth of the Lukan Narrative*, 226; Farris, *Hymns*, 102.

Previews of Jesus' Mission to "Sinners" in Luke

God's salvation plan, which is to be seen in Jesus. Now is the time of fulfillment. The allusions to Dan 9:20–26; 10:7, 12, 16–17 reveal the dawning of Messianic times.[37] For Luke, this dawning of Messianic times is consistent with Old Testament promise (1:70–73) and is to be found in Jesus (2:30). The birth narrative emphasizes Jesus as the "who" of salvation and leaves the "how" to be revealed by Jesus' own preaching and ministry activity. God's salvation in Jesus is to fulfill hopes for both national (1:68–75) and spiritual (1:17, 74, 77) deliverance. An important aspect of salvation for Luke is its religious aspect. This is stated in Luke 1:77 as "knowledge of salvation through forgiveness of sins." Ferris states that this expression is not found in the OT, Jewish literature, or the Dead Sea Scrolls.[38] As will be discussed below, "forgiveness" of sins plays an important role in Luke-Acts.

God's salvation plan will include reversal of societal norms. God's present action in Jesus will bring about reversal of status for many (1:51–53). Jesus will bring about an upheaval in Israel and will reveal the hearts of many (2:34–35). Mark Coleridge observes with regard to Luke 2:22–40 that Jesus brings to light the true divisions within Israel, not only predictable ones, such as those between Jew and Gentile and the "righteous" and the "sinner," but also more covert ones lying at the level of "thoughts." There will be division within Israel, but now the division will be between those who accept Jesus and those who reject him.[39]

In addition, God's salvation plan is universal in scope (2:10, 14, 31, 32) and proper response to God's salvation plan is humble acceptance and faith in God's messengers who deliver the news about God's salvation plan. Proper response is illustrated by Mary who is praised because she believed that what was said by the angel would come to pass (1:45). Other positive responses are seen in the obedience of the shepherds, Simeon, and Anna. Improper response is illustrated by Zechariah and predicted by Simeon. For example, in Luke 1:18 Zechariah asks how he will "know" for certain what the angel said will come to pass. Requests for signs were common in the OT (cf. Abraham, Gen 15:8). The objection of old age is rebutted by the statement of the position and authority of the messenger (1:19).

---

37. Fitzmyer, *Luke I–IX*, 315.
38. Farris, *Hymns*, 139.
39. Coleridge, *The Birth of the Lukan Narrative*, 174.

Zechariah's age is irrelevant because the message comes directly from the hand of God by his special envoy, Gabriel, who stands in the presence of God, having direct access to Him (cf. Dan 7:16; Job 1:6). The Lord will grant the sign, but rebuke Zechariah for unbelief (1:20). He receives a sign but one that is a punishment for his unbelief (1:20–22), which also keeps the message of the promise from the people. As already noted, judicial blindness will play an important role in Luke-Acts.

Finally, joy and peace accompanies God's salvation plan. Joy (χαρά) is a common theme throughout Luke and Acts.[40] John will be a source of joy and rejoicing for his parents (1:14). In the OT, joy and peace are especially associated with the experience of the saving acts of God (Ps 51:10). In Luke 2:10 the angels declare that they bring good news that will bring about great joy (objective gentive) that is for all people. The announcement to the shepherds exemplifies this. In Luke-Acts, joy is seen in the finding of the "lost" (Luke 15:7, 10) and experienced by Jesus' disciples after the resurrection (Luke 24:41) and ascension (Luke 24:52). Joy is experienced where the gospel is proclaimed with success in Samaria (Acts 8:8), the region of Pisidian Antioch (Acts 13:52), and the mission to the Gentiles (Acts 15:3).

According to Luke 1:79, the Messiah is to guide the Lord's people in the way of peace. In 2:14, peace will rest on those on whom God's favor rests. This will be seen to be those who respond properly to God's salvation in Jesus. Simeon fulfills this in Luke 2:29 because he obeyed the Holy Spirit and believed God's promise that he would see the Lord's Messiah. Simeon could depart in peace because his eyes had just seen God's salvation. Peace will be announced on "sinners" in Luke 7:50 and the sick in 8:48. Messianic peace is proclaimed by the crowd of disciples in Luke 19:38 but Jesus declares that the nation has missed the terms of peace because of judicial blindness (Luke 1:68, 78; 19:44).[41] Jesus pronounces peace on his disciples after the resurrection and peace is proclaimed as part of the apostolic message about Jesus (Acts 10:36).

Thus, the birth narrative prepares the reader for the ministry of Jesus and his disciples. Paul Minear observes the relevance of this material for

---

40. Marshall, *Luke*, 57.
41. Tannehill notes the pathos here (*Narrative Unity*, 1:34).

the rest of Luke. He observes Luke's use of common ecclesiological conceptions reflected in his use of terms such as Israel, πᾶς ὁ λαός, οἱ ἅγιοι, and οἱ δίκαιοι.[42] Minear also observes that the prologue clearly anticipates both the conflict within Israel occasioned by the Messiah, and the inclusion within this people of both Israel and the Gentiles. From the first to the last chapters of the Lucan corpus it is the "hope of Israel" that is at stake. This hope is especially relevant to the poor, women, especially widows, those who walk in darkness, lepers and outcasts, sinners who repent, and the righteous who wait in patient expectancy.[43]

The Beginning of the Ministries of John and Jesus

Luke 3:1—4:13 presents the ministry of John the Baptist and the preparation and testing of Jesus. Many of the features have been mentioned in the previous material. The material relevant to the "sinner" discussion will be presented in summary form.

John's mission of preparing a repentant people is presented in 3:1–20. In John's baptism of repentance for the remission of sins, baptism is regarded as an outward ritual signifying the washing away of sins.[44] Repentance was the inward condition, baptism the outward symbol of an inward decision. Water baptism also was to be symbolic of the cleansing of people by the Holy Spirit. Marshall observes that, as a prophetic sign of what was to come, John's baptism was an effective anticipation of this future cleansing and forgiveness.[45]

In John's use of Isa 40, the original context was an address to Jerusalem concerning its emergence from the ashes of its destruction by Babylon. Isaiah 40:2 introduces the theme of forgiveness of sins. Israel is offered double payment for its sins because the Lord has paid the price (Isa 40:2). In Isa 40:3–5 an unidentified voice is heard crying in the wilderness/desert. John steps forward to be that voice. But, just as in the context of Isaiah, the identity of the messenger is of little significance. It is the content of the word from God that matters. The voice cries out "prepare the way (ὁδόν) of

42. Minear, "Luke's Use of the Birth Stories," 116.
43. Ibid.
44. Marshall, *Luke*, 135.
45. Ibid.

The Sinner in Luke

the Lord." The verb "prepare" introduces the idea of the removal of obstructions, which are spelled out in 3:4. In Luke, the image of removing obstruction will be stated in terms of preparing the people through repentance, as indicated in 1:17 by the words "to turn hearts" and "to prepare for the Lord a people made ready."[46] The images of road building in Isaiah become images of repentance. Height and depth are leveled. The crooked and rough roads are straightened and smoothed out. This drastic transformation of a terrain that obstructs travel becomes a symbol of the repentance that the Lord's coming requires.[47]

Robert Tannehill observes that this imagery has already been introduced. The valleys being "filled in and mountains made low" (ταπεινωθησεται, 3:5) may recall the lowering and raising mentioned in Luke 1:52 where God has put down the mighty from their thrones and has exalted the lowly (ταπεινούς). The images of crooked and straight reappear in Acts in the context of repentance or hardening to repentance. For example, in Acts 2:40 Peter warns his listeners to save themselves from the "crooked" generation (cf. Acts 8:21).

In his message to those who came (Luke 3:7–18), John warns against the tendency to think that going through another ritual (e.g., the OT sacrifices; cf. Isa 1:13ff.) would prepare them for the coming of the Lord.[48] His call is for a change of heart that reveals itself in ethical conduct along the lines of proper conduct with one's neighbor as revealed in the Old Testament (Luke 3:8a; cf. Lev 19:10–18, 35–36). John warns against presuming one's connection with Abraham provides protection from the coming wrath of God (3:8b). God can raise stones to worship Him. In Luke 19:38–40, Jesus' disciples praise him as he enters Jerusalem. The Pharisees object and ask Jesus to silence them, but Jesus declares that if they do not worship, even the stones will cry out. It will be those who respond to Jesus whom God will raise up to worship him.

John's message also includes prophetic warning. Judgment is closer than Israel thinks, the axe is already at the base of the tree (3:9). This may be an allusion to Isa 10:33–34, where the Lord is pictured as one who will

---

46. Tannehill, *Narrative Unity*, 1:48.
47. Ibid.
48. Danker, *Jesus and the New Age*, 45.

cut off the top of the tree, Assyria, in judgment. Here the image would be turned toward Israel.[49] This image also appears in Luke 13:1–9 when Jesus warns unrepentant Israel that the fruitless tree is about to be cut down.

Luke gives examples of those who are responding to John's message of repentance (3:1–14). Out of the faceless crowd (ὄχλοι, 3:7, 10) even toll-collectors (τελῶναι, 3:12–13) come in repentance to be baptized.[50] Luke points out this group as an example of those who are responsive (cf. Luke 7:29). John's ministry creates an attitude of Messianic expectation (3:15). He continues his role as forerunner by speaking of the one who would come after him to sift Israel and baptize with the Holy Spirit. John initiates a mission that will continue throughout Luke-Acts and reach out to the world.[51]

The baptism of Jesus in Luke 3:21–22 shows him to be affirmed by God to be the regal Messiah (fulfillment of Ps 2:7) and Messiah-Servant, anointed by the Holy Spirit with power for his task (Isa 42:1). The genealogy of Jesus in 3:23–38 declares him to be from the royal line of David (3:31) and a descendant of Adam (3:38), stressing his identity as the agent of God's universal salvation. Finally, the wilderness experience presents Jesus as the obedient Son of God who has passed the test in 4:1–13. The three quotes from Deuteronomy are derived from passages that remind the reader of tests that Israel failed in the wilderness (Deut 6:13, 16; 8:3).[52] His credentials here are not signs and miracles but absolute obedience to the Father's will as expressed in Scripture.

The Sermon at Nazareth

THE SETTING

In Luke 4:16–21, Jesus enters the synagogue in his hometown of Nazareth. After someone had read at least a three-verse portion of the Law, Jesus stood up to read a portion from the Prophets. On Sabbath mornings, the atten-

---

49. Fitzmyer, *Luke I–IX*, 469.

50. Luke's use of δέ and καί here is intensive, bringing attention to the fact that "even toll collectors" responded. See Green, *Gospel of Luke*, 179. Note the similar use of καί in Luke 6:32–33; 7:29; 18:11; and Acts 10:45, "even on" (καί ἐπί) the Gentiles.

51 Tannehill, *Narrative Unity*, 1:48.

52. Fitzmyer, *Luke I–IX*, 511.

dant would remove a scroll of the Prophets from the ark (*m. Meg.* 4:1–2) and give it to someone appointed to read. The selection of the text was up to the reader. In contrast to the reader of the Law of Moses, the Mishnah states the reader of the Prophets could omit portions and move around in the reading (*m. Meg. 4:4*).

Jesus selected as his reading a portion of Isaiah 61:1–2 combined with Isaiah 58:6 (Luke 4:18–19).[53] The following translation is intentionally literal in an attempt to show the force of the infinitives (Isa 58:6 in italics):

> The Spirit of the Lord is upon me
> because he has anointed me
> to preach good news to the poor,
> he has sent me
> to proclaim to the captives release (ἄφεσιν)
> and to the blind sight;
> *to send forth the oppressed in release* (ἐν ἀφέσει)
> to proclaim the year of the Lord's favor.

The Background of the OT Citation

The Old Testament context of Isaiah 61:1, 2 consists of a declaration by one upon whom the Spirit of the Lord is come because the Lord has "anointed" him for a task of proclamation and release. The identity of the OT speaker is usually understood to be the prophet Isaiah, second or third Isaiah.[54] This is supported by the *Targum Jonathan on Isaiah* 61:1: "The spirit of prophecy from before the Lord is upon me." John McKenzie also points out that although the speaker has the Spirit, like the Servant of Yahweh (40:1), the Servant is never called "anointed."[55] But this does not decide the case for neither is the prophet Isaiah called "anointed." Delitzsch rejects seeing the speaker as the prophet for several reasons: (1) the prophet never refers to

---

53. For a detailed discussion of the issues regarding the source of these texts, the comparison to the LXX, and the combination of these texts see Bock, *Proclamation*, 105–8.

54. McKenzie, *Second Isaiah*, 181. Our position is that Isaiah composed the oracles attributed to him and the men of Hezekiah arranged these in their extant form (cf. *b. B. Bat.* 15a). This is supported by the fact that the Dead Sea Scroll of Isaiah contained all of Isaiah as a unit. For a detailed discussion of the authorship of Isaiah, see Harrison, *Introduction to the Old Testament*, 764–95.

55. Ibid., 180.

Previews of Jesus' Mission to "Sinners" in Luke

himself at such length but stays in the background; (2) in any reference to "calling" by anyone other than Yahweh, it is the Servant of Yahweh of whom and to whom Yahweh speaks (42:1–2; 49:1; 52:13—53:12); (3) the description of the person in 61:1–2 closely parallels the description of the Servant in 42:1–4 and 49:1–11; and (4) it is unlikely that having allowed the Servant to speak for himself with such dramatic directness (48:16b; 49:1–2), the prophet would step forward and describe himself with the same attributes of the one who is to come.[56] Regardless of the identity of the speaker, the herald has clearly portrayed himself in Servant terms.[57] McKenzie observes that the echoes of the Servant Songs (Isa 42:7; 49:9) indicate that the prophet thinks of himself as fulfilling the mission of the Servant, thus he becomes an early interpreter of the Servant Songs. His mission is to declare to the post-exilic community of Israel the arrival of the promised salvation.[58]

This passage is used at Qumran of the promised eschatological salvation. In 11QMelch Isaiah 61:1–3 is combined with both a Jubilee text (Lev 25:13) and Sabbatical year text (Deut 15:2) to proclaim eschatological release through the Messianic figure Melchizedek. 11QMelch II reads as follows:[59]

> *1* [. . .] your God . . . [. . .] *2* [. . .] And as for what he said: *Lev 25:13* <<In this year of jubilee, [you shall return, each one, to his respective property>>, as is written: *Dt 15:2* <<This is] *3* the manner (of effecting) the [release: every creditor shall release what he lent [to his neighbor. He shall not coerce his neighbor or his brother when] the release for God [has been proclaimed] >>. *4* [Its inter]pretation for the last days refers to the captives, about whom he said: *Isa. 61:1* <<To proclaim liberty to the captives.>> And he will make *5* their rebels prisoners [. . .] and of the inheritance of Melchizedek, for [. . .] and they are the inheri[tance of Melchi]zedek, who *6* will make them return. He will proclaim liberty for them, to free them from [the debt] of all their iniquities. And this will [happen] *7* in the first week of the jubilee which follows the ni[ne] jubilees. And the day [of atonem]ent is the end of the tenth

---

56. K&D 7:424–25.
57. Bock, *Proclamation*, 108.
58. McKenzie, *Second Isaiah*, 181.
59. The translation is from García Martínez, *The Dead Sea Scrolls Translated*, 139–40.

> jubilee *8* in which atonement will be made for all the sons of [of God] and for the men of the lot of Melchizedeck. [And on the heights] he will decla[re in their] favor according to their lots; for *9* it is the time of the <<year of grace>> . . .
>
> . . . *18* And the messenger is the [ano]inted of the spirit . . . [And the messenger of] *19* good who announces salv[ation is the one about whom it is written that [he will send him *Isa. 61. 2–3* <<to comfo[rt the afflicted>>, to watch over the afflicted ones of Zion>>.] . . . *25* [. . . Melchizedek, who will fr]ee [them] from the hand of Belial. And as for what he said: *Lev 25:9* <<You shall blow the hor[n in every] land>>.

Several points are relevant to Luke's use of Isaiah 61:1–2 with Isaiah 58:6. First, the text merges Jubilee and Sabbatical year texts and combines them with Isaiah 61:1–3 to refer to the eschatological release of the last days (line 4) just as Jesus in Luke 4:18–19 combines a Sabbatical year text (Isa 58:6) with a jubilee text (Isa 61:2). Second, liberty includes freedom from the "debt of all their iniquities" (line 6). The text connects this eschatological jubilee with the final day of atonement on which atonement will be made for all the sons of God and for the men of Melchizedek. For Luke, the knowledge of salvation comes through the "forgiveness of sins" (Luke 1:77). As will be shown in the discussion that follows, the term used in Isaiah 61:1–2 and 58:6 for "release" will be connected with "forgiveness of sins" in Luke-Acts. Third, liberty is also described as freedom from the hand of Belial (line 25; line 13, not cited here, also speaks of freedom from the hands of Belial and from the hands of all the spirits of his lot). Luke 4:31–44 focuses on the authority of Jesus' message (λόγος, 4:32), which is demonstrated especially by his power to command demons (cf. Luke 13:16; Acts 10:38). Fourth, the end-time messenger is "anointed by the Spirit" (line 18). Jesus is "anointed by the Spirit" (Luke 4:18).

Luke's Understanding of Jesus' Citation

Jesus' identity and mission are presented in Luke 4:18–19. How does Luke understand these statements?

"Spirit-Anointed"

For Luke, the reference is to the Spirit coming upon Jesus at his baptism (Luke 3:21) to empower him for his task.[60] Here the task for which the Spirit empowers is specifically that of the anointed prophet. Jesus is preaching God's message with God's power. He is the Prophet like Moses whom Moses said would come (Deut 18:18; cf. Acts 3:22). Luke clearly links Jesus with the prophets Elijah and Elisha in the midst of the rejection narrative of 4:25–30. As Luke will make clear, Jesus' sending to Israel will consummate the tragic rejection of all Israel's prophets (13:31–35).[61]

However, Luke also understands Jesus' anointing in messianic terms. Joseph Fitzmyer rejects this link because Isaiah 61 is not part of a Servant Song.[62] However, as already noted earlier, the speaker presents himself in Servant language fulfilling Servant functions. Darrell Bock observes that the insertion of Isaiah 58:6 combines a prophetic image (Isa 61) with a liberation image (Isa 58) who is to "set at liberty those who are oppressed." This becomes a figure of one who not only proclaims a message of healing, but effects salvation, a messianic function.[63]

The messianic understanding of Jesus' anointing is also supported by both the prior and immediately following contexts of Luke 4:18.[64] Prior to Luke 4:18, Jesus has been called "Son of the Most High," "holy one," and the Son of God (1:32, 35) who will receive the throne of his father David (1:32). He is explicitly called "Christ the Lord" (Χριστὸς κύριος, 2:11) and Simeon is an eye-witness that Jesus is the Lord's Messiah (2:26–30). The fusion of Psa 2:7 with Isa 42:1 declared by the voice of God at Jesus' baptism has made the link between Son of God, the Anointed, and Servant of Yahweh.

The "Son of God" is a messianic expression that also plays an important role in the temptation narrative (4:3, 9) and the ministry that follows 4:30 (cf. especially 4:41, where the expression "Son of God" is used as a synonym for "the Christ").

60. Fitzmyer, *Luke I–IX*, 529.
61. Moessner, *Lord of the Banquet*, 47.
62. Fitzmyer, *Luke I–IX*, 529.
63. Bock, *Proclamation*, 109.
64. Ibid.

The Sinner in Luke

The final argument supporting a messianic understanding of Jesus' anointing in Luke 4:18 is Jesus' declaration of fulfillment in 4:21. This declaration indicates that his activity is eschatological and messianic.[65] This is demonstrated by Jesus' allusion to Isaiah 61:1 and other Isaiah passages when he defends his messianic credentials to the disciples of John the Baptist (Luke 7:18–23).

"To Preach Good News (εὐαγγελίσασθαι) to the Poor (πτωχοῖς)"

The infinitives in 4:18–19 present Jesus' mission. The first infinitive εὐαγγελίσασθαι is important for Luke. Although the noun εὐαγγέλιον is used only twice by Luke (Acts 15:7; 20:24; Mark [8 times] and Matthew [4 times]), he uses the verb 25 times in (10 times in Luke; 15 times in Acts).[66] It is used to describe the message of angels regarding the birth of John (1:19) and Jesus (2:10). It has also been used of John's preaching activity (3:18). In Luke 4:43, Jesus carries out his task of preaching the good news (the use of δεῖ emphasizes his mission and ἀπεστάλην ties back to ἀπεσταλκέν in 4:18), which is further explained as the good news of the "kingdom of God" and directed to the people in a broad sense. In some sense the expression "preaching the gospel to the poor" may be seen as a general summary describing all of Jesus' mission.[67] But preaching the gospel is also distinguished from "healing" in Luke 7:22 and 9:6, which may help to explain Luke's understanding of other parts of Luke 4:18–19 as related but distinct elements of ministry.

Who are the "poor" (πτωχοῖς)? Luke clearly emphasizes this social class as distinct from the rich (6:20; 7:22; 14:13, 21; 16:20, 22; 18:22; 19:8; 21:3). Some understand Luke's "poor" in completely social and economic terms.[68] Others see the term "poor" in a wide sense of the poor and oppressed as in the OT context of Isaiah 61. This would broaden the term to include all those in need, the hungry, the sick, and the captives.[69] Luke's

---

65. Combrink, "The Structure and Significance," 40–41.

66. This represents 25 of 56 total uses of the verb in the NT. Of the remainder, 22 of the uses are found in the letters of Paul.

67. Jeremias, *New Testament Theology*, 108–109.

68. Fitzmyer, *Luke I–IX*, 248.

69. Jeremias, *New Testament Theology*, 113.

meaning for the term can best be seen in Luke 6:20–23 in the Sermon on the Plain where it is used in direct contrast to the rich but also includes Jesus' disciples who have left everything to follow him. The promises to the poor are stated in eschatological terms such as "kingdom of God" (6:20) and "reward in heaven" (6:23). In the broadest sense, one can even suggest that Luke's poor includes the "sinner" to whom Jesus preaches the good news (7:22, 31–50).[70] This is possible, but care must be given to distinguish the oppression of the hungry from the moral guilt of the sinner. The distinction is illustrated in Luke 19:8, where Zacchaeus, a chief "toll-collector" and "sinner" (19:2, 7) is rich (19:2) and demonstrates his repentance by giving to the "poor." Luke uses the term sometimes in a narrow sense and sometimes in a broader sense in what Bock calls a "soteriological generalization."[71] When viewed this way, the poor are seen as those who depend upon and believe the message from God. For Luke this group represents those most needy of God's help and most responsive and dependent upon him.

"To Proclaim Release (ἄφεσιν) to the Captives"

The captives described in Isaiah 61 are the Jewish captives in exile in Babylon. But physical captivity often took on the connotation of spiritual captivity (Ps 79:11; Isa 42:7). Likewise, in Luke the picture is of release from the spiritual captivity of sin (Luke 1:77; 7:47; 24:47; Acts 2:38; 5:31; 10:43; 13:38; 26:13).[72] The call of Jesus would be a call to come to God on his terms and accept forgiveness as offered through Jesus.

In the LXX, the verb ἀφίημι is used in Genesis 50:17 for forgiveness (נָשָׂא) of the sins (ἀδικίαι) of Joseph's brothers. The first connection of ἀφιέναι to forgiveness of sins (ἁμαρτίαις) is Exodus 32:32 in the context of the golden calf incident. Here Moses asks the Lord to forgive (ἀφιέναι = נָשָׂא) the sins of the people. The use of ἀφιέναι = סָלַח for forgiveness of

---

70. Jeremias, *New Testament Theology*, 113. See also Pilgrim, *Good News to the Poor*, 83.

71. Bock, *Luke 1:1—9:50*, 408.

72. Denova holds that the proclamation of "release to captives" is not carried out in any form by Jesus in Luke because it refers to the release of the exiles that does not occur until Peter's sermon in Acts 2:38 (*Things Accomplished*, 135). However, this narrows the referent in a way that Luke does not, as seen in the use of ἄφεσις and ἀφίημι in Luke-Acts for forgiveness of sins and release from the power of the devil. Jesus clearly makes these pronouncements in the Gospel of Luke (5:2–24; 7:47–49).

sins (ἁμαρτίας) is common in Leviticus in the context of the sin-offering (Leviticus 4:20, 26, 31, 35; 5:6, 10, 13, 16, 18; 6:6 (5:26 MT); 19:22). In Job 42:10, God forgave (ἀφιέναι = עָזַב) the sins of Job's friends.

The Psalms also speak of forgiveness. For example in Psalm 24:18 (25:18 MT), the psalmist declares that the Lord instructs "sinners" (ἁμαρτάνοντας) in his ways (Ps 24:8), he guides the humble in what is right and teaches them his way (Ps 24:9). He then asks the Lord to "forgive (ἱλάσῃ) his iniquity (ἁμαρτία) though it is great" (Ps 24:11) and to "take away (ἀφιέναι = נָשָׂא) all his sins" (ἁμαρτίας, Ps 24:18). In Psalm 31:1, 5 (32:1, 5 MT), the psalmist proclaims those who have their iniquity forgiven are blessed, and he declares that he has acknowledged his own sin (ἁμαρτίαν) and the Lord has forgiven (ἀφῆκας) him (see also 84:2, 85:2 MT).

Isaiah 22:14 is part of an oracle against Jerusalem for failing to repent. This sin (ἁμαρτία) will not be forgiven (ἀφεθήσεται). This has parallels to Luke's passage declaring blasphemy against the Holy Spirit, a sin that will not be forgiven (Luke 12:10).

Isaiah 33:24 is in the context of future hope for the inhabitants of Zion (33:20) for the Lord will save them (33:22). When this occurs, even the lame (χωλοί) will carry off plunder (33:23) and the people dwelling there will not say "I am in pain" for (γάρ) their sin (ἁμαρτία) shall be forgiven (ἀφέθη). This text makes a clear link between healing and forgiveness of sins that is found in Luke 5:17–25.

Isaiah 55:7 is in the context of an invitation from the Lord to Israel to repent and receive pardon and blessing. In 55:3, the Lord promises to those who listen to him an everlasting covenant analogous to the sure mercies of David (cf. Acts 13:34). In 55:4, the Lord declares that he has made David a witness and a leader to the nations (ἔθνοι). David will summon nations not previously known (55:5, the LXX changes this and has the nations calling upon the Lord). In 55:7, the invitation is extended for the wicked (ἀσεβής) to forsake his way and the evil man his thoughts and to turn (ἐπιστέφω) to the Lord and they will find mercy, for the Lord will abundantly pardon (ἀφήσει) their sins (ἁμαρτίας, cf. Acts 3:26).

The noun ἄφεσις is used 44 times in the LXX, translating שְׁמַט seven times, all in contexts dealing with the Sabbatical year of "release" in which the land is "left" (Exod 23:11) and debts are "released" (Deut 15:1,

2 [twice], 3, 9; 31:10). The noun ἄφεσις translates יוֹבֵל 20 times, all in the context of the year of Jubilee (Lev 25:11, 12, 13, 28 [twice], 30, 31, 33, 40 [41 LXX], 50, 52, 54; Num 36:4). It is used for דְּרוֹר seven times, either of the liberty of the Jubilee year (Lev 25:10; Isa 61:1 uses ἄφεσις in this sense) or the Sabbatical year in Jeremiah 34 (41 LXX): 8, 15, and 17 and Ezekiel 46:17. In Jeremiah 34:8, King Zedekiah made a covenant with the people and proclaimed a release (καλέσαι ἄφεσίν). In Jeremiah 34:17, the term is used as irony because the Lord is about to 'release' the nation to judgment. In contrast to King Zedekiah, Jesus as the Davidic *Servant-Messiah* has authority to proclaim "release" and forgiveness of sins to all who forsake their ways and turn to the Lord (Isa 55:3–7; Acts 13:34).

In Isaiah 58:6, ἄφεσις is used the only time in the OT for חָפְשִׁי to speak of the freedom that comes at the Sabbatical year for those Israelites who had to sell themselves into slavery to their countrymen (Exod 21:2, 5; Deut 15:12, 13, 18; Jer 34:9, 10, 11, 14, 16). In 1 Maccabees 10:34 and 13:34, the noun and the verb are both used in a literal sense of Israelites being "released" from tribute, debts, and taxes and of prisoners of war being "freed" from a foreign king Demetrius (1 Macc 10:33).

The terms ἀφίημι and ἄφεσις are important to Luke and serve as an OT link for understanding the "sinner" theme in Luke-Acts. The "release" from the prison darkness of the exiles in Isaiah is interpreted by Jesus to reflect his mission of releasing those held by sin, disease, and the power of the devil.[73]

The term ἄφεσις in Luke is almost always connected to the idea of "forgiveness" of "sins." The following list includes references to Luke:

1) 1:77 speaks of the knowledge of salvation through the "forgiveness" of sins;

2) 3:3 speaks of John's preaching a baptism of repentance for "forgiveness" of sins;

3) 4:18–19 uses ἄφεσις two times with Isaiah as the source and Jesus as the one citing the texts in description of his mission; and

4) 24:47 states that repentance and forgiveness of sins are to be proclaimed in Jesus' name to all nations beginning at Jerusalem.

73. Kingsbury, *Conflict in Luke*, 45.

The Sinner in Luke

The following list includes references to Acts:

1) 2:38 records Peter's exhortation to the crowd at Pentecost to repent and be baptized in the name of Jesus for the "remission" of sins;

2) 5:31 has Peter proclaiming repentance to Israel and "forgiveness" of sins;

3) 10:43 contains Peter's words to the Gentile Cornelius: "all the prophets testify about him that everyone who believes in him receives 'forgiveness' of sins through his name" (cf. Isaiah 53:11);

4) 13:38 has Paul preaching in a synagogue that through Jesus the "forgiveness" of sins is proclaimed to you (diaspora Jews); and

5) 26:18 stands in the context of Paul giving Agrippa a description of his encounter with Jesus on the Damascus Road and Jesus' commission to him to preach to the Gentiles that they may "receive 'forgiveness' of sins and a place among those who are sanctified by faith in me."

The context of the use of the noun ἄφεσις in Luke-Acts is always proclamation. In Luke 1:77, the knowledge of salvation is said to come through "forgiveness" of sins. This is one of the few mentions of how salvation was to be achieved in the opening section of Luke (1:5—4:15). Luke 1:77 roots the hope for forgiveness of sins in the mercy of God and the shining of the Messianic Branch/Sun (1:78). John preaches a baptism of repentance for the "forgiveness" of sins, in Luke 3:3. His message is based upon the authority of a direct message from God (3:2) consistent with the message of Isaiah the prophet (3:4–6). In Luke 4:18–19, Jesus claims the authority to proclaim "forgiveness." Beginning in Luke 24:47 throughout the rest of Acts, "forgiveness" of sins is proclaimed in Jesus' name.

The verb ἀφίημι is also connected to forgiveness of sins in the following passages in Luke: (1) 5:20–24 in which Jesus claims to forgive the sins of the paralytic; (2) 7:47–49 in which Jesus pronounces forgiveness to the "sinful woman"; (3) 11:4 where Jesus' disciples are to pray for "forgiveness" of their sins; (4) 12:10 where all sins are forgiven except blasphemy; (5) 17:3–4 in which Jesus' followers are taught to forgive repentant brethren; and (6) 23:34 where Jesus on the cross prays, "Father, forgive them."

"Sight to the blind"

"Sight to the blind" involves physical healing in Luke 7:22 and 18:35–43, but Luke probably also intends to include the theme of spiritual illumination (Luke 1:77–80; 8:10; 10:23–24; 18:41–43).[74] Luke Johnson comments on the listing of the blind (τυφλοί) in Luke 7:22 with the lame (χωλοί), lepers, deaf, and the dead, and in 14:13, 21 the crippled, and the lame (χωλοί).[75] He sees these as the types of "blemishes" found in Leviticus 21:18 that prohibit participation in the worship of Israel (cf. 2 Sam 5:8: the "blind (τυφλοί) and lame (χωλοί) are not to enter the house of the Lord"). This would suggest that for Luke these are not merely examples of people in misery but people who need to be restored to God.

"Send Forth the Oppressed in Release (ἀφέσει)"

The release of the oppressed is a reference to Isaiah 58:6, which concerns the release of the downtrodden. The term "oppressed' (from θραύω) is used literally of breaking things such as pottery or a skull (Josephus, *Ant.* 8. 390) and figuratively of shattering enemies (Exod 15:6) or oppression (Deut 28:33). The Servant of Yahweh will not be "downtrodden" (θραυσθη-'σεται = רָצַץ, Isa 42:4), but will establish justice. The Servant is God's "chosen one" upon whom he has placed his Spirit (Isa 42:1) and who will bring forth this justice. Luke has already identified Jesus as this Servant at his baptism by the reference to Isaiah 42:1 in Luke 3:22. The mission of bringing "release" to the downtrodden in Isaiah 58:6 (θραύω = רָצַץ) is therefore to be understood not simply as the message of the prophet but the deliverance of the Messiah. The OT passage is in the context of a rebuke to Israel for ritually fasting while practicing injustice (Isa 58:1–5). As already noted, ἄφεσις is used in Isaiah 58:6 to translate חָפְשִׁי which speaks of the freedom that comes at the Sabbatical year for those Israelites who had to sell themselves into slavery to their countrymen. Jesus will do what Israel as a nation was rebuked for failing to do in Isaiah. Jesus will reach out to the

---

74. Bock, *Luke 1:1—9:50*, 408. Walter Pilgrim, *Good News to the Poor*, 68, sees the literal sense as primary. But in addition to the texts emphasizing spiritual sight mentioned here, Pilgrim omits the references in Acts that have literal and metaphorical elements such as the blindness of Paul (Acts 9:8, 18) and Elymas (Acts 13:11).

75. Johnson, *Literary Function*, 133.

needy and give them aid. Injustice will be reversed and liberation will be proclaimed. The use of ἀφέσει here may be tied closely to ἄφεσιν in the previous line and be Luke's way of emphasizing the theme of forgiveness.[76] But the "release" of the oppressed may also be seen in the healings that Jesus performs that reveal deliverance but also underscore his unique authority (Luke 11:14–23, 31–32; 18:38–39; 19:37–38).[77]

"To Proclaim the Favorable Year of the Lord"

The announcement of the year of Jublilee, detailed in Leviticus 25, was the practice of allowing every fiftieth year to be designated as the year of God's Jubilee. During this year the fields rested, persons returned to the homes that they had lost, debts were forgiven, and slaves who had sold themselves to slavery for remission of debts were set free. The promise of Isaiah takes this picture and applies it to the Kingdom of God. God will bring freedom and forgiveness in this coming day. Jesus says that he is proclaiming the Jubilee now. The context in the quotation refers to the time of ultimate salvation.[78] Jesus ends his citation of Isaiah 61 before the reference to judgment in 61:2b, thus emphasizing the present as the proclamation of release. For Luke the ministry of Jesus means the coming of the time of salvation.[79] Jesus in his ministry not only announces the time but also brings about this time through his work of bringing "release."[80]

Jesus sat down after reading the Scripture and delivered the homily (cf. Acts 13:14–15). He sat down in the special preaching seat of the synagogue and instead of a rabbinic sermon delivered a messianic revelation. This is the only report in Luke of the content of a message by Jesus in the synagogue, making this a probable example of the nature of the message he normally delivered.[81]

---

76. Combrink, *Structure and Significance*, 36.

77. Bock, *Luke 1:1—9:50*, 410.

78. Tannehill cites 2 Corinthians 6:2 where in a quotation from Isa 49:8, "acceptable year" is parallel with "day of salvation" and then interpreted by Paul as the "acceptable time" of salvation. See Tannehill, "The Mission of Jesus," 71.

79. Marshall, *Luke*, 185.

80. Tannehill, "The Mission of Jesus," 71.

81. Green, *The Gospel of Luke*, 207.

The Rejection of Jesus as Prophet

When Jesus concluded his words with the declaration that the texts he had read were being fulfilled in their hearing, claiming himself as the fulfillment (4:20–21), Luke states that the entire synagogue congregation began "testifying concerning him" and "marveling" at the words about grace that came from his mouth (4:22a). Then everyone began to say: "Is this not Joseph's son?"

The explanation of the nature of the response of the people is tied closely to Jesus' words in 4:23–27. To their response, Jesus cites a proverb: "You will go on to say to me, 'Physician, heal yourself.'" He then states that the people will begin asking him to do the things that they had heard he had done in Capernaum (4:23).[82] In 4:24 Jesus declares in an "amen" saying that no prophet is welcome (δεκτός) in his own country (a connection with δεκτόν in 4:19). The citizens of Nazareth have missed the Lord's "favor" because they have not "welcomed" his eschatological Prophet, Jesus the Servant-Messiah.[83] The theme of "welcoming" or "receiving" is important in Luke-Acts. In Acts 10:35, Peter states that those of all nations who fear the Lord and do what is right (e.g., respond properly to God's revelation concerning Jesus) are accepted (δεκτός) by him. The verb δέχομαι is used of those who "receive" the word, the gospel (Luke 8:13; Acts 8:14, of the Samaritans; 11:1, of the Gentiles; 17:11). Being receptive to Jesus is tied to being receptive to God (Luke 9:48). This statement by Jesus in Luke 4:24 helps to explain Jesus' understanding of the people's response in 4:22. The first half of the verse is a positive reaction to Jesus' words but the raising of the question about Jesus' heritage shows that they are not "accepting" him as a prophet. Jesus' words are reflective of his authority to know hearts (2:35) and divide people through judgment (2:34; 3:17). When Zechariah expressed doubts concerning the words of Gabriel, he was judged immediately with dumbness (Luke 1:20). Jesus' response is even more authoritative for the reader because Luke has clearly identified Jesus as the Son of God, the Davidic Servant-Messiah. Thus, against the position of Tannehill, the

---

82. This proverb is found in rabbinic sources as "heal your own limp" (*Gen. Rab.* 23) with a similar version in Greek writings (Euripides, *Fragment*, 1071, from Fitzmyer, *Luke I–IX*, 535).

83. Tannehill, "Mission of Jesus," 58.

people are not simply attempting to keep Jesus to themselves but are understood by Jesus to be unresponsive to his pronouncement.[84]

Jesus' response continues in Luke 4:25–27 using the analogy of the prophetic ministries of Elijah and Elisha to declare that like rejected former prophets he will go to others who are responsive. His audience risks missing their chance. In the prophetic ministry of Elijah (4:25–26; cf. 1 Kings 17–18), during the time of famine due to divine judgment, no Israelite widow received benefit from the presence of the prophet, only a widow from Sidon (cf. Luke 7:12–14). During the days of Elisha (4:27; cf. 2 Kings 5:1–14), no Israelite lepers were healed, only Naaman the Syrian (cf. Luke 5:12–14; 7:22; 17:11–19).

What does Jesus intend in this analogy? In Luke 4:25–27, Crockett sees the preview of Jewish–Gentile reconciliation in Acts 10–11.[85] His position is based on seeing clear linkage between the famine described in Luke 4:25 and the famine in Acts 11:28. Elijah is sent to the widow to be fed and she receives the blessing of her son brought back to life. The Jewish believers of Acts receive the ministry of food having shared the word with the Gentiles. However, there is no context of judgment in Acts 11 and Luke's use of the raising of the widow's son focuses not on Jew-Gentile mutual benefit but on Jesus' authority as a great prophet (Luke 7:11–17). Jeffrey Siker argues that Luke 4:25–27 is actually a reversal of expectation that declares that the 'acceptable year of the Lord' is to be proclaimed primarily to outsiders, that is, to Gentiles, and to Jews only as they are able to accept Gentile inclusion.[86] The weakness with this argument is that after the Nazareth rejection, Jesus does not go to Gentiles but to Capernaum (4:31).

Jesus appears to be declaring that the benefits of the favorable year are to go to those who accept his credentials. Just as John warned the crowds against presuming on their Abrahamic heritage (Luke 3:8), Jesus makes it clear that receiving Messianic benefits come only through proper response to his claim of Messiahship. These benefits are intended for all flesh (Luke 3:6) including the oppressed of Israel. But, just as God did in the days of the prophets, those who reject him will miss their opportunity and God

---

84. Tannehill, "Mission of Jesus," 62.
85. Crockett, "Luke 4:25–27," 177–83.
86. Siker, "'First to the Gentiles,'" 73–90.

will take his benefits to others. This is a preview of the rejection of Jesus by the Jews and of the Gentile mission in Acts.[87] But this is not the basis for Gentile mission.[88] Luke has made this clear before Luke 4:16–30 by placing that mission in the context of God's promised universal salvation rooted in Isaiah (Luke 2:31, 32; 3:6).

Importance to Luke

The Nazareth citation of Isaiah is generally accepted to be programmatic for Luke,[89] because of its placement at the beginning of Jesus' ministry in Luke's narrative and because of themes introduced that are repeated throughout Luke and Acts.[90] Luke emphasizes that Jesus is the authority in charge of interpreting his mission and demonstrating how God is fulfilling his salvation promise. Jesus is presented as the Servant-Messiah who not only preaches but brings about deliverance. In the Nazareth proclamation Luke presents the "what" of Jesus' mission but not the "how." This will be revealed in the narrative of Luke.

Summary of the Previews of Jesus' Mission to Sinners

When Luke's reader hears the term ἁμαρτωλός for the first time, he will have already been prepared for the word by Luke's material in Luke 1:5—4:44.[91] The birth narrative has placed the reader in the context of a continuation of the Old Testament activity of the Lord's actions to redeem his covenant people. However, although the national hopes are clearly present, a major emphasis has been the preparation of a repentant people. Salvation includes a knowledge of the forgiveness of sins. As has been seen, the terms "repentance," "forgiveness of sins," and "release" have a narrative history before Luke 5. The fulfillment of God's promised salvation is being revealed before the very eyes of the reader. Shepherds have witnessed it; Simeon and Anna have declared it to be so. God himself has proclaimed

---

87. Tannehill, "Mission," 75.

88. Johnson, *Literary Function*, 95.

89. Talbert, *Reading Luke*, 57.

90. Marshall, *Luke*, 178.

91. Luke 4:31–44 will be discussed in the context of our treatment of Luke 5:1–11 that follows.

Jesus to be his chosen one. Jesus has given his own interpretation of his mission in terms of the fulfillment of Isaiah. Reversal and resistance have already been prophesied and fulfilled with reference to Mary, the lowly virgin as mother of the Davidic Messiah (Luke 1:46–52); the shepherds as witnesses to angelic proclamation (Luke 2:8–20); and the aged Simeon and Anna as prophet and prophetess honored to see the salvation of the Lord (Luke 2:25–38). Simeon has prepared the reader for upheaval. John has preached repentance for forgiveness of sins and has warned about the presumption of being a descendant of Abraham. The reader has seen the kind of people who are responding to John: tax collectors, soldiers, and others. Jesus has been filled with the Holy Spirit and declared to be the "chosen Son" by God at his baptism. Showing himself to be the obedient Son of God through his wilderness testing, Jesus launched his ministry filled by the Holy Spirit. The incident in the Nazarene synagogue has prepared the reader for opposition analogous to the hostility of ancient Israel to the prophets Elijah and Elisha.

The narrative voices of angels, prophets, and even John have stopped. Jesus controls the action. His voice gives authoritative interpretation of the Old Testament and his actions are meant to display fulfillment. Mark Coleridge points out that in Luke's narrative, Jesus is presented as the prime interpreter of himself. Luke's christology is rooted in the Old Testament, but its originality is due to Jesus as interpreter.[92] Coleridge observes that as the initiative in the narrative passes to Jesus, the OT citations and echoes dwindle to almost nothing. Instead of being interpreted by other characters, Jesus interprets himself using his own language and actions. Beginning at Luke 4:1, it is to Jesus that both characters and readers must listen. The display of power through his teaching and miracles following the Nazareth sermon shows the reader that Jesus controls how he fulfills the Old Testament promise of deliverance and release. Salvation is both heard and seen in Jesus to those who are open. The reader is to understand that Jesus himself is the fulfillment of Old Testament promises of salvation. Luke's emphasis on Jesus and his encounter with "sinners" is to be understood as part of this fulfillment, not simply as proof from prophecy, but as part of the proclamation that Jesus is the fulfillment of God's salvation.

92. Coleridge, *The Birth of the Lukan Narrative*, 203.

4

The "Sinner" Texts in the Gospel of Luke

❖ In his gospel, Luke uses ἁμαρτωλός eighteen times:

1) 5:8—the call of Simon Peter (5:1–11);
2–3) 5:30 and 32—the call of Levi and the banquet in his house (5:27–32);
4–7) 6:32, 33, and 34 (twice)—the Sermon on the Plain (6:17–49);
8) 7:34—parable vindicating the ministries of John the Baptist and Jesus (7:18–35);
9–10) 7:37 and 39—the sinful woman (7:36–50);
11) 13:2—warning regarding repentance (13:1–9);
12–15) 15:1, 2, 7, and 10—the lost sheep, lost coin, and the Prodigal Son (15:1–32);
16) 18:13—the Pharisee and the tax collector (18:9–13);
17) 19:7—the story of Zacchaeus (19:1–10); and
18) 24:7—the resurrection.

As this survey makes clear, Luke uses the term ἁμαρτωλός only once (24:7) outside of the central section of chapters 5–19.

Luke 5:1–11

The first use of the term ἁμαρτωλός in the Gospel of Luke is in 5:1–11.[1] However, before turning to examine this account it is worthwhile to note the narrative setting of the material.

---

1. Our concern here and throughout our analysis will be Luke's own narrative. Our comments comparing Luke with the other Synoptic writers will be for comparative rather

Narrative Setting

Several observations can be made regarding the narrative setting of the account. First, Luke 4:14—9:50 presents Jesus' ministry in the Galilean region.[2] I. Howard Marshall sees 5:1–11 as the climactic pericope of the section that includes Luke 4:14—5:11. For Marshall, Luke 5:1–11 reveals the response to Jesus' teaching that began at Luke 4:14.[3] Darrell Bock understands Luke 4:14–44 as an overview of Jesus' ministry and organizes 5:1—6:16 under the theme of gathering disciples. Luke 5:1–11 is the first pericope in this section. The change in thematic emphasis to include calling disciples supports Bock's understanding of the structure.

Second, Luke 4:14–44 presents the launching of Jesus' public ministry immediately following his testing in the wilderness (Luke 4:1–13). Jesus' ministry included teaching in the synagogues and performing miraculous signs (Luke 4:14–15, 23). In 4:14–15, Luke gives a general statement noting Jesus' synagogue teaching ministry and the subsequent spreading of his fame.

Third, Luke 4:16–44 presents two specific instances of Jesus' synagogue ministry. Luke 4:16–30 takes place in a synagogue in Jesus' hometown of Nazareth. This account emphasizes Jesus' preaching, and introduces the themes of hostility and rejection of him. Luke 4:31–37 describes an incident in a synagogue in Capernaum. This story emphasizes the authority of Jesus' teaching, as demonstrated by an exorcism.

Fourth, Luke 4:38–41 introduces Simon to the reader. He is first introduced as the host for Jesus during his stay in Capernaum (4:38). As Tannehill observes, Luke's sequence of events indicate that there was prior contact between Jesus and Simon before Simon is called to follow. Matthew and Mark do not include such a background. The healings in Capernaum, plus the great catch of fish, provide the reader with an understanding of Simon's motivation for leaving all and following Jesus.[4] It is reasonable

---

than source critical or redaction concerns. Luke 5:1–11 is commonly tied to Mark 1:16–20 and John 21:1–14. Joseph Fitzmyer sees three major differences between Mark 1:16–20 and Luke 5:1–11 and concludes that the Lucan account is influenced by Mark but basically independent of it (*Luke I–IX*, 560–61).

2. So also Marshall, *Commentary on Luke*, 7; and Bock, *Luke 1:1—9:50*, 44.

3. Marshall, *Luke*, 175.

4. Tannehill, *Narrative Unity*, 1:203.

The "Sinner" Texts in the Gospel of Luke

to suggest that Luke assumes that Theophilus is already aware of Simon. There is no attempt to identify him further, or to distinguish him from any other Simon (e.g., Luke 7:36–50). Simon's home appears to be a location for Jesus' ministry outside of the synagogue (Luke 4:40–41). Following these verses, Luke records an attempt of some to urge Jesus to remain with them, in their town (4:42). But Jesus responds by reaffirming his divine calling (δεῖ) to preach the good news of the kingdom of God to other towns (4:43). Luke then states that Jesus' synagogue ministry continued and spread to even broader geographical regions of Judea (4:44).

Fifth, and finally, Luke 5:1–11 describes the calling of the first disciples by Jesus. Although James and John are mentioned by name in v. 10, Simon is clearly the focus of the story. Several features of the narrative support this. For example, Jesus selects Simon's boat from which to teach (5:3), and directs his instructions to Simon (5:4–5). It is Simon's reaction that is recorded (5:8). The others are mentioned in terms of their relation to Simon (5:9, 10); and Jesus' words of comfort and commission in 5:10 are directed specifically to Simon (the verbs, "stop fearing" [φοβοῦ] and "you shall be" [ἔσῃ], are singular in number).

This narrative may be divided into two parts: (1) 5:1–3 record Jesus' teaching near the shore and then from a boat at Lake Gennesaret; and (2) 5:4–11 record Jesus' call of Simon. Tannehill divides Luke 5:1–11 into three sub-scenes: (1) Jesus preaching from Simon's boat (5:1–3); (2) the great catch of fish (5:4–7); and (3) Simon's reaction and Jesus' response (5:8–11).[5]

Luke's primary concern in 5:1–11seems to be to introduce Simon Peter, a fisherman, who becomes the leader of the movement associated with Jesus (Acts 1:15; 2:14 et al.). It will be Simon's association with Jesus and Jesus' choice of him as leader from the beginning that will be the basis of his authority (cf. Acts 1:21; 4:13).

Scene 1: Verses 1–3[6]

Luke 5:1 presents Jesus standing by Lake (λίμνην) Genessaret teaching the word of God and the curious crowd (ὄχλον) has begun to press in

---

5. Ibid.
6. The translations are my own based on NA26.

on him.[7] In his opening verse, Luke uses a Septuagintal expression that gives the reader the impression that he is reading a continuation of the Old Testament narrative.[8]

This is the first time Luke has used the expression "word of God" (λόγον τοῦ θεοῦ). The genitive is probably a genitive of source, the word from God or Jesus' message that originates in revelation from his heavenly Father.[9] The expression is used in Acts of the message preached by the early church (Acts 8:11, 21; 11:28). There is continuity between the message from Jesus and the message of his apostles. Marshall states that here the expression "word of God" stresses the significance of the message that Simon will hear.[10]

Verse two presents the solution to the pressing crowd as Jesus sees two boats moored at shore. The fishermen are described as having left (ἀποβάντες, aorist participle) the boats and they are in the process of cleaning (ἔπλυνον, imperfect)[11] the nets (δίκτυα). Earle Ellis states that these boats were open craft some 20–30 feet in length.[12] The mention of two boats fits the kind of fishing that utilizes the large nets (δίκτυα) for night fishing.[13] This mention of two boats also prepares the reader for both the reluctance of Simon (5:5) and the involvement of both boats in the catch (5:4–7).

In v. 3, Luke describes Jesus as he takes the initiative and gets into one of the boats, the one belonging to Simon. He asked Simon to put the

---

7. The ὄχλοι are simply the anonymous audience, as Fitzmyer observes; Luke's stress is on the popularity of Jesus, *Luke I–IX*, 467. Darrell Bock observes that the crowd is not being presented by Luke as responsive but curious, *Luke 1:1—9:50*, 453.

8. The expression "And it came about" is the translation of ἐγένετο δὲ + καὶ + finite verb (indic.) which is a Lucan Septuagintism that is found also in Luke 5:12, 17; 8:1, 22; 9:28, 51; 14:1; 17:1; 19:15; 24:4, 15; Acts 5:7; and 9:19. As Fitzmyer observes, this form most closely represents the Hebrew construction of וַיְהִי . . . וְ which reflects a narrative sequence commonly translated "and" followed by a past tense narrative (*Luke I–IX*, 119; cf., Lambdin, *Introduction to Biblical Hebrew*, 123). LXX examples include 1 Sam 24:17; Gen 4:8; 2 Kgs 19:1; 22:11.

9. Bock, *Luke 1:1—9:50*, 453; so also Fitzmyer, *Luke I–IX*, 5–5.

10. Marshall, *Luke*, 201.

11. Used of "cleaning" clothes in Rev 7:14.

12. Ellis, *The Gospel of Luke*, 102.

13. Marshall, *Luke*, 202.

boat out from shore. Simon's positive response, though not mentioned, is assumed in the second part of the verse because Jesus is described as sitting down and teaching the crowd from the boat. As noted above, Simon has already been introduced to the reader as host for Jesus in Capernaum (4:38). Jesus is in control of the action within the narrative and his selection of Simon focuses the narrative upon him.

The first three verses introduce us to the main characters and the setting. Tannehill notes the connection between Jesus' mission described in Luke 4:43 that continues in Luke 5:1–3. In 5:8–11, Jesus tells Simon of his role in the same mission. Thus the central material dealing with the miraculous catch (5:4–7) is framed by mission material.[14]

Scene 2: Verses 4–7

This scene deals with the miraculous catch of fish that is the basis for Simon's self-confession in v. 8. Verse 4 states that after Jesus finished teaching, he commanded Peter to "'put out' (ἐπανάγαγε, aorist imperative, second singular) into deep water and to 'let down' (χαλάσατε, aorist imperative, second plural) your nets for a catch (ἄγραν)." These are the first recorded words from Jesus to an individual person in Luke. Jesus initiates the drama that unfolds.

Verse 5 describes Simon's response. His initial reply reflects reluctance but the emphasis is on his willingness to obey because of his respect for Jesus. This respect is seen in Simon's initial words to Jesus. Simon addresses Jesus as "Master" (ἐπιστάτα, v. 5), a term used here for the first time by Luke. Luke uses ἐπιστάτα where Mark uses διδάσκαλε (8:45 compare Mark 4:38) or Ῥαββί (9:33, cf. Mark 9:5). In Luke it is used only by disciples (8:24, 45; 9:33, 49; with 17:13 as the exception). The emphasis appears to be on the recognition of Jesus' authority, as evidenced by Simon's wearied but obedient response.[15] This respect for Jesus' authority is further emphasized by Simon's statement that at Jesus' "word" (ῥήματι) he would let down the nets.[16]

---

14. Tannehill, *Narrative Unity*, 1:203.

15. Marshall, *Luke*, 203.

16. See Luke 1:38 where Mary responds in faith to Gabriel's announcement: "Be it unto me according to thy word (ῥῆμα)."

THE SINNER IN LUKE

Charles Talbert observes that Luke 4:31–44 emphasizes the authority and power of Jesus' word.[17] Where Mark 1:22 says that the people were astonished at Jesus' teaching "for he taught them as one who had authority, and not as the scribes" (cf. also Matt. 7:29), Luke 4:32 states that they were astonished at his teaching "for his word (λόγος) was with authority." This statement is followed by an exorcism in 4:33–35 that demonstrates Jesus' authority. Luke records the people's response: "What is this word (λόγος)? For with authority and power he commands the unclean spirits and they come out" (4:36; Mark 1:27 omits "word" and "power").[18] Simon had also witnessed this power firsthand when Jesus healed his mother-in-law by rebuking a fever (4:39). Thus when Simon states his reluctant agreement to obey Jesus' instruction to let down the nets (5:5), his statement "at your word" reflects an authoritative word that both Simon and Luke's reader had witnessed.

Verses 6 and 7 describe the miracle. Verse 6 states that immediately after "doing" (ποιήσαντες, aorist) what Jesus said,[19] they caught such a large number of fish that their nets began to break (διερρήσσετο, the imperfect is inceptive).[20] Fitzmyer notes that this miracle is achieved in response to a willing acceptance of a directive from Jesus.[21] Verse 7 describes Simon calling his partners to help with the catch. The catch is so great that both boats were beginning to sink (βυθίζεσθαι, the present infinitive is best understood as inceptive).[22]

Scene 3: Verses 8–11

Verses 8–10a describe the reaction of Simon and his companions. The focus is on Simon's reaction that is detailed in v. 8. Luke states that Simon fell (προσέπεσεν) at the knees of Jesus (Ἰησοῦ is genitive) and declared to him, "Depart from me for I am a sinner (ἁμαρτωλός), Lord." It is

17. Talbert, *Reading Luke*, 58.
18. Ibid., 59.
19. Note Luke's emphasis on "doing" Jesus' word (6:10, 46–47, 49; 8:21).
20. Marshall, *Luke*, 203.
21. Fitzmyer, *Luke I–IX*, 567.
22. Zerwick describes this present tense in Luke 5:7 as having imperfect aspect, reflecting an unaccomplished tendency, that is, the boats did not sink (*Biblical Greek*, §274).

The "Sinner" Texts in the Gospel of Luke

probable that the importance of the miraculous catch is to bring Simon to the confession of his sinfulness.[23] Simon's call for Jesus to "depart" has a metaphorical meaning with the sense of "leave my vicinity."[24]

Verses 9–10a explain (γάρ) Simon Peter's reaction. Luke states that "fear" or "astonishment" (θάμβος) had gripped both Simon and his companions because of the great catch (ἄγρα, v. 4). Only Luke uses the noun θάμβος in the NT. In Luke 4:36, the term describes the response of those who witnessed the display of power and authority of Jesus over demons. In the only other usage other than Luke 5:9, Acts 3:10 uses the term to describe the amazement of the people at the healing of a crippled beggar by Peter.

The reaction is a common one when humans are exposed to the supernatural.[25] In the *Testament of Abraham* 9:3, Abraham expresses a similar confession when he encounters the archangel Michael. When Abraham saw him he "fell upon his face on the ground" (*T. Ab.* 9:1) and after hearing the message from the angel "with many tears fell at the feet of the incorporeal one" (*T. Ab.* 9:2), just as Simon fell at the knees of Jesus in Luke 5:8.[26] Then before petitioning the archangel, Abraham describes himself as "a sinner (ἁμαρτωλός) and your completely unworthy servant" (*T. Ab.* 9:3).

Simon's reaction to the power shown in the miraculous haul of fish relates Jesus to a realm or sphere to which he himself does not belong.[27] But his reaction is also similar to that of Isaiah "Woe unto me for I am a man of unclean lips" (Isa 6:5).[28] The reaction of Isaiah was in response to the revelation of the Lord as "holy" (ἅγιος, Isa 6:3) and in the immediate context Jesus has been declared the "Holy One of God" (ὁ ἅγιος τοῦ θεοῦ, Luke 4:34). As noted above, Luke emphasizes that Simon's reaction is linked to his "seeing" (ἰδών, Luke 5:8). Simon has a new revelation of Jesus that produces a sudden self-awareness of his moral condition before God.

---

23. Rice, "Luke's Thematic Use," 56.
24. Fitzmyer, *Luke I–IX*, 567.
25. Marshall, *Luke*, 55.
26. The translation is from E. P. Sanders, *OTP*, 1: 886.
27. Fitzmyer, *Luke I–IX*, 567.
28. Ibid. So also Marshall, *Luke*, 205.

The Sinner in Luke

Luke does not minimize Simon's self-confession nor does the angel in Isa 6:6. The angel responded by "removing" Isaiah's transgression (ἀνομίας), cleansing (περκαθάριει) him of his "sins" (ἁμαρτίας, Isa 6:7), and calling him for a specific task (Isa 6:8–9).

Jesus' response to Simon is recorded in vv. 10b–11. He told Simon to "stop fearing" (μὴ φοβοῦ).[29] The expression is used by Gabriel to Zechariah (Luke 1:13) and Mary (Luke 1:30, see also the words to Paul in Acts 18:9). These words provide reassurance and are immediately followed by a direct commission to Simon. The analogy to Isaiah and the reassuring words of Jesus make confession and forgiveness implicit in the narrative. Mercy has been already promised to those who fear the Lord (2:34). This promise is equivalent to forgiveness and enables Simon to stop viewing himself as a "sinner" and to become a follower of Jesus.[30] The commission here has the same elements as those of Isaiah 6:1–10: epiphany-reaction-reassurance-commission.[31]

From this time forward, Jesus declared that Simon would be "catching humans alive" (ζωγρῶν).[32] The expression "catching alive" is made up of two parts, "alive" (ζώος) and "catch" (ἀγρεύω). Luke appears to be making a word play on the term "catch" (ἄγρα) in 5:4 and 9.[33] The metaphor appears to be a description of Simon Peter's role of rescuing people for the kingdom of God. The only other NT use is 2 Timothy 2:26 where Paul describes those who have fallen into the trap of the devil who has taken them "captive." The verb ζωγρεῖν is used in the LXX of saving people alive from destruction that has been declared by the Lord as an expression of his wrath (Num 31:15, 18, the Midianite women who were preserved from destruction; Deut 20:16, the Israelites are commanded to not take any of the Canaanites "alive"). In Josh 2:13, it is used by Rahab in a request to the

---

29. *BDF*, §336 (3).

30. Tannehill, *Luke*, 102.

31. Green, *The Gospel of Luke*, 233.

32. The address is second person singular and is directed specifically to Simon but, as the context shows, it will include his companions (5:11). But as Fitzmyer observes, the emphasis here is on Simon and his unique call (*Luke I–IX*, 568). The use of the present active participle with the future of εἰμί seems to be durative in force, emphasizing a new vocation (BDF §353.7).

33. Tannehill, *Narrative Unity*, 1:203; so also Fitzmyer, *Luke I–IX*, 568.

Israelite spies that she and her family be "preserved alive" in the destruction of Jericho (also Josh 6:25). So Luke uses a word that in the OT emphasizes rescuing someone from destruction. This fits a theme found in the first message delivered by Simon Peter in Acts when he preaches to the crowds at Pentecost: "Save yourselves from this crooked generation" (2:40).

The term "fishing" (ἁλιεύειν) is found only once in the LXX in Jer 16:16. The noun "fisherman" (ἁλιεύς) is found four times: Job 40:26 (LXX), of fishing boats; Isa 19:8, of Egyptian fishermen who will mourn due to God's judgment; Ezek 47:10; and Jer 16:16, which has the closest lexical parallels. The LXX translates the MT:

> Ἰδοὺ ἐγὼ ἀποστέλλω τοὺς ἁλεεῖς τοὺς πολλούς, λέγει Κύριος, καὶ ἁλιεύσουσιν αὐτούς
>
> "Behold, I am sending for many fishers, says the Lord, and they shall catch them" (RSV).

The parallels to Luke 5:10 include the use of the noun ἁλεεῖς (cf. Luke 5:2) and the commission by the Lord for these fishermen to catch people (αὐτούς). However, in the context of Jer 16, the Lord is sending "fishermen" to gather Israelites for judgment through the Babylonian exile (16:15). It is possible that Luke has combined the Jeremiah metaphor but uses ζωγρεῖν to modify the picture from one of judgment to one of rescue from judgment.[34] This would make the mission of "catching humans alive" a double-edged mission of gathering people through repentance but leaving the unrepentant for judgment. This explains how the "good news" that John preached could include warnings of the coming wrath and the soon arrival of a Mightier One who would be coming soon to sort the wheat from the chaff (Luke 3:17–18). This same kind of double-edged mission is seen in Jesus' Nazareth proclamation (Luke 4:18–30) and in the mission of the Twelve. In Luke 9:2–4, the Twelve are sent out to preach the kingdom of God and to heal the sick. However, if they are not "welcomed" (see 4:24), they are to shake the dust off their feet as a testimony against them (9:4).

---

34. Charles W. F. Smith proposed that the Synoptic image of 'fishers of men' originally was rooted in the OT judgment imagery. By the time it was utilized by Luke, the image changed to a pastoral concept. However, the use by Luke here fits more a 'rescue' mission as found in the ministry Peter fulfills in Acts ("Fishers of Men," 187–203).

The Sinner in Luke

The mission by the seventy-two also has the double-edge of proclamation and warning in an eschatological context (Luke 10:12–15).

Another possible OT link is Ezek 47:10, which speaks of fishermen in eschatological Israel whose catch will be bountiful and diverse. The context is the Lord describing to Ezekiel waters that go forth to Galilee (Γαλιλαίαν, 47:8) and heal (ὑγιάσει) the waters (47:8). As a result, every creature on which this water flows shall "live" (ζήσεται, three times in 47:9) and there shall be a "extremely great" (πολὺς σφόδρα) quantity of fish (47:9).[35] Then "fishermen" (ἁλιεῖς) shall come and spread out their nets and there will be an "extremely great multitude" (πλῆθος πολὺ σφόδρα) of fish (47:10). The parallels include references to Galilee (Luke 4:14, 31); the use of "fishermen" (Luke 5:2); emphasis on a large catch; and the emphasis on "alive" or "live" (Luke 5:10); and the theme of "healing" (ὑγιάσει, Luke 4:40; 5:15, 17–25). Zimmerli states that the context in Ezekiel emphasizes the "abundance of holiness on the part of the most holy one" that flows out from the sanctuary and heals what is sick. The image emphasizes the full effect of the presence of God taking up residence in his people's midst.[36]

This Ezekiel background could provide an additional OT connection to Jesus' healing ministry. The concept of healing power flowing from the "Holy One" brings to mind the healing/cleansing of the leper by contact (Luke 5:13), and power flowing "from" Jesus to heal the woman (Luke 8:46). These fishermen could be understood as agents of this kind of ministry in view of their own part in carrying out the same task (Luke 9:1–2; 10:9) with analogous results (Acts 5:15, 16). Verse 11 concludes the narrative by stating that Simon and his companions "left everything and followed him." The idea of "following" is the picture of the disciple (Luke 5:27–28; 9:23, 49, 57, 59, 61; 18:22, 28).[37]

One must ask what is the significance of this narrative for Luke. Since it is the first call to discipleship, Luke presents the reader with the kind of persons Jesus invites to follow him. As a fisherman, Simon is in a low social position in the society and he is a "sinner." Yet Jesus takes the initiative to "rescue" Simon. He is open to Jesus and humble before him. He

35. The adverb σφόδρα is used in Luke 18:23 of the young rich man and in Acts 6:7 of the 'great' increase in the number of disciples in Jerusalem.

36. Zimmerli, *Ezekiel 2*, 509.

37. Fitzmyer, *Luke I-IX*, 569.

acknowledges his sinful condition and Jesus calms his fears and calls him to join him in his mission. Luke has already previewed this positive response by the response of the "toll-collectors" to the preaching of John the Baptist (Luke 3:12). But here Luke presents the ministry of the "Stronger One" (Luke 3:16).

The meaning of this account in Luke's Gospel has been understood in various ways. Joel Green proposes that within Luke's overall narrative strategy, the initial purpose of this story is to secure for Luke's audience the kind of response to the ministry of Jesus that is appropriate.[38] The narrative setting is significant both in location (the first call of disciples) and time (the beginning of Jesus' ministry). William Kurz observes the strong foreshadowing component of the miraculous catch.[39]

For our understanding of the "sinner," Luke emphasizes Simon's awareness of his condition in the presence of the "Holy One" and Jesus' reassurance to Simon who responded in humility. Luke leaves room for the development of the "sinner" concept later in his narrative.[40] But, he has already prepared the reader as to the kind of person Jesus is targeting for ministry.

Luke 5:27–32

The Narrative Setting

Luke's narrative in Luke 5:12–26 turns from the theme of calling disciples (5:1–11) and resumes Jesus' ministry of healing and authoritative teaching. Luke 5:12–16 deals with the healing of a leper and 5:17–26 with the healing of a paralytic. The "cleansing" (καθαρίζειν) of the leper ties into Jesus' words regarding the "cleansing" of Naaman the leper in 4:27. Jesus instructed the former leper to return to the priests to carry out the requirements of the Law of Moses as a "testimony" (μαρτύριον) to them.[41]

In the OT, the only recorded healings of lepers were done by God (Num 12:10) or his prophet Elisha (2 Kgs 5:3–27). In the case of Naaman, Elisha viewed the healing as a sign to let Naaman "know that there is a

---

38. Green, *Luke*, 230.
39. Kurz, *Reading Luke-Acts*, 20.
40. Green, *Luke*, 234.
41. A witness to the presence of Messianic times (Luke 7:22; Bock, *Luke 1:1—9:50*, 477).

prophet in Israel" (2 Kgs 5:8). Jesus' healing of a leper is intended to have an analogous effect on the priests. The manner of Jesus' healing activity is also significant. The birth narrative did not specify how God's salvation would be brought. In the Nazareth proclamation Jesus identified himself as the "who" and his mission of bringing "release" as the "how." Jesus' actions are intended to be seen as fulfillment. Usually, touching a leper transferred the state of uncleanness from the leper to the person who touched him (Lev 5:2–3; 22:4–6). But, Jesus removed the man's uncleanness through his touch. This brings to mind images such as those found in Isa 6:6–7, where the angel removes the uncleanness of Isaiah by touching his lips, and Job 5:18 that declares that the hands of the Lord heal people.

In the healing of the paralytic, Jesus' ministry of healing becomes a means to display his claim to have authority on earth to forgive sins (5:17–26). The narrative begins by focusing on those who are present in the scene, the "Pharisees" and the "teachers of the law" (v. 17).[42] Up to this

42. Neale has described Luke's presentation of the Pharisees as a caricature for literary purposes. Neale suggests that Luke needed a negative background of antagonists or "bad guys" against which to present the hero Jesus (*None But the Sinners*, 18–39, 191–92). He bases his position on two inaccuracies that he sees in Luke's presentation of the Pharisees: 1) Luke presents them as overly influential, but they were actually only a small purity sect; and 2) Luke portrays the Pharisees as rigid legalists. He argues that Luke caricatures the difference between *halakhah* (legal opinions) and *hagadah* (homilies, 192). I agree that Luke's presentation is not the complete picture. There were many admirable qualities of the sect, as demonstrated by Josephus's comment that they were popular among the people (A*nt.* 13.297–98). However, Neale neglects the point that Josephus and the New Testament are our earliest sources for the Pharisees. Both sources agree on the portrayal of both Pharisaic influence and their zeal for the Torah and their interpretations of it. One can compare Josephus' words in *Ant.* 17.2.4 that state there were 6,000 members of the sect and they "valued themselves highly upon the exact skill they had in the law of their fathers" with Luke 6:2 and the Pharisees' question to Jesus: "Why do you do what is unlawful on the Sabbath?" Martin Hengel comments that the number 6,000 only describes those Pharisees who were unwilling to give an oath of allegiance to Herod, therefore the number of Pharisees could be higher (Hengel and Deines, "Sanders," 33 n85). But there is nothing that prevents even 6,000 people zealous for their purpose and actively involved in the worship and teaching of the people through the synagogue to have a significant influence on the people (Hengel and Deines, "Sanders," 32). Steve Mason proposes that Josephus would have been unlikely to have invented the popularity of the Pharisees since he viewed this as an unpleasant fact of life (*Flavius Josephus on the Pharisees*, 375). Mason also observes that Josephus' dislike for the Pharisees is based on their claim of ἀκρίβεια or "accuracy" in interpretation of the laws (Ibid., 373). Therefore what we have in Luke is admittedly not the whole picture, but a historically accurate picture of the sect as it encountered Jesus and his followers.

The "Sinner" Texts in the Gospel of Luke

point Luke has given the reader few comments regarding how the religious or political leaders of Israel are responding to God's salvation plan in Jesus. In the birth narrative, Luke introduced us to the priest Zacharias who was pious but initially unbelieving (1:5–25, 57–80). The amazement over Jesus' questions as a boy in Luke 2:46–47 is the mention of Jesus and the leaders of Israel before Luke 5:17. Luke has not provided any commentary on how the Pharisees are to be evaluated by the reader.[43] But, Luke has prepared the reader for (1) the "scattering" of those who are proud in the "thoughts of their hearts" (διανοία/καρδίας, 1:51); (2) the "falling and rising" (ἀνάστασιν) of many (2:34); (3) Jesus to be a "sign" spoken against (2:34); and (4) Jesus' gift of insight into the "thoughts" (διαλογισμοί) of many "hearts" (καρδιῶν, Luke 2:32).

Luke describes a "paralyzed" man whose friends had carried him to the top of a roof and lowered him into the room in order for Jesus to heal him (5:18–19). Jesus' initial response is not to heal the man but to pronounce that his "sins" (ἁμαρτίας) were "forgiven" (ἀφέωνται). The perfect tense stresses that Jesus has made a pronouncement with abiding force.[44] The use of ἀφίημι with "sins" (ἁμαρτίας) links Jesus' statement to Luke 1:77, which described the "knowledge of salvation . . . through (ἐν) the 'forgiveness of sins' (ἀφέσει ἁμαρτιῶν)." It also links this episode with Jesus' Nazareth proclamation that he is the Servant-Messiah who has been anointed and sent to bring "release" (ἄφεσιν, 4:18). Luke is presenting Jesus as fulfilling these promises in this narrative. The texts from Isaiah 61:1–2 and 58:6 are serving as programmatic for Jesus in the same way Isaiah 40:3–5 served as the program for John (Luke 3:4–18).

The reaction of the Pharisees centers on Jesus' pronouncement (5:21–22). Luke states that they began "thinking" (διαλογίζεσθαι): "Who is this who speaks blasphemy? Who is able to forgive sins but God alone?" Luke uses the term διαλογίζεσθαι three times in these two verses. He is linking this narrative scene to the words of Simeon in 2:35 that Jesus would "reveal the thoughts (διαλογισμοί) of many hearts (καρδιῶν)" in Israel. This is made even clearer by Jesus' question, "Why are you 'thinking in your

---

43. Gowler, *Host, Guest, Enemy, and Friend*, 186.
44. Marshall, *Luke*, 213.

hearts'?" (v. 22). Luke's first introduction of the Pharisees to the narrative presents them as not recognizing his identity or accepting his mission.[45]

As noted above, Jesus' response in v. 22 reveals to the reader that the issue here is a lack of openness to Jesus rather than a positive motivation to protect Israel against a messianic pretender. But Jesus answered the question (v. 21) by demonstrating his authority to forgive sins through healing the lame man. Jesus commanded the man to "rise" and "walk" (v. 23). The paralyzed man was instantly healed and returned home glorifying God (v. 25).[46] Jesus has claimed to have the authority to pronounce sins forgiven. Luke's introduction to the Pharisees presents them as charging Jesus with blasphemy (v. 21). The healing is meant to validate Jesus' claim for the hearers (vv. 22–24). The account ends with the paralytic healed and "everyone" praising God and in awe concerning what they had "seen" (v. 26). Luke did not describe the reaction of the Pharisees. Have they responded favorably to what they have seen and heard? Or, will this be a fulfillment of Simeon's prophecy of Jesus' causing division within Israel (Luke 2:34) and a repetition of the scene in Nazareth?

In Luke 5:27–32 Jesus declares his mission as calling sinners to repentance. The real point of this passage is to show what kind of people Jesus calls and why he calls them. There is a conflict between Jesus and the Pharisees regarding Jesus' associations. The narrative may be divided into two parts: (1) 5:27–28, the call of Levi, the toll-collector; and (2) 5:29–32, the banquet at Levi's house and the Pharisees' protest concerning Jesus' table-fellowship with "tax collectors and sinners."

Luke 5:27–28: The Call of Levi

Luke 5:27 presents Jesus in control of the action within the narrative, so "remarkable things" (5:26) are about to be seen again. Jesus calls a toll-collector (τελώνης) by the name of Levi to be a disciple (5:27–28). The τελώνης in the region of Galilee was responsible primarily to collect customs tolls at borders between provinces or customs duties on goods

---

45. Darr, *On Character Building*, 94.

46. Luke 5:27–32 is closely related to Luke 5:17–26. This will be analyzed in more detail in the discussion that follows.

entering or exiting a town.[47] Capernaum was in Galilee, which was under the authority of Herod Antipas. Toll-collectors, going from province to province, demanded payment of customs that would fill the coffers of the local ruler. The sites would be given to the highest bidder, who would pay the government up front for the year. The toll-collector would then have to make up the amount that he had invested through the customs duties. Anything that he made above the investment was profit.

In rabbinic writings toll-collectors were despised because of their dishonesty and ruthlessness.[48] In the New Testament, toll-collectors were commonly associated with evil people. In Matt 18:11, they are lumped together with robbers, evil-doers, and adulterers; in Matt 21:32 with prostitutes; and in Matt 18:17 with Gentiles.

But Luke's reader has already been introduced to toll-collectors in Luke 3:12. This group is named among those responding in repentance to the preaching of John the Baptist. When toll-collectors came to John the Baptist and asked him how a change of heart would show itself in their daily life, John told them not to take more than was required. The temptation was to take whatever one could extort from a person, using an armed escort to gently persuade the taxpayer. Yet these toll-collectors have been given the "knowledge of salvation for the forgiveness of sins" (1:77) and appear have been "prepared" for the Lord (1:17, 76).

In Luke's narrative, while Levi was working, Jesus approached the toll-booth and invited Levi to follow him (5:27). Levi accepted the invitation. In language identical to the response of Simon and his companions, Levi is immediately responsive. The contrast is that no miracle is involved. Levi began a process of discipleship at that moment. He has left everything to follow him (5:28).

5:29–32: Levi's Banquet

Luke 5:29–32 describes a great banquet hosted by Levi, the toll-collector (5:29).[49] Danker calls this a "farewell banquet."[50] The term "banquet"

---

47. See pages 7–10 above.
48. See pages 7–10 above and the discussion that follows below pages 121ff.
49. BAGD, 206.
50. Danker, *Jesus and the New Age*, 71.

(δοχή) is used in Gen 21:8 LXX for the great feast held by Abraham on the day Isaac was weaned. In Esth 1:3 LXX it refers to the great banquet given by Xerxes for all his nobles and officials. In Dan 5:1 (LXX, Alexandrian version) it is the great banquet given by King Belshazzar for a thousand of his nobles. Luke uses the term in Luke 14:13 in the parable of the great kingdom banquet where it becomes a symbol of fellowship and celebration with God. Although the term is not found here, the scene anticipates the joy associated with repentance for those found by Jesus (Luke 15:7).

The Complaint

Luke 5:30 introduces the reader to the Pharisees again. Their first recorded words in Luke were a charge of blasphemy against Jesus (5:21). In this second narrative, Luke introduces the Pharisees and scribes in the process of grumbling (ἐγόγγυζον, imperfect). The word "grumble" (γογγύζειν) has limited usage in the LXX, referring primarily to the people of Israel grumbling against the Lord or Moses (Exod 16:7; 17:3; Num 11:1; 14:27 [twice], 29; 16:41; 17:5; Ps 106:25, 105:25 LXX). David's enemies "grumble" against him (Ps 59:15, 58:15 LXX). Isaiah uses the verb twice, in 29:24 of those who "complain" but who will one day receive instruction; and in 30:12, Isaiah uses the verb of those who "murmured against" the Lord's instruction through the prophets. The prophet Isaiah declares that "murmuring" is one of the sins that must be done away before the Lord will hear them (Isa 58:9, the noun γογγυσμος).

In Luke's narrative, the reason for the grumbling of the Pharisees and their scribes is Jesus' table fellowship with toll-collectors and "sinners." The Pharisees direct their question to the disciples (5:30), but it is Jesus who responds (5:31–32). What is the reason for the complaint of the Pharisees? Is it based on their own religious prejudice as is commonly suggested?[51] Is the concern political in that Jesus is associating himself with collaborators and traitors?[52] Or, is the concern a moral one with the Pharisees identifying Jesus as breaking the law of God?[53] Or, is the real reason for the Pharisees'

51. This is the view of the first two positions regarding the definition of the "sinner" in Luke as discussed above on pages xiii–xiv, 3–6, and 62–65.

52. As proposed by Norman Perrin (cf. the discussion above, pages xiii, 13–16).

53. As held by Abrahams, Jeremias, and E. P. Sanders (cf. the discussion above on pages xiii, 6–19).

concern irretrievable and irrelevant and only to be understood as symbol and metaphor?[54] The problem of the cause of the offense at the level of history has not been solved.[55] Does Luke provide clues to the resolution of the question?

Toll-collectors and Sinners

As stated in chapter one, one major direction of research in the identification of the "sinner" in Luke and the other Synoptics has been the link between "toll-collectors" and "sinners." Jeremias cites the link between tax collectors and other immoral types and suspected trades to identify the "sinner" as someone at which everyone would point a finger.[56] Perrin links the tax collector to his association with Gentiles, the "sinner" is then identified as those Jews who made themselves as Gentiles.[57] John Donahue clarifies the tax-collecting situation in Israel and helps to support Jeremias' understanding of the τελώνης as despised for moral concerns rather than political association.[58]

J. Gibson argues that the link between tax collectors and prostitutes in Matt 21:31–32 actually supports Perrin's position that the term "sinner" refers to a Jew who made themselves as a Gentile.[59] He makes a case that prostitutes and tax collectors are linked primarily because they are both prime examples of collaborators with Roman forces. Gibson cites Josephus (*Ant.* 19.356) and Rabbinic literature to demonstrate the presence of brothels in Caesarea. Yet these texts do not upbraid the prostitutes for collaboration. In fact, *b. 'Abod. Zar.* 18, which Gibson quotes, ends with a warning to the prostitute because of her iniquity and sins for which she will be judged on the Day of Judgment. She is warned for being in danger of the wrath of God, the same theme found in the sinner material throughout our research. Besides this, even if it is granted that prostitutes are commonly associated with Roman soldiers, this is not an aspect of the offense that is significant

---

54. As proposed by David Neale (cf. above on pages xiii, 19–20, 37–39, 59).
55. Neale, *None But the Sinners*, 129.
56. Jeremias, *New Testament Theology*, 109.
57. Perrin, *Rediscovering*, 94.
58. Donahue, 39–61; see pages 15–16 above for a discussion of Donahue.
59. Gibson, "Hoi Telonai kai Pornai," 429–33.

to Luke. In fact, the "Prodigal son" is associated with harlots and is pictured as a neither a Gentile nor a soldier, but a Jewish sinner (Luke 15:30).

Kathleen Corley argues that the "sinners" associated with toll-collectors are women who are viewed as prostitutes because the terms "sinner" and "prostitute" were commonly associated.[60] She suggests that the women were not actual prostitutes but the label functioned as traditional slander by Jesus' opponents. Corley makes the same mistake here that Jeremias made with respect to the "toll collector" term. She fails to examine Luke's use of the term "sinner" to test her thesis. Two points serve to illustrate that she is incorrect. First, Luke's "sinners" are most often men (Peter in Luke 5:8; the Prodigal Son in Luke 15; the publican in Luke 18:13; and Zacchaeus in Luke 19:1–10). Association with women is made an issue only in Luke 7:36–50 and here Jesus accepts the accuracy of Simon's label of the woman as a genuine "sinner." Second, Corley fails to see that the "sinner" is not labeled such by Jesus' opponents alone. Jesus assumes the label is accurate (Luke 5:27–32; Luke 15) and even widens the application (Luke 13:1–9).

The weakness in the above historical approaches is that they have not been adequately tested against Luke's own usage of the "toll collector." Luke presents the negative image of toll-collectors to be rooted in their dishonesty and corruption (Luke 3:12–14). This is also illustrated by the nature of Zacchaeus' repentance (Luke 19:1–10). The repentance of Zacchaeus addresses the same concerns mentioned in the rabbinic sources concerning toll-collectors who are scorned in the Mishnah on moral grounds rather than ethnic or political grounds.

This is demonstrated by the link in the Mishnah between toll-collectors and other blatantly immoral types: murderers, robbers, extortionists. Mishnah *Nedarim* 3:4 states that men may vow (e.g., to avoid paying) to murderers, robbers, or "toll-collectors" (מוכסין) what they have is a "heave-offering" even though it is not. This is permitted in order to protect themselves from ruthless greed. Mishnah *Baba Qamma* 10:1 prohibits taking change for money at the counter of a toll collector since the money is considered stolen.[61] In the next verse, this same Mishnah links toll-collectors and robbers as examples of people who took something and gave

60. Corley, "Jesus' Table Practice," 444–59.
61. Danby, *The Mishnah*, 346 n1.

the victim something in exchange. The victim can expect to never see his property again (*m. B. Qam.* 10:2).

In addition to the rabbinic perception, the τελώνης was also considered morally suspect in the Hellenistic world. Several examples illustrate this. Livy refers to Posthumius, a tax-farmer (*publicanus*) who was said to have had no equal in dishonesty and avarice (24.3.9). Posthumius almost caused an insurrection because of his "ravaging" the country in Lucania. Livy also spoke of a large disturbance caused by the "violence" (*turbato*) of the publicans (25.4.2). Julius Caesar also spoke of the harshness and extortion of the publicans and their farmers who used military force to impose and exact taxes for their own private gain (*Bell. civ.* 3.32). These references refer to the perception of the tax collectors around 200 BCE. But Tacitus recorded a large public outcry against the publicans and those collecting the indirect taxes during the time of Nero (*Ann.* 13.50). In this passage, Tacitus states the need for measures to be put in place to check the "greed" (*cupidines*) of the publicans.

In the Greco-Roman world, the term "tax-farmer" was a slur. Cicero raises the point in defending his client, Plancio. In addressing Laterensis, Cicero acknowledges that Laterensis assumes that the fact that Plancio's father was a publican is a slur upon him. Cicero attempts to turn this around and make it a positive (*Planc.* 9.23–24). But Cicero also described the corruption related to the profession when he spoke of a female tax collector in Sicily who worked as a prostitute and of the town of Herbita, which was wronged by tax collectors (*Verr.* 2.3.34 §79).

When comparing the perception of the tax collector in the Roman literature with that of the rabbis and the Gospel of Luke, the emphasis is consistent with regard to concerns about dishonesty and oppression. We have demonstrated that the term "sinner" in the OT, the intertestamental literature, and the rabbinic material are consistent in viewing the "righteous/sinner" issue in terms of dealing with God and others in ways appropriate to the relationship. The toll-collectors were in a profession that was open to dishonesty and oppression of their neighbors.[62] As has been demonstrated,

---

62. Contra Neale, who states that toll-collectors were no more prone to degeneration than others (*None But the Sinner*, 115). Although this is correct when speaking of individuals, this does not acknowledge the point that some professions provide more opportunity for taking advantage of others, and persons involved in those professions are assumed to be

in the OT a person guilty of violating God's revealed demands for proper treatment of his neighbor is a "sinner." This type of behavior received the "sinner" designation throughout all stages of the use of the term.[63] As noted above, the rabbis did not chastise the toll collector for his link to Gentiles but because of his suspected dishonesty and oppression. This was the same concern reflected in John the Baptist's instructions to τελωναί in Luke 3:13. The fruit of repentance for the τελωναί would be to take no more than they should by extortion or other means. The key for understanding Luke's view of the "sinner" is clues found within his own narrative. In Luke the toll collector is suspected of dishonesty and connected to others who also are vilified on moral, not political or economic grounds (cf. Matt 21:31–32, toll-collectors and prostitutes).

In conclusion, the toll collector link provides help in identifying the "sinner" in Luke.[64] The historical categories are clearly presented by Perrin, Farmer, Donahue, and Gibson. When tested against Luke's usage, the toll collector is viewed as a "sinner" on moral grounds. Thus for Luke, the "sinners" referred to in the expression "toll collector and sinners" are those comfortable associating with toll-collectors, who are immediately considered to be moral "scoundrels."[65] Thus for Luke, "sinners" are also given the label on moral grounds.

---

dishonest unless shown to be otherwise.

63. See pages 31, 37, 43–44, 48–50 above.

64. Contra Neale, *None But the Sinners*, 117–118.

65. Neale states that viewing the "sinners" as simply those who were not troubled about being seen in the company of toll-collectors is a very loose criterion and from this perspective would not have been a particularly offensive crowd, morally, socially, or religiously (*None But the Sinners*, 117). But Neale also acknowledges that the logic of the narrative demands that Luke present Jesus' actions as radical acts. One need not attempt a reconstruction from the rabbinic lists of despised trades as J. Massyngberde Ford has done in *My Enemy is My Guest*, 72–73. But the link between toll-collectors and prostitutes (Matt 21:32), robbers, evildoers, and adulterers (Luke 18:11) in the Synoptics makes the case that a morally and religiously offensive group is possible. In my view, once toll-collectors are considered real "sinners" in the narrative, the other "sinners" need not be identified in specifics. What is important is that the Pharisees view them as "sinners." Jesus accepts the description at face value and Luke does not debate the label.

The Issue of Table Fellowship

If we are correct in our assessment that the rabbis' concern for "toll-collectors" was a moral concern, then the term "sinner" in the expression "toll-collectors and sinners" is also a moral designation.[66] This is consistent with our findings that the rabbis applied the term "sinner" in a more narrow way to the "wicked," those who have rejected the covenant by ignoring the Law of God. They did not use the term "sinner" for the common people who failed to maintain the Pharisees' level of ritual purity.[67] The issue for the Pharisees against Jesus' table fellowship with "sinners" (Luke 5:30; 7:34; 15:1–2) was not an issue of his being defiled by association with the common people. Table fellowship with the ἁμαρτωλός = רָשָׁע was avoided because the "sinners" violated the Law of Moses not the minutiae of the rabbis.[68] Mishnah *'Abot* 5:7 records the admonition of Nittai the Arbellite, cited as pre-tannaitic by Danby: "Keep thee far from an evil neighbor and consort not with the wicked (רָשָׁע) and lose not belief in retribution."[69] Abrahams rightly argues that the concern over associating with known "sinners" was the tendency to become one, as Psalm 1 warns.[70] This is one reason for the Pharisees' criticism of Jesus. Another reason for avoiding contact with sinners was fear of being swept up in God's judgment against the sinner. This is one aspect of the warning in the Mishnah text cited above. The view is consistent with the psalmist whose attitude toward sinners was to avoid them (Ps 1:1, 5), not dwelling in their tents (Ps

---

66. The expression τῶν τελωνῶν καὶ ἁμαρτωλῶν is conceived of as forming a unity as demonstrated by the use of one article for both nouns (*ZBG*, §184). Jeremias was correct in this observation (see page 10–11 above).

67. See the full discussion on pages 61–65 above.

68 Sanders, *Jesus and Judaism*, 177–94. Sanders is correct in demonstrating that "sinners" were not identical to the *'am ha 'aretz*, the common people. Pharisaic concern for eating their food in a state of purity and for tithing affected the social intercourse between the Pharisees and the common people but on grounds of holiness. Jacob Neusner makes it clear that the pre-CE 70 Pharisaic view of uncleanness was based on ontological (ritual) as opposed to moral (virtue) grounds (See Neusner, "The Fellowship (Haburah) in the Second Jewish Commonwealth," 125–42). Sinners and tax collectors renounced the covenant by their life and attitudes and thus were under the judgment of God.

69. Danby, *The Mishnah*, 799.

70 Abrahams, *Publicans and Sinners*, 57. See the discussion of Abrahams beginning on page 6 above.

84:10=83:10 LXX) or even eating with them (Ps 101:5=100:5 LXX). This warning is also illustrated in Num 16 in which the assembly of Israelites is warned to move away from the tents of the wicked men because of the wrath of God that was about to be poured out against them (Num 16:26). Similar warnings to avoid the sinner have also been found in other Jewish literature (e.g., Sir 8:10; 13:17).[71]

Therefore, the concern expressed by the Pharisees is that Jesus was violating Scriptural injunctions thus invalidating any "messianic" claims and making him a false teacher who could lead Israel astray. This is supported by Jesus' statement that "this generation," including the Pharisees (Luke 7:30, 36), has labeled Jesus a "glutton," a "drunkard" and a "friend" (φίλος) of toll-collectors and sinners (7:34). The context of that statement is the issue of the legitimacy of John as prophet and Jesus as a great prophet or the Messiah (7:16–35). The Pharisees have rejected John and his mission on the grounds he was possessed by demons (7:30, 33). When Jesus uses the label that had been placed on him, it is the explanation for their rejection of his ministry.[72]

E. P. Sanders argues that the criticism against Jesus was caused by his offer of entrance into the Kingdom through faith in him without the accepted requirements for repentance.[73] He argues that all passages including Jesus' calling sinners to repentance are creations by the church or by Luke to emphasize good behavior on behalf of those coming into the church. Bruce Chilton rightly criticizes Sanders on this point.[74] Jesus clearly does include repentance in his call to sinners (Luke 5:32; 13:3; 15:7). Besides this, Jesus is not criticized here for the content of his proclamation but for his choice of association.

Neale objects to the moral basis for the Pharisees' concern for two reasons. First, he cannot imagine any actual circumstances that would have brought different kinds of sinners together in the way suggested by Luke.[75]

---

71. See pages 42–43 above.

72. Note *m. 'Abot* 5:19 mentioned on page 65 above, Balaam is called *the* "sinner" (הָרָשָׁע) for leading others to sin (5:18).

73. Sanders, *Jesus and Judaism*, 204–208.

74. Chilton, "Jesus and the Repentance," 1–18. Also see the discussion regarding the historical reliability of the Synoptic "sinner" tradition beginning on page 72 above.

75. Neale, *None But the Sinners*, 117.

Yet Neale himself states that there is no reason to doubt that such an event actually did occur to give rise to the offense. Luke provides some clues by linking toll-collectors and soldiers in Luke 3:14. As observed in our previous discussion, the nature of the profession linked the groups. Other specific "sinner" types need not be identified, although it is not as difficult to imagine as Neale suggests.[76] Second, Neale argues that it is difficult to imagine how any Jews would have opposed Jesus' attempt to reform sinners.[77] Yet this presupposes that the Pharisees have understood Jesus' mission and accepted his explanation of it. At this point in the narrative, they have been pictured as opposing Jesus rather than being open to him. Luke's use of γογγύζειν also makes connections for the reader between the murmuring of unresponsive Israel and a possible analogous situation in the present.

Jesus Explains His Mission

In Luke 5:31–32, Jesus defends his actions by declaring his mission. In Luke 5:31, he states that the "healthy" (ὑγιαίοντες) have no need for a "physician" (ἰατροῦ) but those having "illness" (κακῶς) do. His words remind the reader of Luke 5:20–25 and the connection between the need for physical healing and Jesus' claim to forgive sins. Jesus then states that he has not come to "call" (καλέσαι) the "righteous" (δικαίους) but "sinners" (ἁμαρτωλούς) to "repentance" (μέτανοιαν, 5:32).

Jesus makes an analogy between the need for physical healing and the need of "sinners" for repentance. The analogy both recalls his claim to have authority to forgive sins (5:20, 24) and the sign of that authority, the physical healing (5:24). This further ties Jesus' claim to "forgive" (ἀφίημι) "sins" (ἁμαρτία) with his mission of "release" (ἄφεσιν) on behalf of "sinners" (ἁμαρτωλούς) (4:18, 19). The mission of Jesus continues to be directly connected to the program of Isa 61.

There is a strong association between disease and sin in the OT. In Gen 20:17, Abimelech is afflicted with illness by God for taking Sarah

---

76. One can imagine a gathering of mafia leaders that would include businessmen, lawyers, and politicians (cf. Ford, *The Enemy Is My Guest*, 72).

77. Ibid., 125. Neale's argument is based on that proposed by Sanders, *Jesus and Judaism*, 203.

as his wife. Miriam becomes leprous because of rebellion (Num 12:13). Moses warns of a curse of various diseases that the Lord would inflict on the Israelites if they disobeyed the covenant (Deut 28:27, 35). The psalmist declares that he has no "health" (ἴασις) in his body because of the Lord's wrath due to his "sins" (ἁμαρτίας, Ps 38:3 [37 LXX]; cf. Pss 6:2 and 41:4 [40 LXX]).

But there is also a strong connection between "turning" to God in "repentance" for "forgiveness" and "healing." In the context of Solomon's dedication of the temple in 2 Chronicles 7:14, the Lord promised that if they "seek his face" and "turn from their wicked ways" that he would "forgive" (ἵλεως) their "sins" (ἁμαρτίαις, cf. Ps 103:3 [102 LXX]). In Isa 6:10, the Lord states that if Israel would turn to him that he would "heal" (ἰάσομαι), a reference to spiritual healing. Luke will refer to the context of this verse in Luke 8:11 but to the specific text itself near the close of his two-volume work in Acts 28:27. The mission of Jesus demonstrates that the fulfillment of the OT promise of spiritual healing is taking place through him.

The OT emphasizes God as the primary agent of physical and spiritual healing. In Luke 5:32, Jesus uses this OT analogy and emphasizes his claim to be God's healing agent. Later the connection between healing and salvation will be stressed (Luke 17:19; 18:42). Jesus is presenting himself as the great healer of spiritual infirmity (Luke 5:32; cf. Ps 103:2).

Jesus' statement that his mission is a call to "repentance" reflects continuity between Jesus' mission and that of John the Baptist (Luke 1:77; 3:3). The mission to call sinners to repentance is also consistent with calls of repentance in the OT. The term "repentance" (μετάνοιαν) in Luke 5:32 is not found in the LXX. The verb μετανοέω usually translates נחם "to change one's mind" and is used primarily of God "changing" his stated intentions to judge (Amos 7:3, 6; Joel 2:13, 14; Jonah 3:9, 10). Jeremiah 8:6 states that there is no one who "repents" (μετανοῶν) from his "evil" (κακίας).[78] The verb μετανοέω is sometimes used in parallelism with "turn" (ἐπιστρέφω, Jer 18:8; Joel 2:14). Isaiah 46:8, a call to repentance, contains the only use of μετανοέω for שוב in the OT:

---

78. The use of κακία for either "sickness" or "evil" makes Jesus' use in Luke 5:31 appropriate for the link between healing and repentance (cf. Jer 18:8).

μετανοήσατε οἱ πεπλανημένοι, ἐπιστρέψαρε τῇ καρδίᾳ.

"Repent, you who have gone astray, turn (or return) in your heart."

The term πεπλανημένοι (those who have strayed) is linked to Isa 53:6 with the image of the prophet who speaks of himself and sinning Israel as sheep who have "gone astray" (ἐπλανήθημεν). This is a possible conceptual link to the shepherd theme in Ezek 34. In the context of denouncing the "shepherd" or leaders of Israel (Ezek 34:4), the Lord rebukes them for not strengthening the "weak" (ἠσθενηκός), caring for the "sick" (κακῶς), "turning back" (ἀπεστρέψατε) the "straying" (πλανώμενον), or "seeking" (ἐζητήσατε) the "lost" (ἀπολωλός).

Neale suggests that Jesus is not launching a new mission but one that the shepherds of Israel should have been launching themselves. Thus, Jesus is upbraiding the Pharisees for their failure and explaining his mission as fulfillment of Ezek 34:16 in which the Lord takes over the shepherd duties himself.[79] Although the allusion to Ezekiel 34 is possible here, any rebuke of the Pharisees' shepherding role must be seen as secondary. If the Ezekiel "shepherd" concept is present in Luke 5:32, the emphasis is on the Pharisees' understanding of Jesus' mission, not a critique of their shepherding duties.[80]

The theme of repentance is found in Luke to be part of the preaching from John the Baptist (Luke 3:3, 8; Acts 13:24; 19:4); Jesus (Luke 5:32; 13:3, 5; 15:7, 10); and his followers (Luke 24:47; Acts 2:38; 3:19; 17:30; 20:21; 36:20). In Luke, repentance is almost always related to the forgiveness of sins.[81] Like the OT use, "repentance" is sometimes expressed by ἐπιστέφω in Luke-Acts (Luke 1:16, 17; Acts 3:19; 9:35; 11:21; 14:15; 15:19; 26:20; 28:27). As mentioned earlier, there are promises in the OT of restoration to those who repent (cf. Joel 2:13, 14; Jer 18:8; 2 Chr 6:37; and 1 Kgs 8:30, 47).[82] However, Jonah appears to be the only actual OT "mission" to sinners (Jonah 3:8, 10).

---

79. Neale, *None But the Sinners*, 131–32.

80. The Ezekiel "shepherd" theme will play an important role later in Luke 15 and 19:1–10. We will examine this link to the "sinner" in more detail there.

81. See the discussion on "forgiveness" in Luke beginning on page 95 above.

82. See discussion on pages 37–39 above.

The Sinner in Luke

Mercy is infrequently offered in direct terms for those designated by the term "sinner" (ἁμαρτωλός). The clearest example is the prophet Ezekiel.[83] In Ezek 33:8, the prophet has become the watchman responsible for sounding the alarm of God's judgment to the "sinner" (ἁμαρτωλός). In 33:9, the "sinner" receives the offer of repentance. In 33:14–16, God offers forgiveness to the repentant sinner. The offer is stated clearly in 33:19: "And when the sinner (ἁμαρτωλός) turns from his iniquity (ἀνομίας), and shall do justice and righteousness, by these he shall live." This is an offer of repentance to "sinners" in Israel. Although the offer of repentance is not new (Joel 2:12–13; Jer 3:12), the call in Ezekiel is unprecedented in its emphasis as an invitation from the Lord and an expression of his desire to offer forgiveness and life to the genuine "sinner." As we will see, Luke will show that Jesus in seeking the "lost" of Israel fulfills the pattern of the seeking shepherd described by Ezekiel.

The mission of Jesus contrasts with the OT parallels in two ways. First, Jesus claims to have the authority to pronounce sins forgiven rather than declaring that "sinners" will be forgiven if they turn to God (5:20; 7:48, cf. Luke 24:47–48 and Acts 2:38; 4:10–12; and 10:43). He parallels Jonah and Ezekiel in offering mercy directly to sinners but is different from them in regard to his claims of authority. Second, Jesus makes direct contact with sinners in his mission to provide "release" (4:31–44), "cleansing" (5:14), and the "healing" of forgiveness (5:24, 25, 27–32). This is unprecedented in the OT and other literature examined.

Neale states that Jesus is not introducing something new but offers what is completely consistent with Jewish thinking.[84] Abrahams makes the same point, saying the difference between the Pharisees' and Jesus' attitude toward sinners was Jesus' act of taking the initiative. The Pharisees took a preventive approach, attacking vice by avoiding it and by aiming at keeping men and women chaste. Jesus approached it from the curative side, aiming to save the dishonest and the unchaste. Yet Abrahams's point that Jesus took the initiative in contrast to the Pharisees admits Jesus' innovation. So does his accurate observation that Jesus approached the "sinners" from the curative side in contrast to the rabbis who took a preventive approach.

---

83. See pages 38–39 above.
84. Neale, *None But the Sinners*, 131–32.

Abrahams concludes by giving examples of rabbinic literature that actually urged men to seek the lost actively, a point also made by Neale. But Neale cites no examples and Abrahams's examples do not actually reflect a mission to "sinners." Abrahams cited *Exod. Rab.* and the parable of Moses seeking stray sheep. But this Midrash does not describe Moses seeking "sinners." The context is God testing Moses' tenderness to see if he will take care of Israel (*Exod. Rab.* 2.1–2).[85] Abrahams tells of Rabbi Aaron who is lauded for rescuing "sinners."[86] But the Mishnah is a statement by Hillel to be like the disciples of Aaron who is described as "loving and pursuing peace," "loving mankind" and "bringing him nigh to the Law" (*m. 'Abot* 1.12). This does not describe a mission to rescue "sinners."

Like Neale, Abrahams proposes that the Pharisees would not have opposed Jesus' mission to reform "sinners." It was the association, especially during meals that violated the Pharisees' understanding of biblical warnings against evil associations.[87] Yet this approach underscores both Jesus' claim to authority and his initiative to fulfill God's salvation. As Bock observes, "Jesus is extending an acceptance that the Pharisees cannot accept, especially since he is seeking them out rather than withdrawing Himself from them."[88]

Jesus declares that he did not come to call the "righteous" (5:32). The term "righteous ones" (δικαίους) is used in direct contrast with the "sinner," consistent with our examination of the two terms in the OT and other literature. Luke has already introduced several people whom he has described as "righteous": Zechariah and Elizabeth (1:6), and the prophet Simeon (2:25). These people have been described as obedient to the Law of Moses and devout, reflecting an understanding of the righteous that is consistent through the literature examined in chapter 3. But Luke also describes Zechariah, Elizabeth, and Simeon in two other important ways: (1) they are longing for the redemption of Israel, and (2) they respond positively to what God is revealing in Jesus. In addition, the reader has heard a repeated emphasis on the humble and the needy, those who acknowledge their need

85. Midrash Rabbah, *Exodus*, 47–49.
86. Abrahams, *Publicans and Sinners*, 60.
87. Ibid., 55.
88. Bock, *Luke 1:1—9:50*, 496.

for God's deliverance through Jesus, thus the term "righteous" has the OT concept of doing what is fitting in respect to God and one's neighbor based on the revelation of God's word and character. The "righteous" in Luke's Gospel have been open to God's new revelation of his salvation in Jesus. Jesus has not declared the Pharisees "unrighteous" but neither has Jesus included them in the category of those needing no repentance.[89]

Jesus does not dispute the Pharisees' designation of those attending the banquet.[90] A common interpretation of the "sinner" in Luke has been based on understanding the term "sinner" as a label put on others that the narrator and Jesus oppose. Neale states that Luke's use of "toll-collectors and others" in 5:29 reflects his desire to show that the label "toll-collectors and sinners" belongs to the Pharisees. It is a label he does not share.[91] However, Jesus' defense does not dispute the designation but assumes its accuracy as the basis for his explanation. It is because they are sinners under God's wrath that he targets them for his mission. God's promise that "all flesh" would see his salvation includes all of Israel, even "sinners" (Luke 3:6).

Jesus' mission is described in terms directly related to the fulfillment of Isaiah 61:1 and 58:6 as presented in Luke 4:18. He has also demonstrated continuity with the ministry of John the Baptist who also preached repentance for forgiveness of sins (Luke 3:3). Jesus appears to be continuing the process of preparing a repentant people. But instead of simply preaching that sins can be forgiven, the anointed Servant-Messiah Jesus claims the authority given to him by his Father to proclaim release from sins. The spiritual aspect of the promised deliverance is the focus of Jesus' ministry in this section (Luke 1:76–77). Those who recognize their needy condition and acknowledge Jesus as God's agent of salvation are realizing the promise that "all flesh" would "see" the salvation of God.

The conflict that was promised in the birth narrative by Simeon (Luke 2:34–35) and foreshadowed by the Nazareth experience (4:22–30) has come to the forefront with the introduction of the Pharisees into the narrative (5:21). Yet it is a mistake to see conflict as driving the narra-

---

89. Contra Neale, *None But the Sinners*, 133.

90. The meal theme is introduced in Luke 5:32 but the image of the kingdom banquet is not introduced until Luke 14. We will examine this theme in the discussion on Luke 15 below.

91. Neale, *None But the Sinners*, 130.

tive. The mission of Jesus' drives the narrative forward as he fulfills his Messianic role as previewed in the birth narrative and detailed in the Nazareth proclamation.

Jesus' Mission of "Release" of the Sinner in Luke 5:1–32

The "sinners" in Luke are the principal story device by which he demonstrates the extent and scope of Jesus' mission.[92] But Luke's "sinner" material does more than serve as a convenient literary device to drive the conflict between Jesus and the Pharisees through the narrative.[93] George Rice has demonstrated that Luke 4:31—5:32 reflects Jesus' mission of "release" outlined in the Nazareth proclamation. Luke 4:31–44 emphasizes the "release" from the power of Satan through the healings and the exorcisms.[94] Luke 5:1–32 emphasizes the call to discipleship through the "release" from sin.[95] Our examination of Luke 5:1–32 confirms Rice's point. The ministry portrayed by Luke in 5:1–32 is directly linked as fulfillment of Isaiah's program declared in the synagogue reading at Nazareth.

This point is further confirmed when Luke's arrangement of his material is compared to Matthew's.[96] Luke 5:1–32 reflects an arrangement of Synoptic material that stresses the "sinner" theme. Note the order of Matthew:

1) 4:18–22, the calling of the two brothers as disciples;

2) 4:23–25, Jesus' ministry in Galilee;

3) chapters 5–7, the Sermon on the Mount;

4) 8:1–4, the healing of the leper;

5) 8:5–34, the centurion's faith, concluding with the Gadarene demoniac; and

6) 9:1–8, the healing of the paralytic and the authority to forgive sins.

---

92. Ibid., 100.
93. Ibid.
94. Rice, "Luke 4:31–44: Release for the Captives," 23–28.
95. Rice, "Luke's Thematic Use," 51–58.
96. This is not a discussion of source relationships but simply an observation regarding the different arrangements of the evangelists' material.

The Sinner in Luke

By comparison, note Luke's arrangement:

1) 5:1–11, the calling of Peter (v. 8: Peter's confession of being a "sinner," ἀνὴρ ἁμαρτωλός; cf. Matthew's #1 above; note that Peter's self-confession is not present in Matthew);

2) 5:12–16, the leper (note the issue of cleansing: "If you will, you can make me clean [καθαρισαι]," suggesting clean from sin; [97] cf. Matthew's #4 above);

3) 5:17–26, the paralytic and the authority to forgive sins (cf. Matthew's #6 above);

4) 5:27–28, the call of Levi, a tax collector (note the close link between ἁμαρτωλοί and τελώνης, Luke 5:30; 15:1; placed in a different position in Matthew, cf. Matt 9:9–13).

5) 5:29–32, the banquet for Jesus by Levi, attended by toll-collectors and sinners. During this banquet, Jesus defines his mission as calling sinners to repentance (v. 32).

One observes a continuity of theme in Luke's arrangement of this section of the Synoptic material. It has been arranged and compressed with particular emphasis on the fulfillment of Jesus' mission of "releasing" sinful people by calling them, cleansing them, forgiving them, and eating with them.

Conclusion

The real point of this passage is to show what kind of people Jesus calls and why he calls them. There is a conflict between Jesus and the Pharisees regarding his associations. Jesus acknowledges the "sinners" condition as under God's wrath, which is clear from his call of repentance. But it is precisely because they are under God's wrath that he is proclaiming the Gospel of the kingdom to them. He can offer them "release." Jesus aggressively builds the relationships from which the challenge about lifestyle can

---

97. The healing of the leper is called a "cleansing," following OT terminology and thus refers to ceremonial cleansing from defilement that excluded one from the community and the Temple (Lev 13:1–5; 45–46). Marshall observes that the concept of cleansing will have been seen in the church as a symbol of the spiritual cleansing from sin that can be affected by Jesus, and to which there is implicit reference in both the preceding and following incidents (*Luke*, 209).

The "Sinner" Texts in the Gospel of Luke

be made. He is on a rescue mission and the heart of it is being laid before the Pharisees.

Luke 6:27–35

The Narrative Setting

The next use of the term "sinner" in Luke is found in the context of the Sermon on the Plain (Luke 6:17–49). The emphasis in this section continues to be the making of disciples. Luke states that Jesus has chosen twelve of his disciples to be "apostles" (6:12–16). Jesus came down from the mountain with the "Twelve" and the rest of the disciples and gathered on a level place with a large group of people who had come from all over Judea and as far away as Tyre and Sidon (6:17). Luke 6:18–19 summarize Jesus' ministry to the people in terms consistent with his Nazareth program (4:18–19).[98]

Luke 6:20–49 is the first extended narrative of Jesus' teaching to his disciples in the Gospel. Luke states that Jesus' comments are directed to his disciples (6:21a). The Pharisees are not present. This is significant in our understanding of the "sinner" in Luke for two reasons. First, the term ἁμαρτωλός in this section is used by Jesus rather than the narrator or by the Pharisees. One weakness in the history of the interpretation of the term "sinner" has been the tendency to limit the examination of it to its use by the Pharisees only. Second, the context is didactic rather than one of conflict. Jesus is not defending his mission.

The Blessings and Woes: Luke 6:20–26

Jesus' instruction begins with a series of blessings (6:20–23) and woes (6:24–26). The blessings include a promise of the Kingdom to the "poor," a link to the "poor" in Jesus' opening message at Nazareth in Luke 4:18 based on Isa 61:1. This supports our earlier point that the "poor" are not to be viewed exclusively in economic terms but also includes spiritual terms. The "poor" being addressed are the "disciples" who have placed their hope in Jesus.[99] The references to the "hungry" and "those who weep" have OT

---

98. Fitzmyer, *Luke I–IX*, 629.
99. Bock, *Luke 1:1—9:50*, 572.

precedents, especially in Isaiah: the "hungry" (Isa 49:10; 65:13; and a conceptual link to Isa 61:1–3);[100] and "those who weep" (Isa 61:2). The promise to the hungry that they will be "satisfied" may allude to the Messianic banquet (cf. Isa 25:6, 8; 55:1–2).[101] Isaiah continues to play an important role in Luke's presentation of Jesus.

Luke 6: 27–31

In Luke 6:27–29, Jesus calls his disciples to demonstrate exceptional love. They are called to love those who have chosen to be their enemies (6:27a), especially those hostile toward them because of their faith in Jesus, and to do good to those who hate them (6:27b). They are to say good things about those who speak badly of them (6:28a) and pray for those who do not wish them well (6:28). They are to turn their cheek if insulted (6:29a; cf. Acts 23:2), and be open-handed in their generosity (6:29b–30). They are to treat others as they want to be treated (6:31). Luke 6:32–36 gives the rationale for the admonitions of 6:27–31.

Luke 6:32–34

In contrast to the behavior he has commanded of his disciples, in Luke 6:32–34, Jesus describes the illaudable behavior of "sinners" (ἁμαρτωλοῖς) in three specific ways: 1) the "sinners" love only when others love them (6:32), in contrast to Jesus' call to his disciples to love even their enemies (6:27a); 2) "sinners" loan only to those who will certainly repay (6:34) in contrast to lending to anyone who has a need (6:30a); and 3) "sinners" do good only to those who do good for them (6:33) in contrast to Jesus' call to his followers to do good to those who hate them (6:27b).

The observations regarding the "sinner" in this pericope will be presented in summary form. First, Jesus views their behavior in terms of eschatological reward. To follow the behavior of "sinners" will not give the disciples "credit" (χάρις, 6:32–34) in the sense of "reward" (μισθός) from God (6:35).[102] Second, instead of ἁμαρτωλοῖς, Matthew uses τελῶναι in Matt 5:46 and ἐθνικοί in 5:47. This reflects the range and flexibility of

---

100. Ibid., 575.
101. Smith, "Table Fellowship," 627.
102. Fitzmyer, *Luke I–IX*, 640.

the terms. Luke has apparently used ἁμαρτωλοῖς to set forth the broader idea that would include the others.[103] It is significant that here the language could fit an Israelite or Gentile "sinner."

Third, the description of the "sinner" fits the OT emphasis that the measure of what is "righteous" is the standard of God's own character and action. God himself is the norm rather than standing under a norm. To be "righteous" is to live in a manner that is appropriate in relationship to God and one's neighbor. And the measure of what is appropriate is the revealed will and character of God (Deut 32:4).[104] The command given by the Lord to Israel in Leviticus 19:18 to love their neighbors as themselves is grounded on the demands of the covenant and the nature of the Lord himself. The command ends with the declaration: "I am the Lord." The "sinner" in the OT was someone guilty of violating the demands of the conduct that the Lord expected in any relationship. Jesus' statement in 6:31 to "treat others as they want to be treated" is rooted in the command of Leviticus 19:18.[105] Just as the Lord did in this OT context, Jesus grounds his demands on the consistent and normative action of God and his character: he is "good" (χρηστός, 6:35) and "merciful" (οἰκτιρμός). The actions of Jesus' disciples toward those who mistreat them are to be based on the revelation of God's character and his actions toward the same kind of people.

Luke displays this OT way of viewing who is "righteous" (δίκαιος) in Luke 10:25–37. A "lawyer" asked Jesus what was required to inherit eternal life. After affirming the scribes' understanding that "loving the Lord" and "loving his neighbor as himself" were the two requirements, the lawyer sought to "justify" (δικαιῶσαι) himself (10:29). Jesus' story of the "good Samaritan" concludes with his question to the lawyer: "Which one was a neighbor to the man who fell into the hands of robbers?"(10:36). The answer was obvious and the lawyer answered: "The one who showed mercy" (ἔλεος, 10:37). The call to love the neighbor was rooted in the mercy of God. According to this definition, the Samaritan's conduct was "righteous," and conduct of the priest and Levite violated the law of the neighbor, and before the Lord the Judge, they were "sinners."

103. Ibid.
104. Ibid.
105. Bock, *Luke 1:1—9:50*, 596.

Another example of this same theme occurs in Luke 11:42 in the context of the six "woes" that Jesus pronounces on the Pharisees and the scribes. Jesus told them that they tithe above and beyond the call of duty, but they neglect "justice" (κρίσιν) and the "love" (ἀγάπην) of God. As demonstrated in our research of the term "sinner," neglecting justice was one of the consistent descriptions of a "sinner."

Fourth, the description of "sinners" is consistent with OT descriptions of the "sinner" as those who oppress others, and look out only for themselves.[106] The abuses related to money are an important theme in the Psalms, the Prophets, and later Jewish literature. And as our research revealed, certain offenses like oppressing the poor and perverting justice made one a "sinner" regardless of one's national identity.

Fifth, the "sinner" term is linked to "enemies," the "ungrateful" (ἀχαρίστους), and the "wicked" (πονήρους, 6:35). In the OT, the "sinner" is often linked to enemies (Ps 3:7, 37:12) and even to the "wicked" (πονηροί, Gen 13:13). Jesus will use πονηρία of the Pharisees (Luke 11:39).

Sixth, the "sinner" in Luke 6:32–34 is not viewed in terms of need but in terms of his characteristics. Thus the disciples who are the "poor" in 6:20 are not to be understood as "sinners" in this context. Here they are to be viewed as opposite the "sinner."[107]

Conclusion

The "sinner" in Luke 6: 32–34 is outside of a Pharisee context and the theme of conflict is absent. Jesus is not defending his mission here, so his use of "sinner" is helpful for our understanding of the term. The use in this pericope has been shown to be consistent with OT themes and possibly broad enough to include Gentiles. The emphasis on the "sinner" here is not his need for mercy but his characteristics, which have been shown to fit the description of the "sinner" portrayed in the OT and other Jewish sources.

---

106. Note that the "sinner" is described as hoarding money instead of sharing it, overthrowing the estate of his neighbor and stealing his property in Sir 29:10, 14.

107. Walter Pilgrim's inclusion of the "sinner" in the category of the "poor" must be carefully qualified by the fact that the "sinner" is a moral category. The "sinner" is needy because he is under the wrath of God; it is this sense in which he is included with the "poor" (*Good News to the Poor*, 83).

The "sinner" is one who acts out of self-interest in his dealings and ignores the needs of others. For the "sinner," even actions of assistance are rooted in a desire for self-gain. Jesus calls his followers to a different standard that includes treating others as one wants to be treated and treating others as God treats them.

Luke 7:34–50

The Narrative Setting

The Issue of Jesus' Identity in 7:11–27

The story of the "sinful" woman and the Pharisee is located in a narrative context that focuses on the identity of Jesus. Is Jesus a prophet, the Messiah, or a false teacher leading Israel astray? In Luke 7:1–10, a centurion reveals confidence in Jesus' authority and asks him to heal his servant. The centurion declares that Jesus can heal the servant simply by his command. Jesus applauds the man's faith as incomparable in all Israel. This reminds the reader of Luke 4:24–27 and the responses of the Gentile woman and the leper during the ministries of Elijah and Elisha. It also prepares for the scene to follow in 7:11–50 by showing that "faith" is the proper response to Jesus. Those who "receive" Jesus properly receive the benefits of his ministry. Those who reject him remain in spiritual "debt" (Luke 7:36–50).

Luke describes the raising of a widow's "only" son in 7:11–17. This is linked to Luke 4:25–26 and the prophet Elijah. As a result of the miracle, the people declared that a "great prophet" had risen among them and that God had "visited" his people (cf. Luke 1:68).

In Luke 7: 18–23, the narrative links the spreading news of Jesus and the issue of his identity as prophet. Luke states that John the Baptist sent a group of his disciples to ask Jesus if he was the "Coming One," the Messiah, or should they look for someone else (7:18–20). This question is the most direct treatment of this issue for Luke up to this point in the Gospel. Jesus responded at first not by words but by actions intended to demonstrate his Messianic credentials (7:21). Jesus' verbal reply links his miracles and preaching directly to the fulfillment of the mission set out in the Nazareth proclamation in Luke 4:18–19 and to the OT promises of Isaiah 61:1. The blind see (Isa 61:1; 35:5); the lame walk (Isa 35:6); lepers are cleansed (2 Kgs 5:14); the deaf hear (Isa 35:5); the dead are being raised (Isa 26:19, Luke 7:14); and the gospel is being preached to the poor (Isa 61:1). Jesus sends John's disciples back to him with the words, "Blessed is the one who does not stumble over me," a possible link to Luke 2:34, Isa 8:14–15 and Isa 28:13–16.

In 7:22, Luke makes a significant point that will be developed in later discussion below. He presents Jesus' preaching to "sinners" as a *proof* of his Messianic credentials. Instead of a reason for rejecting Jesus' Messianic identity, Luke uses OT citations, allusions, and later OT patterns of preaching as evidence that Jesus' actions of "seeking" "sinners" are part of the "fulfillment" that official Israel should grasp.

In Luke 7:24–30, Jesus gave a tribute to John as his forerunner. In 7:29–30, Luke describes the reaction of two groups hearing Jesus' praise of John. The first group includes the people and "even the toll-collectors" who had "listened to John" as revealed in their acceptance of his baptism (7:29). The "toll-collectors" are an example of what a "sinner" is both in the culture and in Luke. But this group "justified" (ἐδικαίωσαν) or "acknowledged God's way as right." They rendered a verdict of approval with regard to God's way of providing forgiveness of sins through his plan of salvation that is being presently revealed.[108] However, the Pharisees rejected God's will for them (7:30). Luke may have an element of irony here, because, in our research, "hardness of heart" and refusal to repent were common characteristics of the "sinner."[109] Here, the "sinners" are open but the "righteous" are unrepentant. This links the narrative to Luke's theme of reversal introduced in the birth narrative.

The Parable of the Children in Luke 7:28–35

Jesus describes the response of the Palestinian contemporaries of John and Jesus in a short parable (7:28–35).[110] The parables present the basis for the

108. Fitzmyer, *Luke I–IX*, 676.

109. See the discussion of Sirach on page 42–43 above.

110. The expression "this generation" is understood to have a strong tone of denunciation as suggested by Fitzmyer, *Luke I–IX*, 679 (see Deut 32:5; Jer 2:31; 7:29).

rejection of John and Jesus. John's asceticism was considered to be demon-possession (7:33). Jesus was viewed as "eating and drinking" instead of fasting, a "glutton," a "drunkard" and a "friend of toll-collectors and sinners" (7:34). This use of "sinner" recalls Luke 5:27–32 and Jesus' encounter with the Pharisees over meal fellowship. As stated in the discussion there, this connection of Jesus to "toll-collectors and sinners" in this context about his rejection confirms our position that this offense was viewed in moral terms and that this association served as a justification for discounting Jesus as the Messiah.

Jesus concludes with another parable in 7:35, stating that wisdom would be shown to be "right" (ἐδικαιώθη) by all her "children." God's wisdom in his plan of salvation will be proved to be right in its "children," which includes the "toll-collectors and sinners" who are favorably responding to the ministries of John and Jesus.[111]

The story of the sinful woman in Luke 7:36–50 appears to be placed here to demonstrate the wisdom of Jesus' mission to "sinners."[112] Luke takes us from "sinners" as a group to an example of Jesus' ministry with a specific "sinner."

Luke 7: 36–39

Immediately following the explanation and defense of the ministries of Jesus and John the Baptist, Luke presents one of the Pharisees in Jesus' audience inviting Jesus to dinner (7:36). Jesus accepted the invitation and he and his host are described as reclining at the table.[113] Luke presents Jesus as open to the Pharisee.[114] However, the reader has been prepared for the narrative by the statement that the Pharisees have rejected the "will of God" for them by refusing to repent at John's preaching (7:30). But the positive response of the "toll-collectors" and the link between "toll-collectors and sinners" in 7:34 has prepared the reader for the "sinful woman" who will

---

111. Fitzmyer, *Luke I-IX*, 679.

112. Marshall, *Luke*, 304; Danker, *Jesus and the New Age*, 99.

113. Dennis Smith suggests that Luke is using the literary form of the Hellenistic symposium in which teaching was expected to occur, "Table Fellowship," 613–38.

114. Bock, *Luke 1:1—9:50*, 700.

respond in repentance. The reader is primed to process this narrative in terms of the reversal foreshadowed in the infancy narratives.[115]

Luke alerts the reader to a woman who was a "sinner" (ἁμαρτωλός) in the village (7:37).[116] He states that after she learned that Jesus was having dinner at the home of the Pharisee, she brought a jar of expensive perfume.[117] In 7:38, she is described as standing by Jesus' feet.[118] As she approached him she began "crying" (κλαίουσα).[119] The woman apparently intended to anoint Jesus' head consistent with custom but was overcome by emotion as she approached.[120] Luke uses the imperfect to describe the woman's actions in progress: she is seen "wiping" his feet with her hair, "kissing" them in a display of reverence and devotion, and "anointing" them with perfume.[121] Jesus did not stop or interrupt the woman and this leads to Simon the Pharisee's unspoken conclusion in 7:39.

The "sinner" in Luke 7:37 is a "sinner" on moral grounds. The narrator first identifies her as a "sinner." She is also acknowledged to be a "sinner" in the village. Simon the Pharisee will describe her as a "sinner" (7:39) and Jesus' comments in the parable and at the end of the narrative are based on the label being accurate. The specific nature of her sin is not identified. She is clearly not simply the wife of a person involved in a despised trade.[122] It is her sins that are the object of forgiveness and the reason for her response. She was most likely a prostitute or an immoral woman, but the specific

---

115. Darr, *On Character Building*, 101.

116. The function of ἰδού is to focus the reader's attention as noted by Marshall (*Luke*, 308).

117. Bock, *Luke 1:1—9:50*, 696.

118. Luke implies that the woman has responded to Jesus' ministry before she entered the home of Simon. This is a gap that Luke expects the reader to fill in from this introduction and the reference to "sinners" in the immediately previous pericope (so Darr, *Character Building*, 18). This will help to solve the interpretive problem of the relationship between her demonstration of "love" and her receiving forgiveness in 7:47. So also Bock, *Luke 1:1—9:50*, 696.

119. See Luke 7:13 and the crying (κλαίω) of the widow.

120. Marshall, *Luke*, 309.

121. Bock cites *Jos. Asen.* 15:11 as evidence that the act of washing and anointing the feet expresses deep reverence (*Luke 1:1—9:50*, 697).

122. Ringe cites this as a possibility, *Luke*, 108.

nature of her sins is not stated.[123] It is clear that she is understood as a "sinner" on moral grounds. She is one "sinner" in Luke's narrative at which everyone could have pointed a finger.[124]

The fact that Jesus permitted the "sinful" woman to continue to touch him raised a question in the mind of Simon the Pharisee that Luke reveals to the reader in 7:39.[125] He said to himself, if "this one" were a prophet, but he cannot be, he would know what kind of woman this is who is touching him, but he apparently does not know that she is a "sinner." This brings out the sense of the Pharisee's question as already being answered in the negative.[126] Simon the Pharisee assumes that Jesus cannot be a prophet because he lacks the necessary discernment.[127] He assumes that if Jesus did know the woman's reputation, as a prophet he would have refused to allow her to touch him.[128] The reader has the same omniscient point of view as Jesus in the narrative. He knows that Simon is wrong on both points. Neale observes that Simon the Pharisee seems completely unmoved by the emotional display of the woman. Luke is emphasizing the insensitivity of the Pharisee toward the plight of the "sinner."[129] He presents Jesus' response in detail in 7:40–50.

Luke 7:40–50

THE PARABLE OF THE TWO DEBTORS

Jesus responded directly to the thoughts of Simon the Pharisee. This links the reader to Luke 2:35 and Simeon's prophecy concerning Jesus' ability to reveal the "thoughts of the heart." The reader already knows Jesus' ability, now Simon learns for himself. Jesus addressed Simon directly and informed

---

123. As Marshall notes, this is the traditional way of seeing the woman (*Luke*, 308).

124. A statement used by Jeremias in "'Zöllner und Sünder,'" 293.

125. The thoughts expressed by the Pharisee are directly a result of "observing" (ἰδών) the womans' continuing actions in 7:38.

126. Zerwick, *Biblical Greek* §313.

127. Bock, *Luke 1:1—9:50*, 697.

128. Marshall, *Luke*, 309.

129. Neale, *None But the Sinners*, 144.

him that he had something to tell him. Simon replied by giving Jesus the respect due to a teacher (7:40).

In 7:41–43 Jesus told a parable of two "debtors" (χρεοφειλέται) who were in debt to the same lender. One "owed" (ὤφειλεν) 500 denarii, the other fifty (7:41).[130] But when neither one was able to repay, the lender "forgave" (ἐχαρίσατο) them both (7:42a). The verb χαρίζομαι means to "bestow graciously" or "give as a favor."[131] In the immediate context, Luke used the word of Jesus "graciously granting" sight to the blind (7:22). It is used of a king bestowing gifts (2 Macc 1:35), or the Lord granting life (2 Macc 3:33). Josephus uses the expression in the sense of "to grant forgiveness" (ἁμαρτήματα χαρίζεσθαι) in the context of God's unwillingness to forgive Saul for his disobedience with the Amalekites.[132] Here it is the gracious forgiveness of debt.

Jesus concludes the parable with a question directed to Simon. He asked Simon which debtor would "love" (ἀγαπήσει) the gracious lender more (7:42b)? The term ἀγαπάω may have the sense of "gratitude."[133] Simon answered the question with hesitation but correctly; the answer was the one who had been forgiven the most (7:43). Based upon Simon's own response, Jesus applied the parable to him in 7:44.

The parable draws an analogy between "sin" and "indebtedness" and between "forgiveness" and "cancellation" of debts. In Deuteronomy 15:1–2, during the Sabbatical year, the Israelites were commanded to "release" (ἀφή σεις) the "debt" (ὀφείλει) of their neighbor. The "release" of the Jubilee becomes a spiritual release in Isa 61:1. The sabbatical year release becomes an image of spiritual release in Isa 58:6.[134] In *1 Enoch*, the sinner is viewed as a debtor. The angel who is the leader is concerned that the rest will back out of their plan to cohabit with human women and leave him alone to become the "debtor" for the great sin (6:4). In the OT, a sinner is a "debtor"

---

130. Marshall states that a Roman denarii had the purchasing power of a day's wage (*Luke*, 310. Bock provides a comparison of two months wages versus twenty months wages (*Luke 1:1—9:50*, 699).

131. BAGD, 876.

132. *Ant.* 6.144

133. Jeremias made this point based on the fact that neither Hebrew nor Aramaic have a distinct word for "thanks" (*The Parables of Jesus*, 127).

134. See the discussion on the Nazareth Sermon starting on page 89–90 above.

to God because sin violates God's righteousness placing him in legal debt to God. The analogy is applied to Simon in 7:44.

THE APPLICATION TO SIMON

Jesus contrasts the actions of the "sinner" with the actions of Simon the host in 7:44–46: (1) Simon gave Jesus no water for his feet but the woman used her very tears to wash them; (2) Simon gave Jesus no kiss of greeting but the woman repeatedly kissed his feet; and (3) Simon did not anoint his head with oil but the woman anointed his feet with costly ointment.[135] Simon is not necessarily being upbraided for being a discourteous host.[136] Jesus is contrasting Simon's minimal courtesy with the lavish display of the "sinner." The contrasting display of hospitality portrays the different way Simon and the "sinner" understood their respective condition before God, the Lender, as well as the identity of Jesus. Simon is the "little sinner" and the woman is the "great sinner." The woman's response reflected her repentance and her ability to perceive the true identity and significance of Jesus. Simon's actions revealed a lack of repentance and spiritual blindness with respect to Jesus.[137] Simon's portrayal as the smaller debtor pictured his own point of view, he had little need for forgiveness. Yet Jesus' application stressed that Simon's display of "little gratitude" demonstrated that the Pharisee had been "forgiven little" because he had not repented.[138]

In Luke 7:47, Jesus directly applies the parable and actions described in 7:40–46 to the present situation with Simon and the "sinner."[139] He states that the woman's sins "which were many" are "forgiven" (ἀφέωνται, 7:47a).[140] Jesus revealed his knowledge of the "sort of woman" she was who had touched him, displaying his credentials as a prophet in answer to

---

135. Darr, *Character Building*, 102.

136. Marshall points out that the actions described here were not customary provisions for guests (*Luke*, 312).

137. Darr, *Character Building*, 102.

138. Ibid.

139. The use of οὗ χάριν links 7:44–46 as the reason for what Jesus is about to say (Bock, *Luke 1:1—9:50*, 703).

140. The use of the perfect supports the argument that the woman had responded to Jesus before entering the meal. As Bock observes, she stands in a present state of "forgiveness" (Ibid.).

The Sinner in Luke

Simon's incorrect conclusion (7:39). The proof that her sins were forgiven is that she expressed great love and gratitude toward him (7:47b).[141] Simon's actions reveal that his debt of sin has yet to be remitted (7:47c).

The Pronouncement

The woman does not speak a word in the entire narrative. However in Luke 7:48, Jesus turned to the woman and addressed her directly: "Your sins are forgiven." The words link the reader to Luke 5:20 and Jesus' same pronouncement on the paralytic. There are also links to 5:27–32 and Jesus' defense of his ministry and association with "toll-collectors and sinners" to the Pharisees. Jesus' declaration here provides the woman with reassurance and comfort but also emphasizes his role as the "Herald" of "release" (7:47; 4:18, 19). A note of irony is suggested in that the "sinful" woman has recognized Jesus as the Herald of release but Simon the Pharisee and his other guests have not.

Jesus' pronouncement brings the same response displayed by the Pharisees in 5:21: "Who is this who even forgives sins?" (7:49). This is a claim beyond any prophet, it is the prerogative of God.[142] As stated at the beginning of this section, the issue of Jesus' authority and identity is still the focus. The answer to the question in 7:49 is left to the reader to provide.[143]

In the context of the guests' confusion, Jesus continued to address the woman. He told her that her "faith" had "saved" (σέσωκεν) her and to go in "peace" (7:50). The term "faith" (πίστις) links the narrative to Jesus' observation of "faith" in the men carrying the paralytic in 5:20. In that context, Jesus' declaration of forgiveness and his subsequent healing are tied to his "seeing" their faith. There is a link also to 7:9 and the great "faith" displayed by the centurion who recognized Jesus' authority. Luke directly links "forgiveness" and "faith."

---

141. The use of ὅτι is causal not in the sense that she is forgiven because of her love but she is *known* to be forgiven because of her love. Zerwick points out that any ambiguity in the grammar is cleared up by the context (*Biblical Greek* §422).

142. See the discussion on Luke 5:27–32, pages 117, 127–32 above.

143. Marshall, *Luke*, 314.

But Luke also links "faith," "forgiveness of sins," and "salvation." This connects the present narrative as an explanation and fulfillment of 1:77 in the birth narrative. Zechariah had promised that Israel would receive the "knowledge" of "salvation" (σωτηρίας) through the forgiveness of sins. Here, the woman received both "salvation" and a verbal assurance from Jesus. There is also a clear link to Jesus' mission of "release" proclaimed at Nazareth in 4:18–19. The imagery of "release" of the sabbatical year and the Jubilee are here fulfilled in spiritual terms. Her debts/sins, which were many, are released (7:47). Jesus told the woman to go in "peace" (7:50). This links his ministry of "release" to the angelic promise of messianic peace in 2:14.

Contribution to Luke's "Sinner" Theme

The context of Luke 7:34–50 links Jesus' mission to "sinners" directly to his credentials as Messiah. Jesus' mission to "sinners" is both the focus of his mission but also a sign of his credentials as the "Anointed Servant-Messiah" who brings "release." This will be important in Acts for Luke because the Gentile mission will not be seen as an afterthought but as proof of Jesus' Messiahship and the fulfillment of Messianic times.

Luke 7:36–50 gives an example of a real "sinner." The use of "sinner" in a moral sense as a person who is guilty and in need of repentance has been confirmed again. The "sinner" is pictured as a "debtor," sin as debt, and forgiveness as "release." This ties in the OT image of the sabbatical year and Jubilee introduced in 4:18–19 based on Isa 61:1 and 58:6. The theme of "forgiveness" is tied directly to the "sinner" theme to explicitly portray the purpose of Jesus' mission.[144] Also, Jesus makes it clear that the repentant "sinner" is to be embraced and welcomed into the fellowship of his followers. This is seen in Jesus' table fellowship with "sinners" and his "welcome" of the woman.

---

144. Neale observes the tightening of the "sinner"-"forgiveness" theme (*None But the Sinners*, 147). Yet he continues to see the "sinner" as primarily an ideological concept, even though he acknowledges that Luke 7:36–50 deals with a specific "sinner."

The Sinner in Luke

Luke 13:1–9

The Narrative Setting

Luke 13:1–9 uses ἁμαρτωλός in a more general sense, as the opposite of the "righteous." Jesus declares that all who do not repent will perish, underscoring the desperate fate of "sinners" (13:3). The term is being used here much in the sense of the "sinner" in the Psalter. This demonstrates that Jesus' sees "sinners" exactly as the OT, and perhaps the Pharisees, with regard to their condition and their fate. The "sinner" is not only a moral category for Luke but also a person who is at great risk of divine judgment. The difference between the Pharisees and Jesus is how he approaches the sinner for redemption.[145]

Between the narrative of the "sinful" woman in Luke 7 and the use of the "sinner" in Luke 13:1–9, the narrator has continued to focus on the issues of Jesus' identity and proper responsiveness to him. Unresponsiveness and resistance to Jesus grows in this section of Luke. On the one hand, he has met with growing popularity (9:7–9) but not with the true repentance that he demanded (10:13–16).[146] Jesus stated that cities known in the OT for their evil ways and God's wrath against them will experience less condemnation than the towns of Israel. Even Sodom, shown to be a symbol of the "sinner" in our research, will fare better "in that day." Jesus rebukes his disciples with words used by Moses to the "unbelieving generation" of Israel (Luke 9:41; Deut 32:5). But he especially criticizes the masses of Israel as an unrepentant, evil "generation" that demands a "sign" (Luke 7:31; 11:29–32, 50–51). The crowd has identified the "finger of God" with the power of the devil (11:14–26). Jesus called this a "wicked" (πονηρά) "generation" in 11:29. In the LXX, the men of Sodom are called "wicked" (πονηροί); and "sinners" (ἁμαρτωλοί, Gen. 13:13).

In response to the request for a "sign," Jesus declared that the "sign" they would receive was the "sign" of Jonah (11:30). In this context, the

---

145 Abrahams, *Publicans and Sinners*, 58. Abrahams states that Jesus essentially shared with the Pharisee a similar view of the "sinner." The difference was in Jesus' taking the initiative in bringing them to repentance.

146. Moessner, *Lord of the Banquet*, 127.

"sign" of Jonah is specifically identified as Jonah's "preaching" (11:32).[147] Jesus stated that "a greater one than Jonah" was present (11:32). As observed in our examination of the "sinner," Jonah was the only example of a "mission" to "sinners" in the OT. Jesus is fulfilling the pattern of the OT prophet. Yet the Gentile "sinners" of Nineveh repented at Jonah's preaching but Israel has not, even though the Messianic Herald is present.

The Pharisees are absent from the narrative from the close of the "sinful woman" narrative in Luke 8:1 through 10:25. When they reappear, a scribe of the Pharisees attempted to test Jesus (10:25–37). In 11:14–54, Jesus condemned the Phariees for "greed," "wickedness" (πονηρίας), and neglecting justice and the love of God (11:39, 42). As shown in the research, these are characteristics of the "sinner" in the OT and Jewish literature. The scribes of the Pharisees are accused of "taking away the key to knowledge" (γνώσεως), a possible link and contrast to Luke 1:77, which speaks of the "knowledge (γνῶσιν) of salvation through the forgiveness of sins" (11:52). They refused to enter and are hindering others from entering (11:52). After this encounter, the opposition of the Pharisees toward Jesus intensified (11:53–54).

At this point in the narrative, Luke describes Jesus as increasingly pointed in his rebuke. In 12:49, Jesus shouts, "I came to bring fire to the earth, and how I wish it were already kindled" (NRSV). Then in an allusion to Mic 7:6 he asked: "Do you think that I have come to bring peace to the earth? No, I tell you, but rather division!" (12:51 NRSV).

Jesus declared that he had come to bring the fire of judgment and cleansing (cf. Luke 3:17). He warned the crowd not to misunderstand their present opportunity. In the tone of an OT prophet, he rebuked the crowds for being able to look at the clouds and recognize rain was coming but failing to look at Jesus and his ministry and comprehend that this is the time of opportunity to respond to God's Messiah (12:54–56). The storm will burst on them shortly. The warning was not to miss this opportunity for salvation. They were to make peace with God by accepting his offer of forgiveness through Jesus, the Messiah (12:57–59).

---

147. Perrin, *Rediscovering the Teaching of Jesus*, 193.

The Sinner in Luke

Luke 13:1–5

Luke 13:1 introduces the narrative scene. As Jesus' warnings about impending judgment are being made, a group arrives and announces some recent news concerning some Galilean worshippers who were killed by Pilate while offering their sacrifices.[148] This would have taken place in Jerusalem in the outer sanctuary where the worshippers laid their hands on their sacrifice before it was offered by the priests. Apparently the blood of the animal and the blood of the worshippers mingled on the pavement. When this incident occurred is difficult to say.[149] The tone of the question suggests that it was recent.

In 13:2, Jesus summarizes the issue that the people raised. He asked the crowd if they thought that these Galileans were greater "sinners" (ἁμαρτωλοί) than the rest of the Galileans because they had suffered these things.

As demonstrated in our research, a consistent theme throughout the use of the term "sinner" is that he is under the wrath of God. The OT does say that God will judge the sinner. Calamity in life was often believed to be the result of past sin.[150] In Job 4:7 Eliphaz asked Job, "Who, being innocent, has ever been destroyed? Where were the upright ever destroyed?" In Exod 20:5 God warns, "I, the Lord your God, am a jealous God, punishing the children for the sin of the fathers to the third and fourth generation of those who hate me." In John 9:1–3, Jesus' disciples, upon seeing a man born blind, asked Jesus, "Rabbi, who sinned, this man or his parents?" The assumption was that someone sinned. The thinking of the crowd in Luke 13:1 seems to be that, since they were not slain, they must be "little sinners" like the Pharisee in Luke 7:36–50. Because they were not slain, they must be safe before God and Jesus' warnings do not apply to them.

In 13:3, Jesus turned the question into a call for repentance: "Unless you 'repent' (μετανοῆτε), you all shall 'perish' (ἀπολεῖσθε)." Jesus corrected their presumption and issued a universal demand for repentance. Only repentance can save them from their own certain destruction. The

---

148. Bock shows that the verb πάρειμι is used not for the crowd's presence but its arrival (*Luke 9:51—24:53*, 1204).

149. The suggested options are given by Marshall (*Luke*, 553).

150. Fitzmyer, *Luke X–XXIV*, 1007.

verb ἀπόλλυμι is used in an active sense meaning "to destroy" or to "kill." It is used of the "destruction" of the flood (Luke 17:27) and Sodom (Luke 17:29). It is the opposite of "saving" a life (Luke 6:9; 9:24). It is used in the passive sense of "perishing" as in Luke 8:24 and the cry of the disciples perishing in the storm. And it is also used of things like wineskins "being ruined" (Luke 5:37) and sheep being "lost" (15:4, 6, 24). In the LXX, ἀπόλλυμι is often associated with the judgment of the Lord upon Israel for sin (Num 16:33; Deut 28:20; 30:18 et al) and is linked to the fate of the ἁμαρτωλοί (Gen 18:24, of Sodom; Pss 37: 20 [36:20 LXX]; 67:2 [66:2 LXX] et al.; Isa 13:9). Jesus warned those in the crowd that they are all "sinners" under the wrath of God. He emphasized the theme by raising another example of people who died in Jerusalem because the Tower of Siloam fell on them (13:4). Jesus repeated his question: "Do you suppose that they were worse "debtors" (ὀφειλέται) before God than all the other people living in Jerusalem?"[151] Jesus declares that the unfortunate were not worse "debtors" and repeats his warning to the crowd (13:5). He warns that the judgment of those listening to him is as certain as the tragic end of those worshippers and tragic bystanders. He attacks the attitude of indifference. Being an unrepentant "sinner" puts one at great risk.

Luke 13:6–9

In Luke 13:6–9, Jesus gives a parable that both warns of judgment and offers mercy for those who respond. He described a farmer who had an unfruitful fig tree growing in his vineyard (13:6–7). The farmer had been "coming" (ἔρχομαι) for three years and now decides to "cut down" (ἔκκοψον) the tree (13:7). The use of ἔκκοψον links Jesus' statement to the words of John in Luke 3:9 regarding the axe approaching the unfruitful tree to "cut" it down (ἐκκόπτεται). The gardener asked for one more year to cultivate and fertilize the tree, after which time if it still failed to bear fruit, then he would "cut it down" (13:8–9).

---

151. The use of "debtors" for "sinners" is consistent with OT thought of God as "righteous Judge." See the discussion in the examination of the "sinful woman" pericope above. This reinforces the "sinner" as a clear moral category in this context.

It is very likely that Jesus had a direct message for Israel here.[152] In the immediately preceding section he quoted from Micah 7 (Luke 12:53). In Mic 7:1, the prophet mourns over the Lord's unproductive fig tree, Israel. In Isa 5:1–7, Israel is described as God's vineyard, producing nothing but bad fruit. In Luke 13:1–9, Israel is reflecting the OT pattern of unresponsiveness. God is giving one more opportunity to respond. The use of the fig tree and vineyard images makes an allusion to Israel probable, especially when this context is linked to the words of John (Luke 3:9).[153] Israel's time is short, God's warning is being given, and his grace is extended for a little while longer.

In the broader narrative context, this narrative is analogous to Jonah's warnings to Nineveh: "Forty more days and Nineveh will be overturned" (see Luke 11:29–32; Jonah 3:4). In the LXX, the number of days becomes "three" days (τρεῖς). The reference to "three" years in Luke 13:7 may be an allusion, admittedly subtle, to the urgency. It is almost too late! Yet one greater than Jonah is here who is offering God's mercy to the "repentant."

Conclusion

In Luke 13:1–9, the term "sinner" broadens to include the entire listening audience of Jesus and, by implication, all Israel and even the reader.[154] The mission of Jesus is linked to the mission of John the Baptist in "preparing a repentant people." This passage demonstrates that Jesus is using OT categories to define the "sinner" as one who is under the wrath of God and in need of "repentance." Up to this point in our examination of the "sinner" in Luke, the term has been understood in moral terms. That this appears to be Luke's understanding of the term is strengthened by the use of it in this non-Pharisee context.

---

152. Contra Sanders, *Jesus and Judaism*, 203.
153. Tannehill, *Narrative Unity*, 1:51, 151.
154. Neale, *None But the Sinners*, 152.

Luke 15:1–32

The Narrative Setting

The following paragraphs summarize the development of Luke's narrative between 13:9—15:1. First, in Luke 13:10–17, Jesus "released" a "daughter of Abraham" from the bonds of Satan through his healing touch. The context is a synagogue and the healing continues the theme of conflict and the division of Israel over Jesus (cf. 2:34). The narrative has links to Jesus' ministry of "release" introduced in Luke 4:18–19. The Nazareth program continues to be fulfilled in Jesus' ministry. The reference to a "daughter of Abraham" may allude to 1:55 and God's mercy being brought to Abraham and his descendents.

Second, in Luke 13:22—15:32 the merging of the themes of "table fellowship" and the eschatological "kingdom banquet" takes place. In 13:22–30, Jesus answered a question about the number of those to be "saved" by emphasizing the need to respond properly to him (13:24).[155] He used the image of a narrow door into a home where a banquet was taking place. Some who came after the door was closed presumed upon their prior "eating and drinking" with the owner to warrant entrance (13:26). But the owner of the house denied any relationship with them and demanded that the "evildoers" leave (13:27). Jesus applied the parable in 13:28–30. Some who expect to be in the kingdom banquet will be excluded (13:28). Some will be present who are not expected, specifically the Gentiles (13:29).[156]

Bock observes that in 13:29, Luke alludes to an OT salvation pattern of the gathering of God's elect and the defeat of the Gentiles. Jesus applies the pattern in a surprising way. The Jewish crowd listening to Jesus becomes those who are excluded while the Gentiles are included in the kingdom banquet, an anticipation of the inclusion of Gentiles in Acts.[157]

Luke 13:22–30 clarifies the role of Jesus' table fellowship with "toll-collectors and sinners." Jesus here describes table fellowship as a symbol of the kingdom. Jeremias views the meal as an acted sermon that proclaimed

---

155. Fitzmyer, *Luke X–XXIV*, 1024–25.
156. Bock, *Luke 9:51–24:53*, 1239–40.
157. Ibid., 1239.

forgiveness and fellowship with God.[158] The table-fellowship was an anticipatory celebration of the end-time feast. Although this is essentially correct, 13:26–27 make it clear that "table-fellowship" was not the symbol of forgiveness already received as much as an offer of forgiveness. Those who "ate and drank" with the owner in 13:26 do not receive admission into the meal. Table-fellowship was not a guarantee of admission. Admission was based on proper response to Jesus before the door was shut.[159] Luke 13:26–27 suggests that Jesus' table fellowship with "sinners" was a means to "invite" all of Israel to repent and experience forgiveness of sins (Luke 5:27–32). Proper response to the "call" resulted in a right relationship with him. For those who responded properly, table fellowship with Jesus became an anticipatory celebration of the kingdom banquet.

Luke 13:30 summarizes Jesus' remarks on the theme of the "kingdom banquet" by stressing the theme of reversal (cf. 1:51–53; 2:34) and reinforcing the warning made in Luke 13:1–6. The theme of reversal continues in Luke 14. In the context of a banquet given by a Pharisee, Jesus instructs the guests regarding whom to "invite" (14:13, 21). They are to "invite" those who cannot repay (14:14). In specific terms they are told to "invite" the "poor," the "crippled," the "lame," and the "blind" (14:13, 21). Luke links the theme of "inviting" (καλέω) to Jesus' table fellowship with "toll-collectors and sinners" and his mission of "calling" (καλέσαι) them to repentance in 5:32. The "invitation" to the "poor," "crippled," "lame" and "blind" links the narrative to 7:21–22 and the blending of Isa 35:5 with Isa 61:1; and to the Nazareth proclamation of 4:18. In the parable, the Pharisees are pictured as those refusing the invitation and as a consequence they remain outside of the banquet. The responsive are included; the unresponsive are excluded.

Luke 15:1–2

The narrative context of Luke 15 includes Luke 14:34 and Jesus' reference to those who have "ears to hear." Luke introduces Luke 15:1 by stating that the "tax collectors and sinners" were all gathering around to "hear" him. Luke, demonstrating that he is not reluctant to use it, uses the term

---

158. Jeremias, *NTT*, 115.
159. Bock, *Luke 9:51—24:53*, 1237.

ἁμαρτωλοί here. However, it is best not to use the "despised occupation" list as an explanation of the identity of the "sinners" here.[160] As Jesus' illustration in 15:11–30 demonstrates, the "sinner" is being understood as a "sinner" on moral grounds. This is further supported by the fact that the "sinners" are viewed as those who are in need of repentance (15:7, 10).

In sharp contrast with the "drawing near" (ἐγγίζοντες) of the "toll-collectors and sinners," Luke 15:2 presents the Pharisees and the scribes "grumbling" (διεγόγγυζον) over Jesus' association with them.[161] The grumbling is made into a specific charge in Luke 15:2: "This one 'welcomes' (προσδέχεται) and eats with sinners." Jesus is doing exactly what he had instructed others to do, he has invited the spiritually needy to the kingdom banquet through the offer of repentance.[162]

We have already seen that "grumbling" (γογγύζειν) is the Pharisees' response to Jesus' table fellowship with "toll-collectors and sinners" in Luke 5:30. The difference in 15:2 is the use of διαγογύζειν. The LXX uses διαγογύζειν ten times. All the uses are found in Exodus to Joshua and refer to the response of the Israelites as follows:

1. Exodus 15:6, the people grumble against Moses because of a lack of fresh water.

2. Exodus 16:2, the whole assembly grumbled against Moses and Aaron because of a need for food.

3. Exodus 16:7, Moses is speaking regarding the people's grumbling against them.

4. Exodus 16:7, 8, Moses declares that the people's grumbling is actually against the Lord.

5. Exodus 17:3, the people grumbled against Moses concerning water.

---

160. Contra Jeremias, *Parables*, 132. Most of these lists postdate the Mishnah. As we have shown in our discussion above, the "sinner" term is applied in the Mishnah only to those who are "sinners" guilty of a specific violation of the Torah. The "toll collector" is associated with the "sinner" on moral grounds.

161. The similar sound of the words may suggest a word play, *BDF* § 488 (2).

162. See the discussion on table-fellowship found in the treatment of Luke 5:27–32, pages 120–121 above.

6. Numbers 14:2, all the Israelites grumbled against Moses and Aaron at Kadesh Barnea.
7. Numbers 14:36, the men responsible for causing the Israelites to grumble at the report concerning Canaan were struck down by the Lord.
8. Numbers 16:11, Korah and others grumbled against Aaron and Moses and are destroyed by the Lord.
9. Deuteronomy 1:27, speaks of the grumbling and rebellion at Kadesh-Barnea.
10. Joshua 9:18, the assembly grumbled against their leaders because of the treaty with the Gibeonites.

It is possible that Luke is making an allusion to the OT background of the word and the pattern of "grumbling" against the Lord's leaders by the Israelites. In addition, since this is the second use of the expression, Luke may use this link to Luke 5:30 to show that the Pharisees continue to be unresponsive in their perception of Jesus. The leaders of Israel continue to "grumble" against God's deliverers (cf. Acts 7:37–39).

Luke 15:3–32: Three Parables

In Luke 15:3–32, Jesus directs three parables to the scribes and Pharisees: the lost sheep (3–7); the lost coin (8–10); and the man with two sons (11–32). The parables are a defense of Jesus' table fellowship with "sinners."[163] As the following layout demonstrates, the parables have several features in common.

15:3–7	v. 4	sheep = ἀπολέσας τὸ ἀπολωλὸς ... εὕρῃ
	v. 5	εὑρὼν ... χαίρων
	v. 6	Συγχάρητέ ... εὗρον ... τὸ ἀπολωλὸς
	v. 7	χαρὰ ... ἁματωλῷ μετανοοῦντι ... μετανοίας

163. Jeremias, *Parables*, 132.

The "Sinner" Texts in the Gospel of Luke

15:8–10	v. 8	drachma = ἀπολέσῃ ... εὕρῃ
	v. 9	εὗρον ... ἀπώλεσα
	v. 10	χαρὰ ... ἁμαρτωλῷ μετανοοῦντι
15:11–32	v. 11	a man ... two sons ...
	v. 17	ἀπόλλυμαι
	v. 18	ἥμαρτον
	v. 19	ἥμαρτον
	v. 23	εὐφρανθῶμεν
	v. 24	my son = ἀπολωλὼς ... εὑρέθη ... εὐφραίνεσθαι
	v. 32	your brother = εὐφρανθῆναι ... χαρῆναι ... ἀπολωλὼς ... εὑρέθη.

The lists above reveal the following links between the three parables:

(1) The "lost" sheep (vv. 4–7), "lost" coin (vv. 8–10), and "lost" son and brother (vv. 11–32).

(2) Lost-found (vv. 4–6, 8–9, 24–25).

(3) Rejoicing: the man (vv. 5–6), the woman (v. 10), the father (vv. 23–24, 32), and heaven (vv. 7, 10).

(4) Link between lost-sinner and found-repentance: the sheep and the man (vv. 4, 6–7), the coin (vv. 8–10), and the son (vv. 17–19, 24, 32).

Each parable uses the verb "lose" (ἀπόλλυμι), which in the passive voice can mean "to perish" or "to lose" one's life (Luke 8:24; 9:24) but also can refer to things being "ruined" (Luke 5:37) or "lost" (Luke 15:4, 6, 24). As noted in our discussion above, the LXX often associates ἀπόλλυμι with the judgment of the Lord. In the context of the parables, joy comes as a result of "finding" the lost item. In the first two parables joy is linked directly to the joy in heaven over one "sinner" who "repents" (15:7, 10). This links the joy directly to the rescue of a "sinner" from "perishing" due to the judgment of God.

This is reinforced in the parable of the son who acknowledges his condition: "I am perishing" (15:17) and links this condition to his "sin" (15:18). This explains the sense in which the term "lost" is to be understood in the previous parables. The prodigal son, then, becomes an example of one who heeded the warning in Luke 13:1–9 to repent and as a result is no longer "lost" or "perishing" but "found" and "alive" (15:32). Jesus defends his mission as rooted in the compassion of God for "perishing sinners." Instead of "grumbling" they should acknowledge the mission of Jesus and "rejoice."

Luke 15:3–7: The Lost Sheep

In 15:3–7, Jesus described a certain man who had one hundred sheep.[164] After discovering he had "lost" one of them, he left the ninety-nine sheep and continued to search until he found it (v. 4). When he found it he picked it up, put it on his shoulders "rejoicing" (v. 5). The emphasis on "joy" continues as the shepherd on his return home invites his friends and neighbors to come and rejoice with him because he had found his "lost" sheep (v. 6). In v. 7, Jesus connects the parable to his ministry to "sinners." He makes a direct analogy (οὕτως) between the "rejoicing" of the shepherd and the "joy" in heaven over the "finding" of one "sinner" and bringing him to "repentance." The joy is greater over the repentance of a sinner than over the "righteous" who assume they need no repentance (v. 7).[165]

---

164. The first two parables each begin with a rhetorical question intended to draw the listeners to affirm Jesus' argument: "Which one of you?"

165. The terms "righteous" and "sinner" continue to be linked in Luke in the way the terms were linked in the OT and other Jewish literature as shown in our research (see the discussion beginning on page 29 above). For our discussion of the "righteous" in Luke see Luke 5:27–32 pages 131–32. Neale proposes that the narrative of Luke 15 views the Pharisees as the "righteous" who need no repentance because to do otherwise would introduce an irony into the narrative that does not exist (*None But the Sinners*, 162). This position is incorrect for several reasons. First, Luke has identified the "righteous" as those who obey the revealed will of God, are looking for the consolation of Israel, and are open to God's saving action in Jesus. The models of Zechariah and Simeon in the birth narrative established the pattern. Second, the Pharisees have been shown to be opposed to Jesus and blind to his identity. Third, the term "grumble" sets their resistance against the OT pattern of the Israelites. It is true that Jesus does not attack the Pharisees as he did in Luke 11. He appears to be appealing to them through these parables. But this does not identify them as the "righteous." The context clearly demonstrates that they are in need of repentance.

The image of the shepherd seeking the lost has links to the OT image of God as the shepherd of Israel (Pss 23:1; 80:1). The emphasis is on his care and protection. Isaiah 40:11 declares that the Lord will "tend his flock like a shepherd and gather the lambs with his arm." In Ezek 34: 31, the Lord told Israel that they were his sheep and he was the Lord their God. But the "shepherd" image is also used of the leaders of Israel. Jeremiah 23:1 speaks of "shepherds" of Israel who "destroy" (ἀπολλύοντες) the Lord's flock but the Lord himself will "gather" (εἰσδέξομαι) his remnant and set them in their pasture.

In the context of Ezek 34, the Lord rebukes the "shepherds" of Israel for looking out for themselves but neglecting his sheep (34:1–10). They have not helped the weak or the sick, or "turned back" (ἀπεστρέψατε) the "straying" (πλανώμενον) or "sought" (ἐζητήσατε) the "lost" (ἀπολωλός, 34:4). In 34:5–6, the Lord declares that his sheep were scattered all over the earth because no one was "seeking them" (ἐκζητῶν) to "bring them back" (ἀποστρέφων, cf. 34:8). In 34:7–10 the Lord stated his opposition to Israel's shepherds. But in 34:11–31, the Lord declared that he himself would "seek" (ἐκζητήσω) the sheep and "visit" (ἐπισκέψομαι, cf. Luke 1:68, 78; 7:16) them (34:11). The "lost" (ἀπολωλός) he will "seek" (ζητήσω) and the "straying" (πλανώμενον) he will "turn back" (ἀποστρέψω, 34:16; cf. 34:12). In contrast to the shepherds of Israel, the Lord stated that he would "save" (σώσω) his sheep (34:22).

A significant development occurs in Ezek 34:23. The Lord states that he will raise up one shepherd over Israel who would "shepherd" them (implying all the elements listed in proper shepherding above, 34:23a). The shepherd is identified as the Lord's "servant" (δουλόν) David who will be their one "shepherd" and a "prince" (ἄρχων = נָשִׂיא) in their midst (34:23b). The many shepherds will be replaced by "one."[166] The Lord will be faithful to his promise given in 2 Samuel 7 to raise up a ruler from the house of David (2 Sam 7:8; Hos 3:5; Jer 30:9–10).[167] Zimmerli observes that the Lord does not satisfy the curiosity of the questioner who would like to know the relationship between the new David and the old. It is enough for them to know that he will be "in their midst" and that this "prince"

---

166. Zimmerli, *Ezekiel 2*, 218.
167. See 2 Sam 7:8 and the reference to David as king and shepherd.

will no longer exist off his sheep but live for his sheep.[168] Luke connects Jesus to the fulfillment of the promises to David in 1:32, 69. Jesus is called "Son of David" in 18:39 in the context of a blind beggar's plea for mercy. Jesus told the beggar that his faith "saved" (from σώζω cf. Ezek 34:21, 22) him. This declaration of Jesus, Son of David, is made immediately prior to the Zacchaeus narrative where the "shepherd seeking the lost" image is linked to the "salvation" (σωτηρία) of a "sinner" (19:9, 10). All of the key terms—"seek," "lost," and "save"—which have been identified in Ezekiel 34 as referring to the role of the future Davidic shepherd-prince, are included as part of the defining elements of the mission of Jesus in Luke.

In Luke 15, the terms "shepherd," "seek," "lost," and "save" link the narrative directly to the Ezekiel shepherd image. Jesus is fulfilling the promise to "seek" the "lost" in terms of bringing "sinners" to repentance. The theme of bringing "sinners" to "repentance" is found in the immediate context of Ezek 34. As noted in our earlier research, mercy is clearly offered to those labeled genuine "sinners" in Ezek 18:20, 27 and 33:12, 19. In Ezekiel 33, the prophet uses ἁμαρτωλός three times. In 33:8, the prophet is specifically charged to warn the wicked. In 33:11, the "sinner" receives the offer of repentance. If the "sinner" (ἁμαρτωλός) turns (ἀποστρέφω) from his way, he shall live (ζῆν, 33:11; 14–19). God offers forgiveness to the repentant sinner. The offer is stated clearly in 33:19: "And when the sinner (ἁμαρτωλός = רָשָׁע) "turns" from his iniquity (ἀνομίας), and shall do justice and righteousness, by these he shall live." The terms "sinner" "turn" "live" and "save" (34:12) are all found in this context to refer to the "salvation" of the "sinner" who is about to "perish" because he had "gone astray" (34:32). The image of "straying" (ἐπλανήθημεν) sheep is also used as an image of sin in Isaiah 53:6.[169]

---

168. Zimmerli, *Ezekiel 2*, 223. Here Zimmerli connects Ezek 34:23–24 directly to Luke 15.

169. The Qumran community used the shepherd image to emphasize the compassion of the "Inspector" of the camp who was responsible to examine potential candidates for admission into the community. According to the Damascus Document 13. 9–10, the Inspector is to have "pity" on the candidates "like a father pities his sons"; he is to "heal" all the "strays" like a "shepherd his flock" (13:9). In 13:10, the shepherd image seems to combine elements from Ezek 34 and Isa 61:1–2. The Inspector is to 'undo all the chains that bind them' (García Martínez, *Dead Sea Scrolls*, 43).

In Luke 15, the role of the watchman and the role of the shepherd merge in the mission of Jesus who "seeks" to "save" the "lost" through "turning" them in "repentance" from their sins so they might "live." In the Ezekiel 34 context, the OT allusion rebukes the shepherds of Israel. In Luke the focus is more on revealing Jesus as the fulfillment of OT promises that the Lord himself would come and "seek" his sheep. The emphasis is on revealing God's salvation and how Jesus fulfills "all the Law and the prophets" (Luke 24:44). Neale seems to understand the allusion to the "seeking shepherd" completely in terms of indicting the religious leaders for their failure to seek the lost.[170] However, the context is clear that Luke uses the image to illustrate Jesus' mission not theirs. It is their blindness to his mission that is at issue.

LUKE 15:8–10: THE LOST COIN

In Luke 15:8–10, Jesus gave another parable emphasizing the appropriateness of "finding the lost" and "rejoicing." The change in the parable consists of a woman as the "seeker" and a coin as the lost item. The essential elements from the first parable are repeated for emphasis: "lose," "find" (v. 8); "found," "lost" (v. 9); "rejoicing," "sinner," "repent" (v. 10). The conclusion of both parables repeats the emphasis on joy in heaven over the repentance of one sinner.

In neither of the stories does Jesus identify himself. But it is clear that he is the seeking one. He is the one fulfilling God's plan to rescue people. The unspoken point is that heaven and the angels rejoice over the rescue of one "sinner" and so should the Pharisees.

LUKE 15:11–32: THE MAN WITH THE TWO SONS

Jesus's final parable deals with a "lost son" or, as the parable proceeds, two lost sons.[171] The parable may be divided into three sections: 1) the sin and return of the younger son (vv. 11–19); 2) the loving forgiveness and joy of the father (vv. 20–24); and 3) the reaction of the older brother to the prodigal's return (vv. 25–32).

170. Neale, *None But the Sinners*, 162.
171. Marshall, *Luke*, 604.

THE SINNER IN LUKE

The Younger Son (15:11–19)

Jesus states that a "certain man had two sons" (v. 11). This prepares the reader for the father's dealings with both sons. The focus of the parable is not the sons but the loving forgiveness and joy of the father at the return of the son.[172] The parable continues to justify Jesus' fellowship with "sinners" (15:1–2).

Jesus tells the story of a man's younger son requesting and receiving his inheritance (v. 12). A father could dispose of his property either by a will to be followed after his death or by a gift to his children during his lifetime (Num 27:8–11; 36:7–9).[173] The oldest son received a double portion. Thus, this younger son received a third of the property.

The young man converted his inheritance into cash, left for a far away country, and quickly "squandered" everything by means of "debauchery" (v. 13).[174] The emphasis is on reckless and immoral pleasure (cf. the description in 15:30).[175] But his circumstances quickly changed when a famine came and he came to be in need (v. 14). The desperate plight of the youth is emphasized as he is forced to take a job feeding pigs (v. 15) and is so hungry that he longs to eat the food of the pigs but no one would give him anything (v. 16).[176]

The crisis described in v. 16 prepares for the repentance in v. 17.[177] The young man "came" to his senses and acknowledged his desperate plight: "How many of my father's hired men get more than enough bread, yet I am here "perishing" (ἀπόλλυμι) with hunger" (v. 17). The verb ἀπόλλυμι connects the youth's plight to the condition of being "lost" in 15:4, 6, 8–9, 24, and 32. The use of ἀπόλλυμι here with "hunger" (λιμῷ) makes a likely allusion to Ezek 34:29, which states in the context of the Davidic shepherd that his sheep shall no more "perish with hunger" (ἀπολλύμενοι λιμῷ).

---

172. Ibid. So also Bock, *Luke 9:51–24:47*, 1309.

173. Fitzmyer, *Luke X–XXIV*, 1087.

174. BAGD suggest that the term "gathered" (συναγαγών) has the sense of "turning everything into cash," (782).

175. Marshall, *Luke*, 608.

176. The use of the imperfects in v. 16 presents an active scene of desperation.

177. Fitzmyer, *Luke X—XXIV*, 1088, who observes that the young man's "realization" and his remorse reflect the beginning of his repentance.

The youth decided to get up and to return to his father, confessing his sin against God and against his father (15:18). He planned to humbly acknowledge his unworthiness and to cast himself upon his father's mercy (15:19).

The Father's Joy (15:20–24)

Luke describes the homecoming in 15:20–24. The young man arose and returned to his father. But while he was still a long distance away, Luke says that the father saw him, was moved with compassion, ran to him, embraced him and kissed him. The picture of "running" emphasizes the father's initiative and love for the son who had left him.[178] The kiss is the expression not merely of emotion but of forgiveness (cf. 2 Sam 14:33, David's kiss of Absalom). The narrative displays in the father's compassion a picture of the love of God for the "lost" that is the rationale for Jesus' ministry to "sinners."

In v. 22, the son declares his confession, but is abruptly interrupted by the rejoicing of his father. The father commands his house servants to hurry, bring out the best robe, and give the son a ring for his hand and sandals for his feet. Instead of a hired day-worker, the lost son becomes the guest of honor, restored to the family and a free man, not a slave.[179] The father commands that a special fattened calf be slaughtered for the occasion. He calls his household to have a feast and "celebrate" (εὐφρανθῶμεν, 15:23). He explains the reason for the celebration, namely, that his son was "dead" and is "alive" again, he was "lost" and has been "found" (15:24). The narrative links directly to the celebration (χαρά) in 15:5–6 over finding the "lost sheep," in 15:9 over finding the "lost coin," and in 15:7 and 10 to heaven's joy over the repentant "sinner." The emphasis is on the point that finding the "lost" calls for celebration. The joy in heaven over the repentant sinner is pictured by the father's joy over his son's return (15:20–24).

The Older Son (15:25–32)

The final section describes the reaction of the older brother to the news of his brother's return (vv. 25–32). The older brother had been in the fields working and now he returns to the sound of music and dancing (vv.

---

178. Fitzmyer, *Luke X–XXIV*, 1089.
179. Bock, *Luke 9:51—24:53*, 1314–15.

25–26). When he asked about the reason for the celebration, a servant explained that his brother had returned and his father had slain the fattened calf because he had him back "safely" (ὑγιαίοντα, v. 27).[180] The servant explained the feast from the point of view of the father.

The older son became angry and refused to go in (v. 28). But the father took the initiative, went out, and pleaded with his son. In the interaction with the father, the elder son responded to his father in a shameful way. He failed to greet his father with respect, described his relationship to his father as "slavery," and complained about the way his father treated him (v. 29).[181] Instead of seeing his brother from the father's point of view as a "son" received back safely (v. 27), the elder brother viewed his "father's son" totally in terms of his sin (v. 30).[182] He was distressed that he had never been treated in such a manner, even though he had never disobeyed his father. He is the picture of the Pharisees who are complaining about Jesus' involvement with sinners (15:1–2).[183]

Jack Sanders sees the parable in Luke 15 in the overall context of Luke-Acts.[184] He views the elder son, who never transgressed his father's commandment (v. 29), as the representative of the observant Jew, whereas the other son who lived in a "distant region" (v. 13) and fed pigs (v. 15), is the "stand-in for the Gentiles."[185] Sanders sees the elder son taking the perspective of the Pharisees found in Acts 15:5.[186] The elder son affirms that he had never transgressed the father's commandments (v. 29). He was unable to welcome the repentant "sinner" home. In the same way, the Pharisees are resentful over Gentile admission without obligation to keep the Law of Moses. They were unable to welcome the Gentiles.

The weakness in this view is that the "young man" never became a "Gentile" but a Jewish "sinner." The issue in Luke is the Pharisees' complaint over Jesus' table fellowship with Jewish "sinners" (15:1–2). The Gentile is-

---

180. See the use of this expression in Luke 5:32 and Jesus' ministry of "healing" "sinners."
181. Gowler, *Host*, 253.
182. The use of οὗτος emphasizes his contempt (Bock, *Luke 9:51—24:53*, 1318 n28).
183. Gowler, *Host*, 253.
184. Sanders, *The Jews in Luke*-Acts, 197–98.
185. Ibid., 108.
186. This position was taken by Augustine and other Fathers, as discussed on pages 2–3 above.

sue raised in Acts 15 is linked to Luke 15 as both a literary and a ministry pattern. But Luke 15 must not be interpreted by Acts 15.

J. Duncan Derrett suggests that the "younger-older brother" image is rooted in the OT theme, especially Esau and Jacob.[187] The older brother's jealousy is like the jealousy of Esau. However, the elder brother in Luke 15 is not viewed as a sensual profligate like Esau. Many of the details Derrett suggests move the point of the parable too far from its clear narrative purpose of justifying Jesus' mission to "sinners." Derrett makes a point that has merit. It is possible that Luke is using a "lesser to greater" argument to make the case that if a human father acts this way, "how much more" will God display his mercy toward the "repentant sinner."[188] Jesus is taking the point of view of God toward the "sinner," this is his rationale for associating with the "lost."

There is another possible OT link in the theme of the "festive meal." As observed, the "kingdom banquet" image is stressed in the preceding context (13:22—14:24) and the issue of Jesus' "receiving sinners" in meal fellowship (συνεσθίει) opens the Luke 15 narrative (vv. 1–2). The "banquet" and "celebration" emphasized in the concluding parable appears to be linked to the banquet image of Isa 25:6 and the theme of rejoicing over the mercy of the Lord in Isa 49:6–13 and over forgiveness in 55:6–13. The term "celebrate" (εὐφρανθῶμεν) associated with "eating" in Luke 15: 23–24, 29, and 32 is linked to χαρά directly in 15:32 and conceptually in 15:5–7 and 9–10. In Isa 25:6, the messianic banquet is described by the term εὐφροσύνη. In Isa 49:13, the prophet declared "rejoice you heavens" (Εὐφραίεσθε οὐρανοί), the earth is to be glad, and the mountains are told to break forth with "joy" (εὐφροσύνην) because God has shown his people "mercy." In Isa 55:6–13, in the context of calling the Servant of Yahweh a "prince" and linking him to David (cf. Ezek 34:24), the prophet called the Israelites to "seek" the Lord, and when they "find" him to "call upon him" (55:6a). When the Lord "draws near" (ἐγγίζῃ, cf. Luke 15:1), they are to leave their ungodly ways and "return" to the Lord and he will abundantly forgive their sins (55:7). The Lord himself gives the explanation for this promise of abundant pardon in 55:8. His "counsels" (βουλαί)

---

187. Derrett, "Law in the New Testament," 56–74.
188. Ibid., 72.

are not their "counsels" nor are his ways, their ways. The "counsels" here are those that include the abundant forgiveness of the Lord. Verses 9–11 emphasize the sovereignty of God and the certainty of fulfilling his word (55:11). In 55:12, the Lord promised that they shall go out with "rejoicing" (εὐφροσύνη) and be taught with "joy" (χαρᾷ) for the mountains and the hills will "welcome" (προσδεξόμενοι, cf. Luke 15:2) them with "joy" (χαρᾷ). In the immediately following context of Isaiah 56:1, his salvation is "near" (ἤγγικε) and his mercy is about to be revealed.

The dual themes of the "celebration" of the kingdom banquet and of "rejoicing" over the forgiveness of sins have possibly merged in this Lucan parable. The Lord's people are told to join the "heavens" in rejoicing because of the matchless "counsels" of the Lord's abundant pardoning mercy. The emphasis in the final parable is the father's "abundant mercies" and the call to "celebrate" at the banquet with the father and the "lost" son who has been found.

The parable ends with the question unanswered: will the older brother go in or not?[189] In the narrative context, the Pharisees and scribes represent the older brother who still has an opportunity to participate in the joy of Jesus' mission. Yet the account ends with a question mark concerning both the elder brother and the elders of Israel.

Conclusion

In Luke 15, Jesus defends his mission to "sinners" by rooting his motivation in the mercy of God. The emphasis is not an attack against the Pharisees' failure to seek the lost but a rebuke against their failure, like the elder brother, to rejoice over Jesus' mission to rescue them. Their blindness to Jesus reflects the hardness of heart pattern found in Israel. Jesus uses parables linked to OT pictures of the promised Davidic Shepherd and the abundant mercy of God. One lost person is worth God seeking him until he repents. There may be a link here to Jesus' assertion in Luke 14:14 that a person is "much more" valuable than a sheep.[190]

---

189. Marshall, *Luke*, 613.
190. Derrett, "Fresh Light," 48.

Luke 18:9–14

The Narrative Setting

In the narrative between 15:32–18:9, Luke presented Jesus' teaching on "wealth" (16:1–15; 19–31), the ten lepers (17:11–19), the coming of the kingdom of God (17:20–37), and the parable of the persistent widow (18:1–8). The catchword "prayer" links 18:1–8 to 18:9–14 but the conceptual connection appears to be requirements for entrance to the kingdom (cf. 17:20–37).[191]

The Setting: Luke 18:9

In Luke 18:9–14, Jesus gave a parable with two main characters. He assumed the role of the narrator and directed the parable to an intended audience described in 18:9 by three things. First, they were "trusting" (πεποιθότας) in themselves. The verb means "to have confidence in, depend on, trust in something or someone."[192] Here Jesus spoke to those who had confidence or trust in themselves. There is a warning in the OT that those who trust in themselves are "fools" (Prov 28:26).

Second, the intended audience is described as those who are confident that they are "righteous" (δίκαιοι). The term "righteous" is used in a legal sense of being right or innocent according to the Law. As shown in our research, in the OT the term especially means to live in a relationship with God and one's neighbor in accordance with the revealed will and character of God. Our examination of the Gospel of Luke has revealed this same meaning. The "righteous" have shown themselves to be obedient to God's will, hoping for the consolation of Israel, and responsive to God's revelation of salvation in Jesus.

The expression describing those who were confident that they were "righteous" links this narrative to Luke 16:14–15. There Jesus addressed Pharisees who "sneered" at him over his teaching about devotion to God and money. Jesus told them they were those who "justified themselves" (δικαιοῦντες ἑαυτούς) before men but that God knew their hearts.

---

191. Marshall, *Luke*, 677.
192. BAGD, 639.

The statement, "trusting in one's righteousness," is probably an allusion to Ezek 33:13 in which the prophet warns the "righteous" one (δι-καίῳ) who "trusts" (πέποιθεν) in his righteousness (δικαιοσύνην) that if he commits iniquity, his former righteousness will not be remembered and he will be judged. In the same context, the "sinner" (ἁμαρτωλός) who repents will live (33:14, 19). Ezekiel 33 provides the OT link to Luke's narrative in 18:9–14.[193]

The third characteristic of Jesus' intended audience is that they "look down" on everyone else (18:9c). They view everyone else with disdain, as nothing.[194] Luke uses the term in Luke 23:11 of Herod's soldiers ridiculing Jesus.

The Parable: Luke 18:10–14

The parable begins in Luke 18:10. Jesus introduced two men who are both going up to the temple in Jerusalem to pray (cf. 18:1). Although the men share the same purpose, they are very different. One is a Pharisee.[195] The other is a "toll-collector."[196] Both are going up to the temple to pray.

Luke 18:11–12 records the Pharisee's prayer. He thanked God that he was not like the rest of men: "swindlers," "unrighteous," "adulterers," or even like "this toll collector" (18:11). He then described his normal routine of "fasting" twice weekly and the "tithing" of everything he owned (18:12).[197]

He stands before God fully confident in himself. He is not like other men. He is confident that in God's court, he stands guilt-free, innocent, and right according to God's standards. He is debt-free before God. The reason he is so confident is that he has been paying in. He fasts twice a

---

193. Bock, *Luke 9:51—24:53*, 1461.

194. BAGD, 277.

195. The picture of the Pharisee here is intended by Luke to reflect an aspect of the Pharisees that Jesus actually encountered and is viewed as censoring (Marshall, *Luke*, 677; Fitzmyer, *Luke X–XXIV*, 1186). This does not mean that this is a model that every Pharisee would seek to follow. But neither is it intended as a caricature (contra Neale, *None But the Sinners*, 167).

196. See the discussion on "toll-collectors" in the section on Luke 5:27–32 above.

197. The importance of "tithing" to the rabbis can be seen in the detailed discussion in *m. Demai* 5.2, 7.2, et al.

week, he gives a tithe of everything. Surely, God has been crediting these things properly to his account (cf. Luke 6:32, 34).

In contrast, Luke 18:13 describe the prayer of the toll collector. In direct contrast to the Pharisee, the toll collector stood far away (cf. 18:11), did not desire to lift up his eyes to heaven (to God), but is seen beating his chest as a sign of deep contrition.[198]

Jesus described the man's prayer in dramatic contrast to the Pharisee. His prayer is simply, "God be merciful to me a sinner" (ἁμαρτωλῷ).[199] The prayer has parallels to Psalm 51 and the Prayer of Manasseh. When he asks for "mercy," he literally asked: "God be propitiated (ἱλάσθητί) to me, a sinner." The word is used in the LXX for "atonement" (Pss 25:11; 34:6). The toll-collector asked God to be merciful toward him by accepting his confession and repentance as an atoning sacrifice. There may be an allusion to the kind of sacrifice that God accepts, a broken and contrite heart (Ps 51:1, 3; cf. 51:17).

This is a powerful illustration of what Jesus means when he uses the term "repentance." The toll collector recognizes the hopelessness of the situation and does the only thing left to do; he throws himself on the mercy of God. The story is addressed to those who had confidence in themselves, trusting their own righteousness, and looking down on everyone else.

Now which person does God accept? In Luke 18:14, Jesus declares the verdict. He states in authoritative terms that "this one" (οὗτος), as opposed to the Pharisee (cf. οὗτος in 18:11), went home "justified" (δεδικαιωμένος).

Then, Jesus broadens the application: "Everyone who exalts himself will be humbled (by God); but those who humble themselves will be exalted." The reversal foreshadowed in the birth narrative has occurred. Mercy has been extended (Luke 1:50), the proud scattered (Luke 1:51), and the humble have been lifted up (Luke 1:52). Luke has given illustrative fulfillment of the "falling" and "rising" of two Israelites (cf. Luke 2:34).

---

198. Bock, *Luke 9:51—24:53*, 1464.

199. The use of the definite article is here simple apposition, Hoerber, "God Be Merciful," 283–86.

The Sinner in Luke

Summary

The parable of the Pharisee and the "toll collector" maintains the understanding of the "sinner" as a moral category in Luke. The links to other "sinners" in 18:11 reinforces this understanding. In addition, the "sinner" is viewed as "repenting" and asking for mercy, which acknowledges the sinful condition of the "toll collector." The development here is the clear reversal of expectation based on the pride or humility of the two men. The "righteous" is declared "unrighteous" and the "sinner" is declared "righteous" both by the authoritative voice of Jesus. Genuine "sinners" may be reinstated to a right standing with God.

Luke 19:1–10

The Narrative Setting

In the narrative preceding Luke 19:1–10, Luke presented Jesus' teaching on the necessity of "receiving" (δέξηται) the kingdom as a child (18:15–17); Jesus' encounter with the "rich ruler" and the emphasis on riches as an obstacle to entrance into the kingdom (18:18–30); the prediction of his death (18:31–34); and the healing of the blind man and the proclamation of Jesus as "son of David" (18:31–43). The narrative context reflects an emphasis on the culmination of the mission of the "Son of Man" (18:31) and the divine necessity of his coming.[200]

This section introduces Luke's final pericope on the "sinner" theme within the central section of his Gospel. It provides a closing climactic account of Jesus and his mission to "sinners" in his rescue of Zacchaeus. Of special importance is Jesus' declaration of his mission in terms of seeking and saving the lost (19:10). The narrative links the reader to many of the themes emphasized throughout the Gospel of Luke. There are links to Luke 5:27–32 and Jesus' table fellowship with "toll-collectors" and "sinners." Zacchaeus will serve as a climax to this theme for he is both a "chief toll collector" and a "sinner." And Jesus will be criticized for his association with Zacchaeus as he has been throughout Luke for his contact with "sinners." Luke 19:1–10 also provides a concluding mission statement that recalls

---

200. Moessner, *Lord of the Banquet*, 168.

Jesus' mission statement in Luke 5:32 at the beginning of his ministry in Galilee. From a broader perspective, this passage will serve as a link to Acts 11:2 and the issue of entering the house of a religious outsider and eating with them.

The Setting: Luke 19:1–2

In 19:1, Luke describes Jesus in the process of passing through Jericho on his way to Jerusalem (cf. 9:51–52). Jericho was a border station between Perea, under Herod Antipas' control, and the province of Judea.[201] Zacchaeus is introduced in 19:2.[202] Luke describes him as a "chief toll collector" (ἀρχιτελώνης) and "rich" (πλούσιος). For Luke's readers, these two terms recall several elements in the Gospel of Luke.

First, Zacchaeus was a "chief tax collector," which meant that he was possibly the owner of the tax franchise surrounding Jericho. He would hire toll-collectors like Levi (5:27) to work at the toll booths. As noted earlier, toll-collectors were linked with the term "sinner" (ἁμαρτωλός, cf. 19:7) because of their reputation for dishonesty and cruelty. But Luke has presented the "toll-collectors" as open and responsive to the ministry of John the Baptist (3:12; 7:29) and the mission of Jesus (5:27–32; 15:1–2). So in Zacchaeus we have a "chief toll collector." To this point, Luke has presented them as open to God's salvation in Jesus.

Second, Zacchaeus is also "rich." Money has been an important theme in Luke. It has been presented as a great obstacle to one's recognition of his spiritual need. As early as the birth narrative, the "rich" are foreseen to be "sent away empty" (Luke 1:53; 6:24). Riches are said to choke out the seed of the word (8:14). The foolish rich man "gained the world" but "lost his soul" (12:13–21). Jesus warned against serving money (16:13). In the parable of the "rich man" and the "beggar," the earthly conditions were reversed in heaven when the beggar went to Paradise and the rich man to hell (16:19–31). In the near context of Luke 19, a "rich" "ruler" (ἄρχων, cf. the

---

201. Safrai and Stern, *Jewish People*, 1:333.

202. The name Zacchaeus is viewed as being stressed by some (Marshall, *Luke*, 696). But as Bock points out, the later context makes nothing of the name (*Luke 9:51—24:53*, 1516). In addition, Luke uses no catchword to remind the reader that the name is being alluded to again. This works against Ravens' use of Zacchaeus' name as support for his view that Zacchaeus is being vindicated rather than rescued, "Zacchaeus," 19–32.

ἀρχι prefix in 19:2) misses the kingdom because of his attachment to his great "wealth" (πλούσιος, 18:23). Jesus responded by using the image of a camel going through the eye of a needle to stress the impossibility for those trusting in riches (πλούσιον) to enter the kingdom (18:25). In the context immediately preceding the story of Zacchaeus, a blind beggar receives his sight and "salvation" because of his faith in Jesus, "Son of David" (18:42). So Zacchaeus is a chief tax-collector but he is also "rich." The narrative of Luke has prepared the reader to be less than hopeful regarding a "rich man" who is not just a tax-collector but the chief tax collector.

Zacchaeus' Quest: Luke 19:3–7

Luke describes Zacchaeus as on a mission (ἐζήτει) to see who Jesus was (19:3–4).[203] The motive is not clear but it seems to be curiosity. But Zacchaeus was hindered by the size of the crowd. The crowd was large, but he was short (19:3). Zacchaeus' actions reflect both desire and creativity. Luke states that Zacchaeus ran ahead of the crowd and climbed a sycamore-fig tree in order "to see" (ἰδεῖν, cf. 19:3) Jesus as he passed by (19:4). When Jesus arrived, he looked up and addressed Zacchaeus by name (19:5a). For Luke, this may suggest Jesus' credentials as a prophet (cf. 7:36–50). Jesus strongly implored him to come down quickly for "today" (σήμερον) it was "necessary" (δεῖ) for him to stay at his house. Luke has used the term δεῖ especially to describe the "necessity" of Jesus' mission: the "necessity" of his doing his father's business (Luke 2:49), the "necessity" of preaching the gospel of the kingdom (4:43; 13:33), and the necessity of the cross (9:22; 17:25; 24:7, 24, 46). Jesus does not say why he must stay with Zacchaeus but the reader has been prepared to link it to his mission.

The entire crowd wanted to see Jesus. Yet Jesus took the initiative and requested hospitality from a man viewed by that crowd as a "sinner" (19:7). This action shows that Jesus was offering fellowship to Zacchaeus and in doing so, was extending an offer of forgiveness.[204]

Zacchaeus responded immediately. He came down from the tree and "received" or "welcomed" (ὑπεδέξατο) Jesus with "joy" (χαίρων, 15:6).

203. The imperfect pictures continual effort.

204. See the discussion on "table fellowship" in the sections on Luke 5:27–32 page 120 and Luke 15:1–32 pages 153–54.

In Luke, δέχομαι and its related verbs often focus on the proper response to Jesus: "receiving" the word (8:13); "receiving" Jesus (9:5; 48); and, "receiving" the kingdom as a child (9:53; 10:8, 10; 18:17). Luke does not use the δέχομαι word group with those who do not respond to Jesus' prophetic voice.[205] The theme of "joy" is common in Luke (1:14; 2:10; 10:17; 13:17;15:5, 7).

Although Zacchaeus rejoiced, the people began to "grumble" (διεγόγγυζον) because Jesus had gone to stay with a man who is a "sinner" (ἁμαρτωλῷ, 19:7; cf. 5:8). Opposition to Jesus' association with "sinners" has been a major theme in the Gospel of Luke (5:27–32; 7:34–36; 15:1–2). In the other opposition contexts, the Pharisees are those "grumbling" (5:30; 15:2). In 19:7, the opposition comes from the "people." The opposition is possibly linked to the OT command not to "dwell" in the tent of "sinners" (Ps 84:10; cf. *1 En.* 97:8). This is important in understanding the identity of the "sinner" in Luke because the attitude revealed in 19:7 makes it clear that the "sinner" is not a sectarian label limited to the Pharisees.[206] In the context, the term "sinner" is linked to his practice as a "toll collector" that has apparently lived up to the bad reputation commonly associated with the trade (cf. 19:8).[207]

The "grumbling" by the crowd links the narrative both to earlier "grumbling" texts in Luke (5:27–32; 15:1–2) but also to the response of Israel to God and his chosen leaders. The people as a whole had not grasped the nature of Jesus' mission anymore than the Pharisees. Yet Zacchaeus had "received" Jesus and according to Luke was to receive a blessing of "peace" and the message of the gospel (9:4 and 10:5, 8).

The Defense: Luke 19:8–10

In Luke 19:8–10, the narrative focuses on justifying Jesus' mission to "sinners" (cf. 5:27–32; 7:36–50; and 15:1–32). Verse 8 records Zacchaeus' response to Jesus. Verses 9 and 10 record Jesus' pronouncement concerning Zacchaeus (19:9) and his mission (19:10).

---

205. Moessner, *Lord of the Banquet*, 133.
206. Contra Dunn, "Pharisees, Sinners, and Jesus," 278–79.
207. Bock, *Luke 9:51–24:53*, 1519.

The Sinner in Luke

Zacchaeus' Response

Zacchaeus stood up, either at the meal or while still in the street with the crowd as an audience. He declared his resolve to give half his possessions to the poor and if he had "extorted" (ἐσυκοφάντησα) anyone, he would repay them four-times what he had taken (19:8).[208] Zacchaeus' attitude has changed toward the poor whom he had apparently oppressed.[209] The people from whom he had "extorted" money, he resolves to repay four times the amount required in Exodus 22:1 for sheep rustlers.

Zacchaeus is the model of John the Baptist's call for fruit to accompany one's change of heart (Luke 3:12–14). John had warned the Israelites not to presume that they were safe from God's coming wrath because they called "Abraham their father" (3:8). They are to produce fruit reflective of their change in heart (3:8–9, cf. Luke 13:1–9). When Zacchaeus promises to "give" half of his possessions to the "poor," in Luke's narrative this reflects a change of heart toward "wealth" that is a sign of repentance, something the "rich ruler" did not display (Luke 18:22–23). As Bock states, Zacchaeus is an example of one "rich" man who made it through the eye of the needle. He has done so because he has responded properly to Jesus.[210]

Zacchaeus' resolve to restore those whom he had "extorted"[211] recalls John's prohibition of συκοφαντήσητε in 3:14 as a demonstration of the

---

208. The verbs "give" and "repay" are both present tense which has brought the suggestion that Zacchaeus is not stating resolve to do something but proclaiming a defense against the charge of being a "sinner." Ravens, mentioned earlier, suggested that the normal use of the present tense demands this interpretation ("Zacchaeus," 24). The issue is not dependent upon the verb tense here as much as how one understands the context. There is no case in the "sinner" contexts in which the narrative aim is to vindicate the "sinner" before other people. In Luke 5:27–32, 7:36–50; and 15:1–32, Jesus' defense in each case presumes the accuracy of the "sinner" designation to justify his mission of bringing them to repentance. There is nothing in the Zacchaeus narrative that hints that he had known or responded to Jesus prior to this setting. In addition, the use of "receive" to describe Zacchaeus' response, and Jesus' declaration that "today" "salvation" has come to this house links his salvation, not his vindication, to the present scene.

209. Zacchaeus' statements of repentance follow Jesus' acceptance of him just as the prodigal son's confession followed his father's acceptance in 15:20–21. See York, *The Last Shall Be First*, 159 n. 3.

210. Bock, *Luke 9:51—24:53*, 1514.

211. The use of the aorist particple ἐσυκοφάντησα with the first class condition reflects Zacchaeus' awareness that he had defrauded others (*BDF* §371, 1). See Rom 5:17; Col 2:20,

fruit of repentance.[212] His attitude and behavior changes are seen here as natural products of a changed heart. Jesus had "called" him, Zacchaeus had "received" him, and the evidence of repentance is a new desire to "love his neighbor" as God's will had expressed.[213]

John York describes Zacchaeus' repentance in terms of honor gained and lost.[214] He explained that "riches" in Luke were not the real issue but the honor associated with them. The "wealth" of the "rich ruler" became an obstacle to kingdom entrance because he could not "humble himself" and lose his status of honor. In contrast, the disciples had "left everything" for the sake of the kingdom and had cast their honor status totally upon Jesus' promise. Zacchaeus as the "rich" "toll collector" and "sinner" is demonstrating that wealth is no longer his measure of honor.

Jesus' Response

Jesus responded to Zacchaeus directly, just as he had pronounced "forgiveness of sins" to the paralyzed man in 5:20 and the "sinful woman" in 7:50.[215] He told him that "today salvation had come" to this house because he too was a "son of Abraham" (19:9). The expression "today" (σήμερον) begins Jesus' statement and is clearly emphatic.[216] It recalls his initial invitation to Zacchaeus (19:5) but also his Nazareth declaration of fulfillment in 4:20, 21 (cf. 2:11; 13:32–33).

The arrival of "salvation" (σωτηρία) recalls the promise that God's people would receive the knowledge of "salvation" (σωτηρία) through "forgiveness of sins" (1:77) and Simeon's declaration that when he saw Jesus he had seen God's salvation, which was to be for all people (2:30).[217] This allu-

---

3:1; and Bock, *Luke 9:51—24:53*, 1521.

212. The fact that συκοφαντέω is found in the NT only in Luke 3:14 and 19:8 strengthens the case that Luke intends a strong narrative link.

213. This reflects the consistent findings in our research that "righteousness" was linked to the "neighbor law" of Leviticus 19, which is rooted in the will and character of God (cf. Luke 6:27–36; 10:27–28, 37).

214. York, *The Last Shall Be First*, 158–60.

215. Contra Marshall, *Luke*, 698.

216. Fitzmyer, *Luke X–XXIV*, 1225.

217. The other uses of σωτηρία in the Gospel of Luke relate to national salvation (1:69, 71). In Acts, the term is used of salvation associated with forgiveness

sion to Isa 40:5 is repeated in Luke 3:6, repeating the promise that "all flesh" would see the "salvation" of God. The context that follows in Luke 3:7 is a revelation of God's salvation to the "all flesh" of Israel, emphasizing repentance for the forgiveness of sins. In that narrative, the scope of what "all flesh" meant for Israel was reflected by the response of "even the toll-collectors" who were the only ones identified as actually being baptized. The "call" of Levi the "toll collector" also underscored the scope of Jesus' mission of "release" at the beginning of his Galilean ministry (5:27–32). Jesus' declaration of "salvation" to Zacchaeus the "chief toll collector-sinner" reflects a narrative fulfillment of the Isa 40:5 promise to Israel within the Gospel of Luke and serves as a climax to the ministry of Jesus prior to Jerusalem.

Jesus explained that this "salvation" was extended to Zacchaeus because he was a "son of Abraham." This recalls the birth narrative's emphasis on the covenant with Abraham (1:73) and God's present action to bring help by being merciful to Abraham and his "descendants" (1:54–55). The reference to "son of Abraham" also links the present narrative to John's declaration that true children are seen by their repentance (3:7–9). Jesus' mission of "release" is also directed to a "daughter of Abraham" in 13:10–17. In 19:9, Jesus affirms Zacchaeus not only as the intended focus of his mission based on fulfillment of OT promise, but also as an example of a true "son of Abraham" reflected in his repentance.

Jesus broadens the explanation of his declaration of salvation in 19:10.[218] He spoke here of himself in the third person: "The Son of Man 'came' (ἦλθεν) to 'seek' (ζητῆσαι) and to 'save' (σῶσαι) the 'lost' (ἀπολωλός)." The statement is a summary and justification of his entire mission to "sinners." The use of ἦλθεν recalls Jesus' statement in 5:32 that he had "come" (ἐλήλυθα) to call "sinners" to repentance. But the image of "seeking" and "saving" links Jesus' mission statement to the promise in Ezek 34 of the Davidic Shepherd who would "seek" the "lost" of Israel. This also links the present narrative to Luke 15 and combines his role as the Messianic Servant and Herald of "release" with the image of the "seeking" Davidic Shepherd-Prince.

---

through Jesus (4:12; 13:26, 47; 16:17).

218. The use of γάρ looks back to 19:9 (Bock, *Luke 9:51—24:53*, 1521).

Ezekiel 33–34 as Background for Luke 15—19:10

Luke appears to have used Ezek 33–34 as the OT pattern for the ministry of Jesus in Luke 15:1–19:10. The "seeking shepherd" image of Ezek 34 is clearly evident in Luke 15 and Luke 19:8–10. But Ezek 33 provided the OT background for the rebuke of those "confident of their righteousness" in 16:15, and for the parable of the Pharisee and the toll collector in 18:9–14. The Pharisees' rejection of the ministry of Jesus means they stand rebuked. Ezekiel 33 also provided an OT link to Jesus' offer of "forgiveness of sins" to those who repented like the "lost" son, the "toll collector," and Zacchaeus.

Summary

The Zacchaeus narrative summarizes and justifies Jesus' mission to "sinners." The identity of the "sinner" here is not ideological but specific. The "sinner" is Zacchaeus and he is morally guilty of sins against his neighbor consistent with OT categories. The "sinner" in Luke continues to be understood in moral terms. However in this account, it was not the assessment of the Pharisees but the people. This corrects those definitions of the "sinner" that rely almost completely on identifying the "sinner" as simply a label used by the Pharisees. The Zacchaeus narrative also used the OT image of the Davidic "Seeking Shepherd" to explain why Jesus took the initiative in the rescue of the "lost."

Luke 24:7

The context of Luke 24:7 is the burial tomb of Jesus on the morning of the resurrection. Two men in dazzling apparel remind the visiting women that Jesus had told his disciples that he would be delivered (παραδοθῆναι) into the hands of "sinful men" (ἀνθρώπων ἁμαρτωλῶν). This passage is parallel in wording to Mark 14:41 and Matt 26:45 though the setting for Mark 14:41 and Matt 26:5 is in Gethsemane at the approach of Judas and the soldiers who arrested Jesus.

The term ἁμαρτωλῶν may be used here in the sense of "heathen" or "Gentiles."[219] This interpretation is supported by the allusion in Luke 24:7 to Jesus' prophecy in Luke 18:32 that he would be delivered

---

219. Danker identifies these "sinful men" as Gentiles in *Jesus and the New Age* (246).

(παραδοθήσεται) to the Gentiles (ἔθνεσιν). Our examination of the "sinner" in the Old Testament revealed a similar use in the LXX of Isa 14:5 in a taunt against the king of Babylon: "The Lord has broken the staff of the wicked (ἁμαρτωλοί), the scepter of rulers." The wicked here are the Gentile kings. In the Apocrypha, the term ἁμαρτωλός is used in reference to Gentile rulers in Tob 13:8 and 1 Macc 1:34. The usage in Luke 24:7 may be similar to these references. In Luke 23 Jesus is handed over to Pilate and Herod who decide his fate. Both of these men could be described in this Old Testament sense (cf. Acts 4:27 and the application of Ps 2 to Pilate and Herod).

Although the expression ἀνθρώπων ἁμαρτωλῶν may be a reference to Gentiles, the statement by the two heavenly messengers specifically mentions Galilee (Luke 24:6), thus connecting to Jesus' earlier references to these events in his instructions in Galilee (Luke 9:22 and 9:44). The statement by the messengers has several links to Luke 9:22, the reference to the "son of man" (τὸν υἱὸν τοῦ ἀνθρώπου), the use of the divine "must" (δεῖ), and the mention of "rising on the third day." In Luke 9:22, the agents of Jesus' demise are identified as the elders, chief priests, and the scribes. Luke 9:44 also includes a reference to "the son of man" and an explicit reference to being "delivered into the hands of men" (παραδίδουσθαι εἰς χεῖρας ἀνθρώπων), the agents being left identified in very general terms, but no reference to resurrection. Therefore, it seems likely that in Luke 24:7, the reference to Jesus' instructions most explicitly ties to Luke 9:22.[220]

From a narrative perspective, the reader hears the words of the divine messengers from the point of view of the fulfillment of Jesus' prediction. Although Luke 24:7 is the only use of ἁμαρτωλός in the passion narrative, the agents of Jesus' demise who "delivered" Jesus have been identified in the narrative as the scribes and chief priests (20:19–20); Judas (22:4, 6, 21–22, 48); Pilate (23:25); and the chief priests, the rulers, and the people (23:25).

Rather than limiting the expression "sinful men" ἀνθρώπων ἁμαρτωλῶν to only Gentiles, the messengers reflect the point of view of divine judgment that Luke shares.[221] The "sinful men" includes the religious and political leaders of Israel and even the people of Israel who

---

220. Fitzmyer, *Luke X–XXIV*, 1545.
221. Green, *Gospel of Luke*, 838.

participated in the events. This is made clearer in Acts. In the message at Pentecost, Peter speaks of "this man who was handed over by the hands of "lawless" men (ἀνόμων)" (Acts 2:23). Although the narrative of Acts never uses the term ἁμαρτωλός, both Israelites worshipping in Jerusalem (Acts 2:23; 3:13–15) and the members of the Sanhedrin (Acts 4:10; 5:30; 7:52) are accused of killing Jesus, the "Holy and Righteous One." In Acts 7:52, Stephen elevates the accusation against the Sanhedrin, calling them "murderers" (φονεῖς).

Thus, the final use of ἁμαρτωλός in Luke-Acts is used not of those at the center of Jesus' mission as found in Luke 5–19, but of those guilty of rejecting Jesus and participating in his death. This prepares the reader for the conceptual link to this theme in Acts. This use of the "sinner" concept reinforces the idea that the "righteous" and the "sinners" in Luke are evaluated by their response to Jesus. The irony in Luke-Acts is that Jewish "sinners" and Gentiles, usually understood as "sinners" by Jews (cf. Gal 2:15), who respond properly to God's program of salvation in Jesus are right with God. The religious leaders, Jewish and Gentile rulers, and Jews and Gentiles who reject Jesus find themselves "fighting against the Lord and his Anointed."

Conclusion

In conclusion, the following summary points may be made regarding the "sinner" in Luke. First, the "sinner" for Luke is a moral category rooted in OT concepts. The "sinner" is one who violated the revealed will of God in respect to God or his neighbor and is guilty. Luke presents this condition as perilous. The "sinner" is one who is spiritually sick and is in need of a physician (Luke 5:27–32); one who is in great debt to God (7:36–50); one who is in danger of impending disaster (Luke 13:1–9); one who is lost and needs to be found (Luke 15; 19:1–10); and one who stands in great need of mercy (Luke 18:9–14).

Second, for Luke the key antonym, "righteous," includes those who are obedient to the law of God, waiting for the consolation of Israel, and open to Jesus.

Third, for Luke, Jesus' mission to "sinners" reveals Jesus as Messiah and confirms his credentials. Jesus is presented especially as the Servant-

Herald of Isaiah and the Davidic Shepherd of Ezekiel. Therefore, Jesus' mission to "sinners" contributes to Luke's aim of narrating "fulfillment" and providing "assurance" (Luke 1:1–4; 7:21–23).

Fourth, Luke portrays the Pharisees as resistant to Jesus' ministry because of his extraordinary claim to forgive sins and his association with "sinners." Yet for Luke, this is also part of the fulfillment of the theme of reversal. Those who viewed themselves as "righteous" have their hearts revealed. They grumble and are unresponsive to Jesus, revealing that these "righteous" are actually "sinners" and remain in great danger.

Fifth, Jesus' ministry to "sinners" is unprecedented in biblical and Jewish literature. He does not simply warn "sinners" of God's judgment and call them to repent. Jesus claims that he has authority to declare "release." Jesus is also unique in the model of his ministry. He actively seeks out "sinners," eats with them and stays in their homes, all with the single purpose of "seeking and saving the lost."

Sixth, the final use of the term "sinner" in Luke 24:7 is outside of the mission section and in the context of Jesus' passion and resurrection. As the final use of the term in the Lucan corpus, the term provides the divine point of view regarding those who rejected Jesus and participated in his death. This text prepares the reader for how to understand these characters as they are later introduced in Acts.

5

The "Sinner" in Luke

The Identity of the "Sinner"

❧ THE FIRST QUESTION our study set out to address was the identity of the "sinner" in Luke. Our research has demonstrated that for Luke the term "sinner" is primarily a moral category. The key antonym "righteous" served to demonstrate that Luke followed OT categories in defining the "sinner." Basic to the understanding of the term is its association with guilt. The language is legal language of guilt and innocence. Our research has demonstrated that a consistent characteristic of the "sinner" is that he is under the wrath of God. This was true in both Hellenistic and Jewish sources and Luke's usage is consistent with this.

Of special significance is the fact that in the OT God himself serves as the standard that determines who fits the "sinner" or "righteous" labels. God is the judge of all people and nations. The specific standards against which people and nations are measured include the revealed ways and will of God. For Israel, the ways and will of God were displayed in his saving actions, the covenant, and the law. The covenant relationship with Yahweh marked the boundaries for proper human conduct and as a result influenced the notions of "sinner" and "righteous." In the OT and Jewish material, the will of God as revealed in the law served as a primary standard by which one was considered to be a "sinner" or "righteous." Luke's "sinner" is viewed in consistent OT categories as one guilty of violating God's revealed will. The development comes in Luke's understanding of "righteous" to include a proper response to God's action of salvation in Jesus.

The theme of mercy for the "sinner" is present but infrequent in the OT and early intertestamental Jewish literature. The theme became much more frequent in later Pseudepigrapha. Luke's emphasis on a mission to bring forgiveness to "sinners" is unprecedented in the history of the "sinner" concept.

For Luke, the "sinner" is guilty of transgressing the Law and stands under the wrath of God. The "sinner" needs the "knowledge of salvation" that comes through the "forgiveness of sins" by means of repentance. Luke's "sinner" texts have reinforced the identification of the "sinner" in moral terms. First, in Luke 5:1–11, Simon declared himself a "sinner" in direct response to the miraculous catch. The confession is to be understood in moral terms in a context analogous to Isaiah 6.

Second, in Luke 5:27–32, Jesus eats with toll collectors and "sinners." The Pharisees first applied the label but Jesus used the accuracy of the label as the basis for his mission statement that he had come to call "sinners" to repentance. The need for repentance reinforces the understanding of "sinners" as a moral category.

Third, in Luke 6:31–35, in the context of the Sermon on the Plain, Jesus' use of the term "sinners" emphasized characteristics commonly ascribed to "sinners" in the OT. They are self-focused and violate the call to love their neighbor as themselves. The term is used here in a moral sense.

Fourth, in Luke 7:34–50, the term "sinner" is used in the expression "toll collectors and sinners" in 7:34 and of the woman who is clearly identified as a "sinner" on moral grounds in 7:36–50. She was a person in great moral debt to God but one who had received forgiveness.

Fifth, in Luke 13:1–9, the "sinner" term is applied in universal terms and viewed clearly in OT moral categories as a person under wrath and in need of repentance.

Sixth, in Luke 15, the "sinner" is viewed as "lost" and in need of repentance. The illustration of the prodigal son demonstrates a Jewish "sinner" as violating the law of God in moral terms and in need of repentance.

Seventh, in Luke 18:9–14, the toll collector acknowledged himself to be a "sinner" and in need of mercy.

Eighth, in Luke 19:1–10, Zacchaeus was identified as a "sinner" by the "people," demonstrated repentance through his actions, and was declared by Jesus to have been one of the "lost" who had received "salvation."

Ninth, Luke 24:7 speaks of "sinful" men who are guilty of crucifying the Servant-Messiah. These men are "sinners" because they violated the

Law and the expressed will of God. They murdered Jesus who was not only an innocent man, but also the Lord's Anointed (cf., Psalm 2:1, 2; and Acts 4:27). The "sinful men" include the religious and political leaders of Israel and even the people of Israel who participated in the events. This prepares the reader for the conceptual link to this theme in Acts.

In view of our understanding of the "sinner" in Luke as a moral category rooted in OT concepts of the "righteous" and the "sinner," it is now appropriate to give a summary response to the various definitions of the "sinner" introduced in chapter one.

1. The "sinner" is not a synonym for the *'am ha-'areṣ*.[1] The key antonym for the *'am ha-'areṣ* was the *ḥasid*, or the pious, those members of the Pharisees who kept the strictest adherence to the regulations regarding tithing and food laws. Consistent with OT usage, the "sinner" in the Mishnah was opposite of the "righteous." E. P. Sanders was correct in his point that the term "sinner" was not used by the Pharisee as a label for the *'am ha-'areṣ*. As our research has shown, Jeremias was incorrect in proposing that the Pharisees would use the term "sinner" to apply to them.

2. The term "sinner" is not to be understood as merely a sectarian label used by the Pharisees.[2] Although the word was found on occasion in a sectarian context in some intertestamental literature, this was infrequent. The examination of the term "sinner" in the Mishnah also supports the point that the Pharisees applied the label based on violations of the Torah. More importantly, in the Gospel of Luke, when the Pharisees use the term "sinner," Jesus does not reject the term but uses it as a basis for his explanation of his association with them.

3. The expression "toll collectors and sinners" was shown to be helpful in understanding the "sinner" as a moral category but the "despised trades" lists used by Abrahams and Jeremias cannot be used as a basis for filling in the picture of the "sinner" in the Synoptics.[3] The use of the link between "toll collectors and sinners" in the Mishnah is im-

---

1. See the discussion on pages x–xi, and 64–67 above.
2. See the discussion on pages xi–xiii above.
3. See the discussion on pages xiii and 121–24 above.

portant because it is shown to parallel the NT link of "toll collectors" with "sinners," "prostitutes," Gentiles, and others understood to be "sinners" on moral grounds. However, the NT does not make such a link with shepherds, fishermen, or tanners.

4. The term "sinner" cannot be limited to Perrin's definition of a "sinner" as a Jew who made himself as a Gentile.[4] Although the Apocrypha and Pseudepigrapha revealed a great concern over Hellenization, the issue of Gentile association is not raised in the Pharisee "sinner" contexts in Luke.

5. The "sinner" term is also not a technical term for those who "sinned willfully and heinously and would not repent."[5] The "sinner" is guilty of violating the expressed will or character of God in regard to God or one's neighbor. Although it is true "sinners" rarely repented in the OT and Jewish literature examined in our research, it is better to say that the "sinner" stands in great need of repentance. This is Luke's emphasis.

6. The use of the word "sinner" as merely a literary device ignores its links to OT categories of the "righteous" and "sinner."[6]

Luke's "Sinner" and the Mission of Jesus in the Gospel of Luke

The second question our study set out to answer was how understanding Luke's concept of the "sinner" clarified his portrait of Jesus and his mission.

When Luke uses the term "sinner," he uses it from a variety of viewpoints. First, there is the viewpoint of a "would be" disciple, Simon Peter (Luke 5:1–10). He identifies himself as a "sinner" in language similar to Isaiah's vision of the Lord and Abraham's response before Michael, the angel, in the Testament of Abraham 9:3. He knew that he was in the presence of the divine and that made him aware of his own unworthiness. Yet, Peter is still welcome because Jesus came as the Messiah, Servant-Herald, who came to bring "release" to "sinners." The beginning point for becoming a

---

4. See the discussion on pages xiii, 13–16, and 126–130 above.
5. See the discussion on pages xii, 16–19, and 160 above.
6. See the discussion on pages xiii, 19–20, 37–41 above.

disciple of Jesus appears to be the self-perception of one's condition as a "sinner" in need of forgiveness (cf., Luke 7:36–50).

Second, there is the viewpoint of the Pharisees in a specific type-scene: a meal in which Jesus is dining with "tax collectors" and "sinners" (Luke 5:31–32; 7:36–50; 15:2). One of the weaknesses of "sinner" research in the Synoptics has been the problem of limiting the "sinner" discussion to the point of view of the Pharisees. There are nine "sinner" pericopes in Luke, and in five of them Pharisees are not found in the context (5:1–10; 6:31–35; 13:1–9; 19:1–10; 24:7). The Pharisees see the "sinners" as transgressors of the Law and thus to be avoided, especially during meal times. Their reaction was based upon warnings found in the OT, especially the Psalms. The warnings were reinforced in other intertestamental Jewish literature and later found in the Mishnah. The Pharisees viewed the "sinners" as people to be avoided.

Third, there is the viewpoint of Jesus. Jesus clearly understood "sinners" in consistent OT terms as the "guilty" in need of repentance. But Jesus' ministry and message focused on "sinners" from the point of view of their need for salvation. Jeremias was correct in his observation that "sinners" needed to be viewed from Jesus' perspective.[7]

Fourth, there is the viewpoint of the crowd (Luke 19:1–10). In this passage it is the people who designate Zacchaeus a "sinner." Luke's use of the word "grumble" was a link to OT narratives about Israel's pattern of resistance to God's chosen deliverers and their missions. Here, the people are like the Pharisees (Luke 5:30; 15:2) and reflect resistance to Jesus and his mission.

Fifth, there is the viewpoint of our trustworthy narrator, whom we identify as Luke. He presents "sinners" as identifiable types, acknowledged "sinners." He identified the "pious" (Luke 1–2: Zechariah, Elizabeth, Simeon, Anna) in terms of obedience to the law and hope in the consolation of Israel. In contrast, the "sinner" is presented as in need of repentance. Luke knows the difference between the common people (laoi&) and the flagrant "sinner."

Luke presents the "sinner," however, as part of the group Jesus targets for mission and with whom he associates in order to bring them the gospel.

---

7. Jeremias, *New Testament Theology*, 112.

He also includes "disciples" in that category (Peter [Luke 5:8] and Levi [5:27–32]). "Sinners" are often a cause for conflict between Jesus and the Pharisees during which his mission is justified (Luke 5:27–32; 7:35–50; 15:3). The "sinner" also serves to illustrate Luke's theme of reversal. Those who viewed themselves as "righteous" have demonstrated that they are "sinners" by their lack of response to God's salvation plan as revealed in Jesus. In sharp contrast, the "sinners," who rarely repented in the OT and intertestamental literature, reflected openness to John the Baptist and to Jesus. As a result, they receive the "knowledge of salvation," namely, the forgiveness of sins. But Luke especially viewed the "sinner" in terms of fulfillment.

Outside of the mission narrative of Luke 5–19, the final use of the term "sinner" in Luke 24:7, reflects the perspective of both fulfillment of Jesus' predictions and divine judgment upon those who participated in the rejection and death of Jesus. The application of the term "sinner" to the priests, rulers, and even the people, prepares the reader for the material in Acts, in which Peter (Acts 2–5) and Stephen (Acts 7) will directly accuse these groups with this crime against God.

The Pharisees' Objections to Jesus

The third question addressed by our research was the reason for the Pharisees' objection to Jesus' association with "toll collectors" and "sinners." Our research has demonstrated that Pharisaic opposition was rooted in the biblical requirements to avoid such types. Jesus' association with "sinners" caused him to be treated with suspicion. How could he be a prophet if he broke the law by associating with the "wicked"? In the eyes of the "righteous," his role as prophet was inconsistent with his conduct.

The "Sinner" and Fulfillment in Luke

A fourth question addressed by our research is the role the "sinner" theme plays in Luke's understanding of fulfillment. Luke presented Jesus as the fulfillment of God's promised salvation by proclaiming his mission in terms of OT salvation themes and images. Luke portrayed Jesus as the Messianic Servant of Yahweh who was the Anointed Herald of "release." The "sinner" was in need of the "release" of forgiveness of sins (Luke 5:8, 27–32). Jesus claimed the role not of simply a prophet promising release, but the

Anointed One who had authority on earth to proclaim the year of Jubilee and the release of the debt of sin (7:36–50). Luke portrayed Jesus also as the Davidic Seeking Shepherd of Ezekiel who sought "sinners" who were the scattered "lost" sheep of Israel. Both the image of Shepherd and of Anointed Herald could be seen in Jesus' view of "sinners" as the "sick" in need of the medicine of repentance that only he could offer (Luke 5:27–32). But Jesus also fulfilled the role of Jonah, warning that unless "sinners" repented, they would perish (13:1–5). In contrast to Jonah who directed his warning to the Gentiles of Nineveh, Jesus reversed the expectation by addressing his warning to everyone in Israel, broadening his category of "sinner" to include even the Pharisees (18: 9–14).

Luke saw Jesus as the fulfillment of everything written in Moses, the Psalms, and the Prophets (Luke 24:44). Luke viewed the "sinner" as a way to reveal the scope and nature of the fulfillment of God's promised salvation. It is appropriate to conclude, in view of the use of the term "sinner" in all the literature and tested against Luke's use, that he understood Jesus' mission to "sinners" to be a summons to real "sinners" inviting them into the kingdom of God. Jesus' preaching the gospel to "sinners" is a "sign" that the Messianic times have arrived (Luke 7:22).

Jesus' table fellowship with "sinners" was a special emphasis for Luke. He viewed meal fellowship as an occasion for Jesus' offer of forgiveness of sins. Proper response to Jesus granted forgiveness and entrance into the Kingdom. Table fellowship then became a preview of the Kingdom banquet. As stated earlier, Pharisaic opposition to Jesus' association with "sinners" was rooted in biblical requirements to avoid them. Yet Jesus came as One greater than Jonah to real "sinners" within Judaism, and he ministered to them from the point of view of God's mercy. Jesus claimed unique authority in his offer of forgiveness, not on the authority of OT promise but on the authority of his role as Prophet and Anointed Herald of Isaiah, the Servant of Yahweh. How could he be a true prophet if he broke the law by associating with the "wicked"? The answer is that Jesus viewed the "sinner" from the viewpoint of redemption. He took the initiative in calling "sinners" because he had come to seek and to save those who were lost.

Finally, the use of "sinner" in Luke 24:7 reflects an intra-narrative fulfillment within Luke that will become part of the standard preaching formula in the early chapters of Acts. Jesus' rejection was previewed in the prophecy of Simeon that Jesus would cause the rising and falling of many in Israel and would become a sign spoken against (Luke 2:34). Jesus made explicit statements predicting his rejection and death beginning in Luke 9:22 (cf. 9:44; 18:31–32), later tying this prediction to the writings of the prophets (18:31). In the early chapters of Acts, those who participated in the rejection and death of Jesus are accused directly by Peter for their complicity (Acts 2:22–23; 3:13–15; 5:30–31) but informed that these events were part of God's plan and foreknowledge (Acts 2:23) and the means of fulfilling the prophets (Acts 3:18-26). Paul repeats this theme in the sermon at Pisidian Antioch (Acts 13:27).

The Role of the "Sinner" in Luke-Acts

The final issue addressed by our research was the role the "sinner" theme plays in Luke-Acts. As Denova suggests, Luke appears to use Isaiah as a general outline for the presentation of the fulfillment of God's salvation in Jesus in Luke-Acts.[8] He uses Isaiah for his general theological guide, revealing many themes, all under the primary emphasis expressed in the words "all flesh shall see the salvation of God" (Isa 40:5). This emphasis can be outlined as follows.

1) Preparing a repentant people (Isa 40:3–5)

   a) Within Israel (Isa 40:3–4): Luke 1:17, 76–77; 2:30; 3:3–6; 24:47; Acts 2:38–40; 3:19–23; 5:31

   b) From all nations (Isa 40:5; 59:8): Luke 24:47; Acts 11:18; 20:21; 26:20–23; 28:28

2) Granting release to those in darkness (Isa 61:1,2; 58:6; 59:5; 35:5)

   a) Within Israel (Isa 61:1–2; 58:6): Luke 4:18–19; 6:20–21; 7:22; 9:1–6; 10:1–9; Acts 2:38; 3:19; 5:31)

   b) To all nations (Isa 59:5; 35:5): Luke 24:47; Acts 10:43; 26:18.

3) Sifting of Israel based on response to Jesus (Isa 8:14; 5:1–7): Luke 2:34; 12:51–53; 13:6; 14:15–24; 20:18 (cf. Luke 3:17 and Isa 30:24)

---

8. See page xv above.

4) Judicial condemnation and hardening of the unrepentant (Isa 6:9, 10): Luke 8:10; Acts 28:26

5) Suffering of the Servant-Messiah (Isa 53): Luke 11:22, 22:37; 23:43; 24:25; Acts 3:13; 8:32

6) God's salvation "seen" by the Gentiles (Isa 40:5; 42:6; 49:6; 52:10): Luke 2:30–32; 3:6; 24:47; Acts 1:8; 28:28

7) Restoration of Zion by the Messiah (Isa 52:9): Luke 2:25, 38; 24:21; Acts 1:6; 3:21

The "sinner" texts within the Gospel of Luke serve as illustrations and as proclamation of the fulfillment of the first four themes listed above. Luke 5:1–32 emphasizes the first three themes. Luke 6:32–36 is found in the larger context of the Sermon on the Plain, which is directed to Jesus' followers and fits primarily under the first theme of preparing a repentant people. Luke 7:36–50 and 15:1–32 fall under theme one but especially theme two of granting release. Luke 18:9–14 and 19:1–10 illustrate and proclaim fulfillment under theme two, but especially theme one. Luke 24:7 falls under themes three (sifting Israel), four (judicial condemnation), and five (suffering of the Messiah). Theme four and theme five are part of the preaching in Acts. Theme six (Gentile salvation) is introduced in Luke but fulfilled in Acts. Theme seven (restoration of Zion) is also promised in Luke and restated as unfulfilled promise in Acts (Acts 1:6; 3:21).

The theme of fulfillment is introduced in Luke's prologue as one of his purposes in writing (Luke 1:1–4). The content of this fulfillment included the "knowledge of salvation through the forgiveness of sins" (Luke 1:77). In Luke 2:29–32, upon seeing Jesus, Simeon declared that his eyes had seen the Lord's salvation. This salvation had been prepared in the sight of all people. It was to be a light for revelation to the Gentiles and for glory to the Lord's people, Israel. Simeon went on to tell Mary that her child would be destined to cause the falling and rising of many in Israel, and a sign that will be spoken against, so that the thoughts of many hearts will be revealed (Luke 2:34, 35).

The words of Simeon highlight themes of universal mission and Jewish opposition. The theme of opposition begins in Luke (here in Luke 2:34, 35 and Luke 4:22–30) and continues in Acts (Acts 4:1–3; 5:17–40).

However, although the universal mission is prophesied in Luke (cf., 3:6, "*All flesh shall see God's salvation*"; 24:47), Jesus' ministry in the Gospel of Luke focused upon "the people of Israel."

In his sermon at Nazareth in Luke 4:16–18, Jesus set forth his mission in terms of the fulfillment of Isaiah 61:1–2. Robert Tannehill demonstrates that this passage sets the course for Jesus' mission in Luke and the broadening mission in Acts.[9] It is in the "sinner" material that Luke presented several key mission statements (Luke 5:27–32; 19:10). Links are made that will be repeated in Acts. Several expressions are made that become key to understanding Jesus' mission for Luke: "preaching the gospel (εὐαγγελίζομαι) to the poor"; "preaching (κηρύσσω) "release" (ἄφεσιν) to the captives"; and "recovering sight for the blind." Jesus' proclamation of his mission to bring release (ἄφεσιν) to the captives in Luke 4:18 (ἄφεσιν) becomes expressed in offering forgiveness of sins to Jewish and later to Gentile "sinners" (5:20–24; 7:47–49; 24:47; Acts 2:28; 5:31; 10:43; 13:38; 26:18).[10]

When the synagogue crowd began asking, "Isn't this Joseph's son?" apparently with a tone of rejection, Jesus created a mob scene when he cited Old Testament precedents for both the rejection of God's prophets by Israel and the extension of God's favor toward Gentiles (Luke 4:22–27). The Nazareth sermon emphasizes themes of fulfillment, preaching the gospel, forgiveness, rejection, and Gentile mission that provide a link between Jesus' mission in Luke and the pattern of the apostles' mission in Acts. When Jesus began his Galilean ministry, one aspect of his mission of "release" was taking the gospel to "sinners" in need of repentance and forgiveness *within* Judaism (Luke 5:8, 20–26, 27–31). And though Jesus applauds the faith of a Gentile centurion in Luke 7:1–10, he does not launch a Gentile mission in Luke. Yet his affirmation of Gentile faith in the Gospel of Luke provided a link for Luke's readers in Acts 10, when another centurion becomes the first official Gentile to be admitted into the church.

An examination of Peter's vision and the ministry to Cornelius in Acts 10–11 reveals many of the same key issues related to the Pharisees' opposi-

---

9. Tannehill, *The Narrative Unity of Luke-Acts*, 1:160–73.
10. Ibid., 1:60–68, 103–108.

tion to Jesus' association with "sinners" and toll collectors. Table fellowship plays a key role in the controversy. Elliott is correct when he states:

> Household scenarios and domestic imagery serve the unfolding of distinctively Lucan christological, soteriological, and ecclesiological themes: Jesus Christ as exalted Servant and Benefactor; salvation for the lost and the lowly, women and outcasts, Gentiles and sinners; repentance and forgiveness; almsgiving and mercy; hospitality and table-fellowship. The household, in fact, functions as Luke's prime metaphor for depicting social life in the kingdom of God.[11]

In Luke 14:13, Jesus' invitation to the kingdom banquet included the "poor, the crippled, the lame, and the blind." In Luke 13:29, Jesus declared, "People will come from east and west and north and south, and will take their places at the feast in the kingdom of God." Outcasts (the crippled, lame, blind) and even Gentiles will enjoy the kingdom banquet.[12] As stated, Jesus' table fellowship with "sinners" was an invitation to receive forgiveness of sins and a place at the kingdom banquet. As observed in our discussion of Luke 15, there are clear narrative links to Luke 13 and 14. When the Gentiles are included in Acts, this promise was partially fulfilled.

There are other links between Jesus' mission in Luke and the mission to the Gentiles in Acts. As noted, in Jesus' opening statement of his mission in the sermon at Nazareth in Luke 4, the listeners sought to kill Jesus when he used the Elijah and Elisha stories to demonstrate God's mercy toward Gentiles (Luke 4:25–29). When Paul described his ministry to the Jews in Acts 22, the crowd sought to take Paul's life when he stated that he had been commanded by the Lord to take the message far away to the Gentiles (Acts 22:21–22).

In Luke, Jesus' preaching of the gospel to "sinners" is a "sign" that Messianic times had arrived (Luke 7:22). In the same way, in Acts, Gentile inclusion is not simply seen as a judgment upon unbelieving Israel. Gentile mission is also a sign that the day of eschatological release has arrived (Acts 15:14–18). As a result, "all flesh," both Jewish "sinners" in Israel and Gentiles at the "ends of the earth," would "see the salvation of God" (cf. Acts

---

11. Elliott, "Temple versus Household," 117.

12. Marshall agrees that this is a reference to the fact that Gentiles can qualify for admission to the kingdom banquet (*Commentary on Luke*), 568.

15:16–17). With Paul's ministry, the theme of "light to the Gentiles," first introduced in Luke 2:32, finds its fulfillment in Acts 13:47 and 26:23.

A Proposal Regarding the Role of the "Sinner" in Luke-Acts

Our proposal is that Jesus' mission to "sinners" and his comments about Gentiles in Luke prepare the reader for the mission to Gentiles in Acts. J. T. Sanders draws a similar conclusion by noting that the place of the toll-collectors and "sinners" in the Gospel (Luke) is taken by the Gentiles in Acts.[13] He observes that the "sinners" in Luke's Gospel are pictured as those who respond to Jesus in contrast to the religiously devout who reject Jesus. In Acts, the Gentiles are presented as those who respond in faith in contrast to the unresponsiveness of the Jews.[14] Luke uses a term that, according to our research, referred to Jewish "sinners" and to Gentiles in general. Luke provided a subtle linkage in the readers' mind to demonstrate how a Jewish religious sect made up fishermen, toll collectors, and "sinners," which claimed to have found the Messiah, became a religion with a wide Gentile following. Luke's answer is that the "repentant Jewish sinners" and "repentant Gentile" followers of Jesus represent fulfillment of God's promise of universal salvation.

As demonstrated in our analysis of the birth narrative, Isaiah 40:3–5 played an important role in defining the nature and scope of God's new salvation plan inaugurated through Jesus. The central text was Isaiah 40:5: "All flesh shall see the salvation of God." Luke used the term "sinner" to define those within Judaism who were included in the notion "all flesh." Jesus revealed this salvation to all whose eyes and heart were open to see it. Even "toll collectors" and "sinners" were welcome to the banquet. In Acts, the notion "all flesh" would broaden in scope to include the Gentiles. The OT promise regarding Gentiles was to be fulfilled in the mission of Jesus' apostles (Luke 24:45–49; Acts 1:8; cf. Isa 49:6). The book of Acts closes with an allusion to Isaiah 40:5. Paul had just quoted Isaiah 6 to his Jewish visitors, warning them of the consequences of unresponsiveness. He then declared that the "salvation of God" had been sent to the Gentiles (Acts 28:28). Acts ends with Paul following the pattern that Jesus established in

13. Sanders, *The Jews in Luke-Acts*, 134.
14. Ibid., 135.

the Gospel. Jesus "welcomed" "sinners" as a means of inviting them into the kingdom. Luke used this as his closing image in Acts. Paul "welcomed" all who came to see him and he preached to them about the kingdom of God and taught them about the Lord Jesus Christ (Acts 28:30–31). Part of the purpose of Luke in writing to Theophilus was to set forth this fulfillment of God's saving plan "in order" (Luke 1:1–4).

Luke's final use of ἁμαρτωλός is found in Luke 24:7, in the context of the resurrection narrative. As stated in the beginning of our study, the emphasis on this term in the Gospel of Luke makes its absence in Acts curious at the least. However, the use in Luke 24:7 may provide a clue for a major reversal in Acts. In Acts, those who participated in the rejection and death of Jesus are culpable before God and called upon to repent. Although the term "sinner" is not used, terms such as "lawless," "betrayer," and even "murderer" are applied to them. Luke will provide labels and descriptions of characters who would be clearly viewed as "sinners" by his readers. For example, "murderers" would fit the sinner label not only in the Old Testament, but also in the Greek and Roman world (cf., Acts 5:28, 30; 7:52). The absence of the term ἁμαρτωλός in Acts appears to be due to a narrative strategy in which Luke describes individuals in such a way that invites his readers to apply the term. Luke intends his readers to view certain people in Acts as "sinners," without directly labeling them as such.

One example of this is evident due to the fact that in our research a consistent implication of being a "sinner" in Jewish and Greek literature was being under the wrath of God or the gods.[15] In Acts, those who participated in Jesus' demise are in danger of judgment and must repent (Acts 2:36–40; 3:13–15, 19). Luke's statement regarding Judas' "bowels bursting" (Acts 2:18) would communicate to his readers that Judas had died under divine judgment.[16] In addition, those who oppress or harm those preaching the gospel experience divine judgment. For example, in Acts 9:8, Saul experienced judicial blinding for opposing Jesus, just as Elymas did in opposing Paul's preaching in Acts 13:11. In Acts 12, Herod Agrippa

---

15. See chapter two of this study.

16. Death linked to divine judgment and "bowels" is found in the death of King Joram (2 Chr 21:18–19); the death of Antiochus Epiphanes (2 Macc 9:5–7, 9–10, 28); the death of Aristobulus (*J.W.* 1.70-84); and the death of Herod the Great (*J.W.* 1.654–665; Acts 12:23).

I executed James, arrested Peter, and is dealt a death blow by an angel from God (12:23). Although Luke does not use the term ἁμαρτωλός, because of the exercise of the wrath of God, the reader of Acts would have understood him as such. In contrast, Luke makes it clear to the reader that Paul the evangelist and his associates are innocent of crimes, wrongs, evil, temple robbing, blasphemy against the gods, causing riots, having such innocence declared by Roman officials (Acts 18:14; 19:37). That Paul was not a "sinner" under the wrath of God/gods is also illustrated in Acts 28:4 which describes the island inhabitants of Malta, after Paul was bitten by a poisonous snake, declaring him to be a murderer whom the gods had not permitted to escape justice. Because Paul suffered no ill effects, the people viewed him no longer as a criminal but as a god (Acts 28:6).

A second example is based upon our research on the "sinner" in the Psalms. One specific category of "sinner" in the Psalms was anyone who resisted or treated God's anointed unjustly.[17] In Acts 4:25–26, Luke has Peter quote the LXX of Ps 2:1–2 precisely. In Acts 4:27, Peter identifies those fighting against the Lord and his anointed as Herod Antipas, Pilate, the Gentiles, and the people of Israel who had gathered against the Lord's holy servant Jesus, whom the Lord had anointed (cf., the danger of "fighting against God" as stated directly to the Sanhedrin by Gamaliel in Acts 5:39). Luke has explicitly linked the concept of harming God's anointed to the events of the passion, reflecting the assessment of the divine messengers in Luke 24:7 that those identified are indeed "sinners." Again, although the term "sinner" is not used here, Luke has provided a conceptual link that invites this label to be understood by his readers.

If the above point is correct, Luke's portrayal of Saul in Acts can be understood in this light. Saul is introduced in the context of Stephen's execution in which Saul participates (Acts 7:58; 8:1). Stephen had just charged the Sanhedrin with resisting the Holy Spirit (Acts 7:51) and betraying and murdering the Righteous One (Acts 7:52). This narrative is preceded by Saul's mentor Gamaliel warning the Sanhedrin of the danger of finding themselves "fighting against God" (Acts 5:39). Immediately after Stephen's death, Saul launched his attempt to "destroy the church" (Acts 8:3). When Jesus encountered Saul on the road to Damascus, Saul is questioned regard-

---

17. For example, Pss 2:10–12 and 37:20. See the discussion on pages 30ff. above and Croft, *Identity*, 46.

ing his persecution (διώκεις) of Jesus (Acts 9:4–5).[18] From the narrative perspective, Saul had resisted the Holy Spirit, fought against God, and persecuted Jesus, the Lord's Anointed. Although Luke does not use the "sinner" term, the use of the term in the Psalms and Luke 24:7, and the link to Ps 2:1 in Acts 4:25–27 all imply that the term should be applied to Saul by the reader.[19]

In the final chapter of Luke-Acts, Paul defends his innocence before God and before Rome to the local Jewish leaders in Rome (Acts 28:17–19). After his personal defense, Paul testified to them concerning Jesus as Messiah (Acts 28:23). As the readers have come to expect, the leaders were divided in their response (cf. Luke 2:34; 4:19–30; 8:9). Paul cites Isa 6:9 warning his hearers of the danger of divine judicial hardening for unresponsive.

Conclusion

A contribution of our research toward Lucan studies is the clarification of a key concept in Luke's presentation of Jesus and his mission. Who is the "sinner" in Luke? The "sinner" is a person who is guilty of violating the will of God as revealed in the law and thus under the danger of God's wrath. This definition of the "sinner" in Luke helps our understanding of Jesus' mission directed to "sinners." He presented himself as the Anointed Servant-Herald who came to announce liberty and to bring "release" to "sinners." This "release" included forgiveness of sins. For the Pharisees, Jesus' association with "sinners" was a reason to be suspicious of his credentials as a prophet. For Luke, Jesus' mission to "sinners" served to reveal and validate his credentials as Messiah. Jesus was the fulfillment of OT promises of salvation. This salvation was universal in scope. For Luke, Isaiah's promise that "all flesh" would see God's salvation included genuine "sinners" within Israel and even Gentiles at the "ends of the earth." In conclusion, our research has shown that Luke used the term "sinner" to present the nature, target, and

---

18. Luke uses διώκεις six times, all in Acts in the context of Paul's encounter with Jesus (9:4, 5; 22:7, 8; 26:14, 15).

19. This has implications for the debate regarding whether to view Saul's experience on the road to Damascus as a "conversion" or "call" or both. Krister Stendahl championed the now common view that Saul is simply being called since he does not change religions (Stendahl, *Paul Among the Jews*, 7-23). If our reading of the narrative is correct, then the event should be viewed as a "conversion-call" story (cf., Luke 5:1-11; Barrett, *Acts*, 1:444).

scope of Jesus' mission in the Gospel of Luke, and to prepare his reader for the widening mission through the apostles to the Gentiles in Acts.

Although the term "sinner" is not found in Acts, Luke uses descriptions that invite his readers to apply the label. The final use of ἁμαρτωλός in Luke–Acts, Luke 24:7, provides the conceptual bridge to Acts in which the rejection of Jesus or opposition to the preaching about Jesus is described as opposing God and placing one under his wrath. The great irony of Luke-Acts is that Jewish "sinners" and Gentiles who respond to the gospel (Acts 28:28–29) receive the promised salvation. But those who reject God's program of salvation in Jesus as expressed in the gospel message of Peter and Paul stand in danger of divine wrath and as a consequence would be worthy of the "sinner" label from the narrative perspective.

Bibliography

Abrahams, Israel. *Studies in Pharisaism and the Gospels.* 2 vols. Cambridge: Cambridge University Press, 1917, 1924. Reprint, New York: Ktav, 1967.

Alexander, Loveday. *The Preface to Luke's Gospel: Literary Convention and Social Context in Luke 1.1–4 and Acts 1.1.* SNTSMS 78. Cambridge: Cambridge University Press, 1993.

Anderson, A. A. *Introduction and Psalms 1–72.* NCB. Grand Rapids: Eerdmans, 1972.

———. *Psalms 73–150.* NCB. Grand Rapids: Eerdmans, 1972.

Aristophanes. *Thesmorphoriazusai.* Edited by T. E. Page. Translated by Benjamin Rickley Rogers. LCL. Cambridge: Harvard University Press, [1924] 1955.

Aristotle. *The Nicomachean Ethics.* Edited by T. E. Page. Translated by H. Racham. LCL. Cambridge: Harvard University Press, [1926] 1956.

Augustine. *The Works of Saint Augustine.* Vol. 4. Translated by Edmund Hill. Brooklyn: New City, 1992.

Barrett, C. K. *A Critical and Exegetical Commentary on the Acts of the Apostles.* Vol. 1: *Acts I–XIV.* ICC. Edinburgh: T. & T. Clark, 1994.

Bauer, Walter. *A Greek-English Lexicon of the New Testament and Other Early Christian Literature.* Translated by William F. Arndt and F. Wilbur Gingrich. 2d ed. Revised and augmented by F. Wilbur Gingrich and Frederick W. Danker. Chicago: University of Chicago Press, 1979.

Blass, Friedrich, Albert Debrunner, and Robert W. Funk. *A Greek Grammar of the New Testament and Other Early Christian Literature.* Chicago: University of Chicago Press, 1961.

Bock, Darrell. L. *Proclamation from Prophecy to Pattern: Lucan Old Testament Christology.* JSNTSup 12. Sheffield: Sheffield Academic Press, 1987.

———. *Luke 1:1—9:50.* BECNT 3A. Grand Rapids: Baker, 1994.

———. *Luke 9:51—24:53.* BECNT 3B. Grand Rapids: Baker, 1994.

———. "Scripture and the Realisation of God's Promises." In *Witness to the Gospel: The Theology of Acts,* edited by I. Howard Marshall and David Peterson, 41–62. Grand Rapids: Eerdmans, 1998.

Boeckh, August, Johannes Franz, Ernst Curtius, and Adolf Kirchoff, editors. *Corpus inscriptionum graecarum.* 4 vols. Berlin: Akademie der Wissenschaften, 1828–77.

Bonsirven, Joseph. *Palestinian Judaism in the Time of Jesus Christ.* Translated by William Wolf. New York: McGraw-Hill, 1964.

Borg, Marcus. *Conflict, Holiness and Politics in the Teachings of Jesus.* New York: Mellen, 1984.

Bouwman, G. "La pécherese hospitalière (Lc., 7, 36–50)." *ETL* 45 (1969) 172–79.

Bowker, John. *Jesus and the Pharisees.* Cambridge: Cambridge University Press, 1973.

Brawley, Robert L. *Luke-Acts and the Jews: Conflict, Apology, and Conciliation.* SBLMS 33. Atlanta: Scholars, 1987.

Brown, Colin, editor. *New International Dictionary of New Testament Theology.* Grand Rapids: Zondervan, 1975–85.

Brown, Francis, S. R. Driver, and Charles Briggs, editors. *A Hebrew and English Lexicon of the Old Testament.* Oxford: Clarendon, 1979.

Bruce, F. F. *New Testament History.* Garden City, NY: Doubleday, 1969.

Buchanan, George W. Review of *Studies in Pharisaism and the Gospels* by Israel Abrahams. *CBQ* (1968) 415–16.

Büchler, Adolf. *Der galiläische 'Am-ha 'Areṣ des zweiten Jahrhunderts.* Vienna: Holder, 1906.

———. "The Levitical Impurity of the Gentile." *JQR* 17 (1926) 1–81.

Burridge, Richard A. *What Are the Gospels? A Comparison with Graeco-Roman Biography.* SNTSMS 70. New York: Cambridge University Press, 1992.

Bussby, Frederick. "Did a Shepherd Leave Sheep upon the Mountains or in the Desert? A Note on Matthew 18.12 and Luke 15.4." *ATR* 45 (1963) 93–94.

Cadbury, Henry J. *The Making of Luke-Acts.* New York: Macmillan, 1927.

Caesar, Julius. *Civil Wars.* Translated by A. G. Peskett. Edited by G. P. Goold. LCL. Cambridge: Harvard University Press, [1914] 1979.

Calvin, John. *Commentary On A Harmony of the Evangelists, Matthew, Mark, and Luke.* Translated by William Pringle. 2 vols. Edinburgh: Calvin Translation Society, 1845.

Charlesworth, James H. *Jesus Within Judaism.* Garden City: Doubleday, 1988.

———, editor. *The Old Testament Pseudepigrapha.* 2 vols. New York: Doubleday, 1983–85.

Chilton, Bruce D. "Jesus and the Repentance of E. P. Sanders." *TynBul* 39 (1988) 1–18.

———. "Announcement in Nazara: An Analysis of Luke 4:16–21." In *Studies of History and Tradition in the Four Gospels,* edited by R. T. France and David Wenham, 147–72. Gospel Perspectives 2. Sheffield: JSOT Press, 1981.

Cicero, *Against Verres.* Translated by N. H. Watts. Edited by G. P. Goold. LCL. Cambridge: Harvard University Press, [1923] 1979.

———. *Pro Cnaeo Plancio.* Translated by N. H. Watts. Edited by G. P. Goold. LCL. Cambridge: Harvard University Press, [1923] 1979.

Coleridge, Mark. *The Birth of the Lukan Narrative: Narrative Christology in Luke 1–2.* JSNTSup 88. Sheffield: JSOT Press, 1993.

Combrink, H. J. B. "The Structure and Significance of Luke 4:16–30." *Neot* 7 (1973) 40–41.

Corley, Kathleen E. "Jesus' Table Practice: Dining with 'Tax Collectors and Sinners,' including Women." In *SBLSP,* edited by Eugene H. Lovering, Jr., 444–59. Atlanta: Scholars, 1993.

Crockett, Larrimore C. "Luke 4:25–27 and Jewish-Gentile Relations in Luke–Acts." *JBL* 88 (1969) 177–83.

Croft, Steven J. L. *The Identity of the Individual in the Psalms.* JSOTSup 44. Sheffield: JSOT Press, 1987.

Cyril. *Commentary on the Gospel of Saint Luke.* Translated by R. Payne Smith. *N.p.* Studion, 1983.

Bibliography

Dahl, Nils A. "The Story of Abraham in Luke-Acts." In *Studies in Luke-Acts*, edited by Leander E. Keck and J. Louis Martyn, 139-158. Philadelphia: Fortress, 1966.

Danby, Herbert, translator. *The Mishnah*. New York: Oxford University Press, 1933.

Danker, Frederick W. *Jesus and the New Age: A Commentary on St. Luke's Gospel*. St. Louis: Clayton, 1972.

Darr, John A. *On Character Building: The Reader and the Rhetoric of Characterization in Luke-Acts*. Louisville: Westminster John Knox, 1992.

Delorme, Jean. "Luc v. 1–11: Analyse Structurale et Histoire de la Rédaction." *NTS* 18 (1972) 331–50.

Denova, Rebecca I. *The Things Accomplished Among Us: Prophetic Traditions in the Structural Patterns of Luke–Acts*. JSNTSup 141. Sheffield: Sheffield Academic, 1997.

Derrett, J. Duncan M. *Jesus's Audience: The Social and Psychological Environment in which He Worked*. New York: Seabury, 1973.

———. "Law in the New Testament: The Parable of the Prodigal Son." *NTS* 14 (1967) 56–74.

———. "Fresh Light on the Lost Sheep and the Lost Coin." *NTS* 26 (1979) 36–60.

Diodorus Siculus. Translated by C. H. Oldfather. Edited by T. E. Page. LCL. Cambridge: Harvard University Press, 1916.

Dittenberger, Wilhelm, editor. *Orientis graeci inscriptiones selectae*. 2 vols. Leipzig: Hirzel, 1903–5.

Dodd, C. H. *The Founder of Christianity*. New York: Macmillan, 1970.

Donahue, John R. "Tax Collectors and Sinners." *CBQ* 33 (1971) 39–61.

Donohue, John J. "The Penitent Woman and the Pharisee: Luke 7:36–50." *AER* 142 (1960) 414–21.

Drexler, Hans "Die grosse Sünderin Lucas 7:36–50." *ZNW* 59 (1968) 159–73.

Dunn, James D. G. "Pharisees, Sinners, and Jesus." In *The Social World of Formative Christianity and Judaism*, Edited by Jacob Neusner, 264–89. Philadelphia: Fortress, 1988.

Elliott, John Hall. "Temple versus Household in Luke–Acts: A Contrast in Social Institutions." *HvTSt* 47 (1991) 88–120.

Ellis, E. Earle. *The Gospel of Luke*. NCB. Grand Rapids: Eerdmans, 1966.

Evans, Craig A. *Life of Jesus Research: An Annotated Bibliography*. NTTS 13. Leiden: Brill, 1989.

———. *Jesus*. Grand Rapids: Baker, 1992.

———. *The Gospel of Luke*. NIBCNT 3. Peabody, MA: Hendrickson, 1990.

Farmer, William R. "Who are the 'Tax Collectors and Sinners' in the Synoptic Tradition?" In *From Faith to Faith: Essays in Honor of Donald G. Miller on His Seventieth Birthday*, 167–74. PTMS 31. Pittsburgh: Pickwick, 1979.

Farris, Stephen. *The Hymns of Luke's Infancy Narrative*. JSNTSup 9. Sheffield: JSOT Press, 1985.

Feldman, Louis H. *Jew and Gentile in the Ancient World*. Princeton, New Jersey: Princeton University Press, 1993.

Finkelstein, Louis. *The Pharisees: The Sociological Background of Their Faith*. Philadelphia: Jewish Publication Society, 1938.

Bibliography

Fitzmyer, Joseph A. *The Gospel According to Luke I–IX.* AB 28. Garden City, NY: Doubleday, 1981.

———. *The Gospel According to Luke X–XXIV.* AB 28a. Garden City, NY: Doubleday, 1985.

Ford, J. Massyngberde. *My Enemy Is My Guest: Jesus and Violence in Luke.* Maryknoll, NY: Orbis, 1984.

García Martínez, Florentino. *The Dead Sea Scrolls Translated.* 2d ed. Translated by Wilfred G. E. Watson. Leiden: Brill, 1994.

Gibson, J. "Hoi telōnai kai hai pornai." *JTS* 32 (1981) 429–33.

Giblin, Charles Homer. "Structural and Theological Considerations on Luke 15." *CBQ* 24 (1962) 15–31.

Gowler, David B. *Host, Guest, Enemy, and Friend: Portraits of the Pharisees in Luke and Acts.* ESEC 2. New York: Lang, 1991.

Grabbe, Lester L. *Judaism From Cyrus to Hadrian.* 2 vols. Minneapolis: Fortress, 1992.

Green, Joel B. *The Gospel of Luke.* NICNT. Grand Rapids: Eerdmans, 1997.

Harrison, R. K. *Introduction to the Old Testament.* Grand Rapids: Eerdmans, 1969.

Harvey, A. E. *Jesus and the Constraints of History.* Philadelphia: Westminster, 1982.

Hengel, Martin, and Roland Deines, "E. P. Sanders' 'Common Judaism', Jesus, and the Pharisees." *JTS* 46 (1995) 1–70.

Henry, Matthew. *Matthew to John.* An Exposition of the Old and New Testament 5. Chicago: Fleming Revell, 1721.

Hoerber, Robert George. "'God Be Merciful to Me a Sinner': A Note on Luke 18:13." *CTM* 33 (1962) 283–86.

Homer, *The Illiad.* Translated by A. T. Murray. Edited by T. E. Page. LCL. Cambridge: Harvard University Press, [1924] 1965.

Jeremias, Joachim. *Jerusalem in the Time of Jesus.* 3d. ed. Translated by F. H. Cave and C. H. Cave. Philadelphia : Fortress, 1969.

———. *New Testament Theology.* Translated by John Bowden. New York: Scribner, 1971.

———. *The Parables of Jesus.* 2d ed. Translated by S. H. Hooke. New York: Scribner, 1954.

———. "Zöllner und Sünder." *ZNW* 30 (1931) 293–300.

Johnson, Luke T. *The Literary Function of Possessions in Luke-Acts.* SBLDS 39. Missoula, MT: Scholars, 1977.

Josephus. *Against Apion.* Translated by H. St. J. Thackeray. Edited by G. P. Goold. LCL. Cambridge: Harvard University Press, 1926.

———. *Jewish Antiquities, Books IX–XI.* Translated by Ralph Marcus. Edited by G. P. Goold. LCL. Cambridge: Harvard University Press, 1927.

———. *Jewish Antiquities, Books XII–XIV.* Translated by Ralph Marcus. Edited by G. P. Goold. LCL. Cambridge: Harvard University Press, 1936.

———. *Jewish Antiquities, Books XV–XVII.* Translated by Ralph Marcus. Edited by Allen Witgren. LCL. Cambridge: Harvard University Press, 1927.

———. *The Jewish War, Books I–III.* Translated by H. St. J. Thackeray. Edited by G. P. Goold. LCL. Cambridge: Harvard University Press, 1939.

———. *The Jewish War, Books IV–VII.* Translated by H. St. J. Thackeray. Edited by G. P. Goold. LCL. Cambridge: Harvard University Press, 1939.

Bibliography

———. *The Jewish War, Books I–III*. Translated by H. St. J. Thackeray. Edited by G. P. Goold. LCL. Cambridge: Harvard University Press, 1939.

———. *Life*. Translated by H. St. J. Thackeray. Edited by G. P. Goold. LCL. Cambridge: Harvard University Press, 1926.

Juel, Donald. *Luke-Acts: The Promise of History*. Atlanta: John Knox, 1983.

Justin Martyr. *First Apology*. Ancient Christian Writers 56. Edited by W. Burghardt, J. J. Dillon, and D. D. McManus. New York: Paulist Press, 1997.

Kasovsky, Chayim. *Thesaurus Mishnahe* 4. Jerusalem: Massadah, 1960.

Kee, Howard Clark. *Christian Origins in Sociological Perspective*. Philadelphia: Westminster, 1980.

Keil, C. F., and F. Delitzsch. *Biblical Commentary on the Old Testament*. Translated by J. Martin et al. 25 vols. Edinburgh, 1857–1878. Reprint, 10 vols. Peabody, MA: Hendrickson, 1996.

Kilgallen, John J. "John the Baptist, the Sinful Woman, and the Pharisee." *JBL* 104 (1985) 675–79.

Kingsbury, Jack Dean. *Conflict in Luke: Jesus, Authorities, Disciples*. Minneapolis: Fortress, 1991.

Klein, Günter. "Die Berufung des Petrus." *ZNW* 58 (1967) 1–44.

Koch, Klaus. "חָטָא" In *TDOT* 4:309–319.

Koehler, Ludwig, Walter Baumgartner, and J. J. Stamm. *The Hebrew and Aramaic Lexicon of the Old Testament*. Translated and edited under the supervision of M. E. J. Richardson. 5 vols. Leiden: Brill, 1994–2000.

Kurz, William S. *Reading Luke-Acts*. Louisville: Westminster John Knox, 1993.

Landman, Isaac. "Am Ha-Aretz." In *UJEnc* 1:217.

Lapide, Cornelius. *St. Matthew's Gospel I–IX. The Great Commentary of Cornelius A' Lapide* 1. 6th ed. Translated by Thomas W. Mossman. Catholic Standard Library. Edinburgh: John Grant, 1908.

Lattimore, Richard Alexander. *Themes in Greek and Latin Epitaphs*. Urbana: University of Illinois Press, 1942.

Leaney, Robert. "Jesus and Peter: the Call and Postresurrection Appearance (Lk 5,1–11 and 24,34)." *ExpTim* 65 (1953–54) 381–82.

Levine, Lee I., editor. *The Galilee in Late Antiquity*. Cambridge: Harvard University Press, 1992.

Liddell, George Henry, Robert Scott, and Henry Stuart Jones. *A Greek-English Lexicon*. 9th ed. with new supplement. Oxford: Clarendon, 1977.

Lightfoot, John. *Horae Hebraicae et Talmudicae*. Translated by Robert Gandell. 4 vols. Oxford: Oxford University Press, 1859.

Livy. *Livy, Books XXIII–XXV*. Translated by Frank Gardner Moore. Edited by T. E. Page. LCL. Cambridge: Harvard University Press, 1940.

Maddox, Robert. *The Purpose of Luke-Acts*. Edinburgh: T. & T. Clark, 1982.

Magriso, Yitzchak (ben Moshe). *Avoth MeAm Lo'ez*. Translated by David N. Barocas. Edited by Aryeh Kaplan. New York: Maznaim, 1979.

Malina, Bruce J. *The Social World of Jesus and the Gospels*. New York: Routledge, 1996.

Marshall, I. Howard. *Luke: Historian and Theologian*. Grand Rapids: Zondervan, 1970.

———. *The Gospel of Luke*. NIGTC. Grand Rapids: Eerdmans, 1978.

Bibliography

Mason, Steve. *Flavius Josephus on the Pharisees*. StPB 39. New York: Brill, 1991.
McKenzie, John L. *Second Isaiah*. AB 20. Garden City, NY: Doubleday, 1968.
McNamera, Martin. *Palestinian Judaism and the New Testament*. Wilmington, DE: Michael Glazier, 1983.
McKnight, Scot. *A Light Among the Gentiles: Jewish Missionary Activity in the Second Temple Period*. Minneapolis: Fortress, 1991.
Meyer, Ben F. "A Caricature of Joachim Jeremias and His Scholarly Work." *JBL* 110 (1991) 451–62.
Meyer, Heinrich August Wilhelm. *Critical and Exegetical Handbook to the Gospel of Matthew*. Translated by Peter Christie. New York: Funk and Wagnalls, 1884.
———. *Critical and Exegetical Handbook to the Gospel of John*. Translated by William Urwick. New York: Funk and Wagnalls, 1884.
Michel, Otto. "τελώνης." In *TDNT* 8:88–105.
Minear, Paul S. "Luke's Use of the Birth Stories." In *Studies in Luke-Acts: Essays Presented in Honor of Paul Schubert*, edited by Leander E. Keck and J. Louis Martyn, 111–30. Nashville: Abingdon, 1966.
Moessner, David. P. *Lord of the Banquet. The Literary and Theological Significance of the Lukan Travel Narrative*. Minneapolis: Fortress, 1989.
———. "'Eyewitnesses,' 'Informed Contemporaries,' and 'Unknowing Inquirers': Josephus' Criteria for Authentic Historiography and the Meaning of ΠΑΡΑΚΟΛΟΥΘΕΩ." *NovT* 38 (1996) 105–22.
Montefiore, C. G. *The Synoptic Gospels*. 3 vols. London: Macmillan, 1909.
Neale, David A. *None But the Sinners*. JSNTSup 58. Sheffield: JSOT Press, 1991.
Neusner, Jacob. *From Politics to Piety: The Emergence of Pharisaic Judaism*. Englewood Cliffs, NJ: Prentice-Hall, 1973.
———. "The Fellowship (*Haburah*) in the Second Jewish Commonwealth." *HTR* 53 (1960) 125–42.
———. *Rabbinic Literature and the New Testament*. Valley Forge: Trinity, 1994.
———. Review of *Jerusalem at the Time of Jesus* by Joachim Jeremias. In *JAAR* 39 (1971) 201–2.
Oppenheimer, Aharon. *The 'Am Ha-aretz: A Study in the Social History of the Jewish People in the Hellenistic-Roman Period*. Translated by I. H. Levine. ALGHJ 8. Leiden: Brill, 1977.
Origen. *Contra Celsum*. Translated by Henry Chadwick. Cambridge: Cambridge University Press, 1953.
O'Rourke, John J. "Some Notes on Luke xv. 11–32." *NTS* 18 (1972) 431–33.
Owen, John J. *A Commentary, Critical, Expository, and Practical on the Gospels of Matthew and Mark*. New York: Leavitt and Allen, 1864.
Parsons, Mikeal. C. and Richard I. Pervo. *Rethinking the Unity of Luke and Acts*. Minneapolis: Fortress, 1993.
Parsons, Mikeal C. and Joseph B. Tyson, editors. *Cadbury, Knox, and Talbert: American Contributions to the Study of Acts*. Atlanta: Scholars, 1992.
Perrin, Norman. *Rediscovering the Teachings of Jesus*. NTL. London: SCM Press, 1967.
———. Review of *Studies in Pharisaism and the Gospels. First and Second Series*, by I. Abrahams. *JR* 50 (1970) 118–19.

Bibliography

Pervo, Richard I. *Profit With Delight: The Literary Genre of the Acts of the Apostles.* Philadelphia: Fortress, 1987.

Pilgrim, Walter E. *Good News to the Poor: Wealth and Poverty in Luke-Acts.* Minneapolis: Augsburg, 1981.

Porton, G. "Diversity in Postbiblical Judaism." In *Early Judaism and Its Modern Interpreters,* edited by Robert Kraft and George W. E. Nickelsburg, 57–80. Philadelphia: Fortress, 1986.

Powell, Mark Allan. *What Is Narrative Criticism?* GBS. Minneapolis: Fortress, 1990.

———. *What Are They Saying about Acts?* New York: Paulist, 1991.

Rad, Gerhard von. *Old Testament Theology.* Translated by D. M. G. Stalker. 2 vols. New York: Harper and Row, 1962.

Ravens, D. A. S. "Zacchaeus: The Final Part of a Lucan Tryptych?" *JSNT* 41 (1991) 19–32.

Radbertus, Pascasius. *Pascasii Radberti Expositio in Matheo Libri XII.* Edited by Bedae Paulus. Corpus Christianorum, Continuatio Mediaeualis 56. Turnholt: Brepols, 1984.

Rengstorf, Karl H. "ἁμαρτωλός." In *TDNT* 1:317–35.

Rice, George E. "Luke's Thematic Use of the Call to Discipleship." *AUSS* 19 (1981) 51-58.

———. "Luke 4:31–44: Release for the Captives." *AUSS* 20 (1982) 23-28.

Ringe, Sharon H. *Luke.* Westminster Bible Companion. Louisville: Westminster John Knox, 1995.

Rivkin, Ellis. "Defining the Pharisees: The Tannaitic Sources." *HUCA* 40–41 (1969–70) 205–49.

Safrai, Shemuel, and Menahem Stern. *The Jewish People in the First Century: Historical Geography, Political History, Social, Cultural and Religious Life and Institutions.* 2 vols. CRINT. Assen: Van Gorcum, 1974–76.

Salom, A. P. "Was Zacchaeus Really Reforming?" *ExpTim* 78 (1966–7) 87.

Sanders, E. P. *Jesus and Judaism.* Philadelphia: Fortress, 1985.

———. "Defending the Indefensible." *JBL* 110 (1991) 463–77.

Sanders, Jack T. *The Jews in Luke-Acts.* Philadelphia: Fortress, 1987.

———. "Tradition and Redaction in Luke xv. 11–32." *NTS* 15 (1968–69) 433–38.

Sarason, Richard S. *Demai.* The Talmud of the Land of Israel 3. Chicago: University of Chicago Press, 1993.

Schrenk, Gottlob. "δικαιοσύνη." In *TDNT* 2:192–210.

Schürer, Emil. *The History of the Jewish People in the Age of Jesus Christ.* Revised and edited by Geza Vermes and Fergus Millar. Edinburgh: T. & T. Clark, 1987.

Siker, Jeffrey S. "'First to the Gentiles': A Literary Analysis of Luke 4:16–30." *JBL* 111 (1992) 73–90.

Sloyan, Gerald. *Jesus in Focus: A Life in Its Setting.* Mystic, CT: Twenty-Third, 1983.

Smith, Charles W. F. "Fishers of Men." *HTR* 52 (1959) 187–203.

Smith, Dennis. "Table Fellowship as a Literary Motif in the Gospel of Luke." *JBL* 106 (1987) 613–37.

Snaith, Norman H. *The Distinctive Ideas of the Old Testament.* London: Epworth, 1944.

Sokoloff, Michael. *Dictionary of Palestinian Aramaic of the Byzantine Period.* Ramat-Gan, Israel: Bar-Ilan University Press, 1992.

BIBLIOGRAPHY

Stein, Robert H. *Luke*. NAC 24. Nashville: Broadman, 1992.
Stendahl, Krister. *Paul Among Jews and Gentiles*. Philadelphia: Fortress, 1976.
Sterling, Gregory E. *Historiography and Self-Definition: Josephos, Luke-Acts and Apologetic Historiography*. NovTSup 64. Leiden: Brill, 1991.
Strack, Hermann L., and Paul Billerbeck. *Das Evangelium nach Markus, Lukas und Johannes und die Apostelgeschichte*. Kommentar zum Neuen Testament aus Talmud und Midrasch 2. Munich: Beck, 1924.
Talbert, Charles H. *Literary Patterns, Theological Themes, and the Genre of Luke-Acts*. SBLMS 20. Missoula, MT: Scholars, 1974.
———. *Reading Luke*. New York: Crossroad, 1982.
Tacitus, *Annals. Books XIII–XVI*. Edited by T. E. Page. Translated by John Jackson. LCL. Cambridge: Harvard University Press, 1957.
Tannehill, Robert C. *Luke*. ANTC. Nashville: Abingdon, 1996.
———. *The Narrative Unity of Luke-Acts*. 2 vols. Philadelphia: Fortress, 1986.
———. "The Mission of Jesus According to Luke 4:16–30." In *Jesus in Nazareth*, edited by Walter Eltester, 51–75. BZNW 40. Berlin: de Gruyter, 1972.
Thomas Aquinas. *Saint Luke*. Catena Aurea: Commentary on the Four Gospels Collected out of the Works of the Fathers 3. Translated and edited by John Henry Newman. Southampton, NY: Saint Austin, 1997.
Tiede, David. *Luke*. ACNT. Minneapolis: Augsburg, 1988.
Trollope, William. *Analecta Theologica: A Critical, Philological, and Exegetical Commentary on the New Testament*. 2 vols. London: Gilbert and Rivington, 1842.
Tromp, Johannes. "The Sinners and the Lawless in Psalm of Solomon 17." *NovT* 35 (1993) 344–61.
Tyson, Joseph B. *Images of Judaism in Luke-Acts*. Columbia: University of South Carolina Press, 1992.
Vermes, Geza. *Jesus and the Jew: A Historian's Reading of the Gospels*. London: SCM, 1973.
———. "Jewish Literature and New Testament Exegesis: Reflections on Methodology." *JJS* 33 (1982) 361–76.
Walker, William O. "Jesus and the Tax Collectors." *JBL* 97 (1978) 221–38.
Walls, A. F. "'In the Presence of the Angels' (Luke xv 10)." *NovT* 3 (1959) 314–16.
Watson, Nigel M. "Was Zacchaeus Really Reforming?" *ExpTim* 77 (1965–6) 282–85.
Wilson, Stephen G. *The Gentiles and the Gentile Mission in Luke-Acts*. SNTSMS 23. Cambridge: Cambridge University Press, 1973.
Wood, Herbert G. "The Use of *agapao* in Luke VII, 42,47." *ExpTim* 66 (1954–55) 312–20.
York, John O. *The Last Shall Be First: The Rhetoric of Reversal in Luke*. JSNTSup 46. Sheffield: JSOT Press, 1991.
Zimmerli, Walther. *Ezekiel 2*. Hermeneia. Translated by James D. Martin. Philadelphia: Fortress, 1969.